NEMIROVSKY AND YUDIN
Problem Complexity and Method Efficiency in Optimization
(*Translated by E. R. Dawson*)

PALMER
Graphical Evolution: An Introduction to the Theory
of Random Graphs

PLESS
Introduction to the Theory of Error-Correcting Codes,
Second Edition

SCHRIJVER
Theory of Linear and Integer Programming

TOMESCU
Problems in Combinatorics and Graph Theory
(*Translated by R. A. Melter*)

TUCKER
Applied Combinatorics
Second Edition

**Introduction to
the Theory of
Error-Correcting Codes**

Introduction to the Theory of Error-Correcting Codes

Second Edition

VERA PLESS
University of Illinois at Chicago Circle

WILEY

A Wiley-Interscience Publication
JOHN WILEY AND SONS
New York · Chichester · Brisbane · Toronto · Singapore

Library of Congress Cataloging-in-Publication Data:

Pless, Vera.
  Introduction to the theory of error-correcting codes/Vera Pless.
—2nd ed.

    p. cm.—(Wiley-Interscience series in discrete mathematics)
  "A Wiley-Interscience publication."
  Bibliography: p.
  Includes index.
    1. Error-correcting codes (Information theory)   I. Title.
II. Series.

QA268.P55   1990
005.7′2—dc20   89-5700   CIP

ISBN 0-471-61884-5

Printed in the United States of America

10 9 8 7 6 5 4 3 2

To my children
Nomi, Ben, and Dan

Preface

This revised book is intended for a two-quarter sequence or one semester course in error-correcting codes at an advanced undergraduate or beginning graduate level. The only requirement is a course in linear algebra although other modern algebra courses would be helpful. In fact, it is a good idea to take this course in conjunction with a modern algebra course as the coding course provides motivation and many concrete examples for the algebra course.

Since the first edition was written, practical uses of error-correcting codes have proliferated. In addition to many uses in communication systems, error-correcting codes are widely used in modern memory devices, have many uses in computer systems, and also provide the high fidelity on many compact disc players. Although the technology is changing rapidly, the fundamental principles of coding remain the same.

I am gratified that many people have used this book as a text. Several of these people or their students have been kind enough to tell me about mistakes, omissions, and topics they would like included or other ways the text could be improved. I have kept track of these comments. As I have taught this course myself and thought about these things, there were items I wanted to change and I also found better ways of presenting some topics. In this revision, mistakes were corrected. Several sections were added including three new sections on B.C.H. codes, one on Reed-Muller codes, and a hand decoding of the binary Golay code. Many new topics or new ideas have been added to existing sections. Greater emphasis has been placed on non-binary codes. There is more material on cyclic codes. As before the intention is to present proofs or approaches in as elementary a fashion as possible. In this regard there is a simplified proof of the MacWilliams identities due to Brualdi, Pless and Beissinger [32] and the presentation of quadratic residue codes has been much simplified. There is a new proof of the uniqueness of the Golay code in part due to an idea of Koch [36]. Many new problems have been added throughout.

In addition to texts on coding mentioned in the first edition, several new or revised books are now available. The ones I have used are Blahut [31], Hill [34], Lin and Costello [39] and van Lint [40]. The texts mentioned that have not been superseded by revised versions, such as MacWilliams and Sloane, are still valuable references. There is much updated material on codes in Conway and Sloane [33].

I want to thank all who read the original text and offered comments. I particularly want to thank Noburu Ito for his meticulous reading of the text, finding mistakes, and offering improvements. I also want to thank John Baldwin, Joel Berman, Lincoln E. Bragg, Richard Brualdi, Netiva Caftori, Peter Landweber, Fred Smith and Glenn Weller for their useful comments. I have tried to make the changes or additions suggested. I would appreciate comments on this revised edition also. Finally, I want to thank Maria Taylor of Wiley Interscience for all her help with this revision.

VERA PLESS

University of Illinois at Chicago Circle
June 1989

Preface to the First Edition

This book arose out of a two-quarter sequence in error-correcting codes that I taught at the University of Illinois Circle Campus and a similar one-semester course at Dartmouth College. It is intended for undergraduates in mathematics, computer science, or electrical engineering. The only requirement is an elementary course in linear algebra. An appendix, which covers some of the linear algebra needed, is provided to supplement such a course. A modern algebra course is not necessary but would probably be helpful. If the algebra course is taken concurrently with the coding course, the latter could provide motivation and many concrete examples. I have had undergraduates, from sophomores up, and graduate students in this course. The instructor can determine the pace at which to proceed from the backgrounds of the students.

The theory of error-correcting codes started as a subject in electrical engineering with Shannon's classic papers in 1948 and 1949. It has since become a fascinating mathematical topic, and part of the fascination has been the use of many varied mathematical tools to solve the practical problems in coding. This book attempts to demonstrate this process. Understanding how one might go about finding mathematical techniques to solve applied problems is useful to students who might encounter such problems some time. Because the subject is relatively new, there are many open problems in coding, some of which are mentioned in this book. Whenever possible, the most elementary proofs or approaches are used.

This book is about linear block codes, and general background material is given in the first two chapters, including an introduction to such specific linear codes as Hamming codes and Golay codes. Chapter 3 raises the problem of how to correct double errors, which leads to the necessity of using finite fields, the topic of Chapter 4. Chapter 5 covers the important class of cyclic codes. Chapter 6 talks about an interesting family of cyclic codes, quadratic residue codes, and also about the group of a code. Chapter 7 discusses the practical B.C.H. codes. Chapter 8 is on weight distributions, particularly of self-dual codes, which leads to designs in codes in the next chapter. The last chapter uses the designs in some codes to give a new proof, due to J. H. Conway, that the Golay code is unique. This chapter also includes some new material about gluing codes together. This is my choice of material for a two-quarter or one-semester course in coding. If more time were available, I would also cover Reed-Muller codes, majority logic decoding, convolutional codes, and nonlinear codes and would say more about bounds on the information rates of codes.

The books that I have used the most and put on reserve for students are: E. R. Berlekamp's *Algebraic Coding Theory* [2], J. H. van Lint's *Coding Theory* [9], F. J. MacWilliam's and N. J. A. Sloane's *The Theory of Error-Correcting Codes* [15], and W. W. Peterson's and E. J. Weldon, Jr.'s, *Error-Correcting Codes* [19]. Other useful general books on codes are: I. F. Blake's and R. C. Mullin's *The Mathematical Theory of Coding* [4], S. Lin's *An Introduction to Error-Correcting Codes* [11], and R. J. McEliece's *Theory of Information and Coding* [18].

I wish to thank the students and faculty at both the University of Illinois Circle Campus and Dartmouth and others who have helped me by finding mistakes, suggesting portions of the text that should be clarified, and providing new problems. In particular, for their valuable comments, I thank Deborah Bergstrand, Ken Bogart, Reza Heydarpour, Noburu Ito, Will Polik, Joshua Rabinowitz, and Ann Street. I also thank Shirley Roper and Nancy French for their patience in typing and retyping.

VERA PLESS

University of Illinois at Chicago Circle
August 1981

Contents

Introduction to
the Theory of
Error-Correcting Codes

1

Introductory Concepts

1.1 INTRODUCTION

The subject of error-correcting codes arose originally in response to practical problems in the reliable communication of digitally encoded information. Claude Shannon's paper "A Mathematical Theory of Communication" [28], written in 1948, started the discipline in electrical engineering called information theory, and also the branch of it called error-correcting codes. Since then algebraic coding has developed many connections with portions of algebra and combinatorics. Sophisticated mathematical techniques have proven useful for coding and coding problems, and the results have interested mathematicians. Now algebraic coding is also a mathematical topic with the feature that it has recent practical origins which have provided motivation for many of its main concerns.

We here think of a message as a block of symbols from a finite alphabet. A commonly used alphabet is the set of two symbols 0 and 1, and so we start with that. A possible message is 1001. This can represent a number such as 759, a letter such as *A*, or a complete message such as, "The yellow cat is sick." This message is then transmitted over a communications channel that is subject to some amount of noise. The object of an error-correcting code is to add redundancy to the message in an analytic fashion so that the original message can be recovered if it has been garbled. This is commonly done in ordinary speech where people repeat things in many different ways in order to be properly understood. Consider now the diagram of the communications channel (Figure 1.1).

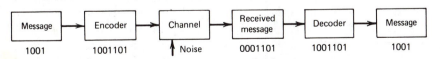

Figure 1.1 The communications channel.

The first box contains the message, in our case 1001, which we say represents, "The spacecraft is approaching from the north." This message then enters the encoder where the redundancy digits 101 are added so that the message can be corrected if it becomes distorted when communicated. The message is then transmitted over the channel, where it is subject to noise. When noise hits the message, a 0 is changed to a 1 or a 1 to a 0. In our message the first digit was changed by noise. Then the receiver is either completely confused—possibly 0001101 does not stand for any message—or else she is misinformed—0001101 could represent the message, "The spacecraft is approaching from the east." Then the received message enters the decoder where, due to the redundancy added, the original message can be recovered. Error-correcting coding is the art of adding redundancy efficiently so that most messages, if distorted, can be correctly decoded.

We can think of the communications channel as a real communications channel or as data stored in a computer that deteriorates with time. Furthermore, although we think the channel's reliability is quite good, our need for reliable communications is great. For example, in communicating with a satellite any mistake could be disastrous.

Communications channels where error-correcting codes are used are too numerous to mention. Codes are used on telephone lines and computer links. Black and white pictures were transmitted from several Mariner space probes using error-correcting codes, as were color pictures from recent Voyager journeys. Error-correcting codes give the high fidelity on compact discs. Errors arise from a variety of causes, some of which are human, equipment failure, lightening, interference, or scratches on discs. Error-correcting codes are also used for data compression. Indeed, their uses are ever expanding.

We make a distinction between detecting and correcting errors. It is much easier to detect errors than to correct them, and at times even detection is useful. For example, if there is a feedback channel and enough time, we can ask for the message to be sent again. This is not always possible, as with data stored on magnetic tape. In many real-time communications, it is often necessary to correct errors, and that is our emphasis here.

One of the simplest channels is the binary symmetric channel (B.S.C.). It has no memory and it receives and transmits two symbols, 0 and 1. The B.S.C. has the property that with probability q a transmitted digit will be received correctly, and with probability $p = 1 - q$ it will not be. This can be illustrated as shown in Figure 1.2. We call p the *symbol error probability*.

In order to see the problems we face, we now attempt to construct some simple codes. Suppose our message is 1001. If we add no redundancy and transmit this message and an error occurs, there is no way to detect it. If we start with the modest aim of detecting single errors, we could begin by

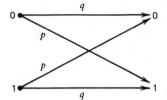

Figure 1.2 Binary symmetric channel.

repeating our message once; 10011001. If an error occurs and we receive, say, 10010001, then by comparing the two parts we can detect it. Still we do not know whether the error is in the first or second rendition. Also, we are transmitting twice as many digits as we need, and if we merely wish to detect single errors, we can do better than this by using the *overall parity check*. A parity check is accomplished by adding an extra digit to the message. It is a 0 if there are an even number of 1's, and a 1 if there are an odd number of 1's. Then we transmit the message 10010, and if we receive, say 10000, we can detect that an error has occurred since we see an odd number of 1's. The overall parity check is widely used in computers and elsewhere.

In error correcting our first aim is to correct single errors since these are the most probable. We will then correct double errors, and then triple errors, and so on, correcting as many as we can. If we now make a naive attempt to correct single errors, we could transmit our message three times; 100110011001. Then if an error occurs and we receive 100100011001, we can take a majority count of the disagreeing digits $1, 0, 1$, and decide that most likely a 1 was sent. However, we have now transmitted three times as much as we need, although we can correct some double and triple errors (which ones?). A significant improvement occurs with the Hamming $(7, 4)$ code. We describe this code by the following four codewords.

1	2	3	4	5	6	7
1	0	0	0	0	1	1
0	1	0	0	1	0	1
0	0	1	0	1	1	0
0	0	0	1	1	1	1

We think of the first four positions as the information positions and the last three as the redundancy positions. The first codeword represents the message 1000, the second represents the message 0100, and so on. We write each codeword either as a block of seven 0's and 1's, say 1000011, or in the more usual vector form as $(1, 0, 0, 0, 0, 1, 1)$. We can obtain more codewords by adding these four vectors where in each addition we add corresponding components mod 2. So, for example, $(1, 0, 0, 0, 0, 1, 1) + (0, 1, 0, 0, 1, 0, 1) = (1, 1, 0, 0, 1, 1, 0)$. This codeword represents the message 1100. In this fashion we can encode all $2^4 = 16$ messages consisting of four symbols, each either 0 or 1. In order to decode this code, we consider the following three decoding sequences:

$$\mathbf{a} = 0001111,$$
$$\mathbf{b} = 0110011,$$
$$\mathbf{c} = 1010101,$$

and we use the inner product of two vectors $\mathbf{x} = (x_1, \ldots, x_7)$ and $\mathbf{y} = (y_1, \ldots, y_7)$ defined by $\sum_{i=1}^{7} x_i y_i \pmod 2$. If our message is 1011, we encode it as $\mathbf{x} = 1011010$. Suppose an error occurs and we receive $\mathbf{y} = 1010010$. We form the three inner products $\mathbf{y} \cdot \mathbf{a} = 1$, $\mathbf{y} \cdot \mathbf{b} = 0$, and $\mathbf{y} \cdot \mathbf{c} = 0$. In this order the symbols represent the binary number $100 = 4$. From this we conclude that the fourth digit is in error. This procedure is known as Hamming decoding, and it corrects any single error. Note that we do not even transmit twice the number of information digits.

Suppose that we are transmitting on a binary channel and that q, the probability of correct transmission, is .90, so that p, the probability of an error, is .10. Then the probability that a four digit message would be transmitted correctly without any coding is $q^4 = .6561$. If the Hamming code is used, then the probability of correctly decoding a received vector is q^7(no errors) + $7pq^6$(one error) = $.4783 + .3720 = .8503$, a considerable improvement.

The word error rate P_{err} for a particular decoding scheme is the probability of incorrectly decoding a received message. For the Hamming code we see that P_{err} is $1 - (q^7 + 76q^6) = .1497$.

Hamming decoding is so easy that it can be done quickly without a computer. Yet many intelligent people have worked for years to devise decoding schemes for other codes or classes of codes that will operate efficiently on computers. One of the codes that has received such attention is the famous Golay (23, 12) code. Here each codeword has 23 digits of which 12 are the information digits and 11 are the redundancy digits. It is known that this code can correct one, two, or three errors, but its decoding requires a computer and people have worked on numerous decoding schemes. To see why such effort is needed, consider the Hamming code repeated three times. Break any string of 12 information digits into three portions of four digits each, then encode each of these portions using the Hamming code. We can consider this as a code with 12 information digits and 9 redundancy digits, 2 fewer than the Golay code, and we can decode it

Table 1.1 Some Binary Codes

1	2	3	4	5
7	4	1	16	128
23	12	3	4,096	8,388,608
47	24	5	16,777,216	140,737,488,355,238

Column 1—length of code, n.
Column 2—number of information symbols, k.
Column 3—number of errors code can correct.
Column 4—number of messages in code $= 2^k$.
Column 5—total number of messages $= 2^n$.

using Hamming decoding for each set of 7 digits. Decoding is easily done by hand. This code can only correct single errors and some double or triple errors if they occur in separate Hamming blocks, whereas the Golay code can correct double or triple errors wherever they are distributed. Larger codes that can correct more errors are more useful because the errors can be distributed in more ways, but they are harder to decode.

We can see some of the reasons for this from Table 1.1. In the first code, the Hamming code, we have a possible 128 received vectors and we must decide which of the 16 codewords was sent. This is much more difficult for the second code, the Golay code, which has 8,388,608 possible received messages, which are to be decoded into one of 4096 codewords. The last code, which we see later, is a quadratic residue code; it presents even more difficulty. Often, for practical purposes, codes are needed whose lengths are in the hundreds.

The *rate* of a code is defined as the ratio of the number of information digits to the length. Thus the codes above have rates $4/7$ for the first, $12/23$ for the second, and $24/47$ for the third; all numbers close to $1/2$. A very important result in coding is the surprising theorem of Claude Shannon. We cannot state it precisely without defining more concepts, but roughly it says that if the code rate is less than a number called "channel capacity," which measures the amount of information that a channel can transmit, then it is possible to transmit information with an arbitrarily small probability of error by using long enough codes. However, Shannon proved this theorem by probabilistic methods, not constructive ones, and one of the outstanding problems in coding is constructing families of codes with known properties that are as good as the theorem predicts. A "good" code is a code that can intrinsica ly correct many errors. For practical purposes, however, it is also important to be able to decode efficiently.

Since Shannon's theorem, coding theorists have constructed many good codes, devised ingenious decoding algorithms, and developed the theory of codes. A number of these good codes will be described in later chapters but we will not be able to cover all the known ones. The recent construction of new, good codes using methods of algebraic geometry has created much excitement in the coding community. Unfortunately their study requires an extensive knowledge of algebraic geometry.

In this book we are concerned primarily with linear or algebraic codes where the errors are randomly distributed. Shannon's theorem is about nonlinear codes, but an analogous theorem has been demonstrated for linear codes so there are good reasons for studying them. Much more is known about them and this knowledge can be used for decoding and storage. There are special codes for correcting bursts of errors, but even there the more general case provides useful information. There are codes where the messages are not broken into blocks but form a continuous stream. These are called convolutional codes and they often find practical applications. We do not study them here as their structure is apparently quite different from block codes and possibly not as well understood.

Another interesting topic is how the original information is assigned its block of digits. There might be reasons based, for example, on frequency of occurrence for such assignments. This topic is called source encoding and is not pursued here. We do, however, study linear codes with elements from any finite field.

1.2 BASIC DEFINITIONS

In the last section we saw a specific binary code, the Hamming code, described by its generator matrix. We now define a linear code and describe two common ways to give such a code, one by a generator matrix and the other by a parity check matrix. Since we are often concerned with binary codes, we sometimes state our definitions separately for that case.

In order to define a binary linear code, we consider the space V of all n-tuples of 0's and 1's with addition of vectors componentwise mod 2. So, for example, $(1, 0, 0, 0, 1, 1) + (0, 1, 0, 1, 0, 1) = (1, 1, 0, 1, 1, 0)$. An (n, k) *linear, binary code* is the set of all linear combinations of k independent vectors in V. The word linear means that if two (or more) vectors are in the code, so is their sum. A *nonlinear code* is just a set of vectors. As we are mainly concerned with linear codes, the word code means a linear code. We could also define an (n, k) binary code C by saying C is a k-dimensional subspace of V.

In the general case we let F be $GF(q)$, the finite field with q elements. This is described thoroughly in Chapter 4. We include it here for completeness. Then it is known that q must be a power of a prime. If q is itself a prime p, say $q = 2$ or 3, then F can be thought of as the set of p elements $0, 1, \ldots, p - 1$ with the arithmetic operations performed mod p. A binary code is a code over $GF(2)$. The reader who has not encountered finite fields should think of these cases when $GF(q)$ is mentioned. An (n, k) *code over* $GF(q)$ is a k-dimensional subspace of F^n, the space of all n-tuples with components from $F = GF(q)$.

Clearly an (n, k) binary code has 2^k vectors or codewords in it. Since a code is a vector subspace, it can be given by a basis. The matrix whose rows are the basis vectors is called a *generator matrix*. As a subspace has more than one basis, so a code has more than one generator matrix.

Consider, for example, the $(5, 3)$ binary code C_1 whose generator matrix is G_1.

$$G_1 = \begin{pmatrix} 1 & 0 & 0 & 1 & 1 \\ 0 & 1 & 0 & 0 & 1 \\ 0 & 0 & 1 & 1 & 1 \end{pmatrix}.$$

All the codewords in C_1 can be gotten from the linear combinations of these three vectors. A codeword in C_1 has three information positions. Any three positions where the columns of G_1 are independent can be taken as information positions. The first three positions certainly can be, but there are others. C_1 has $8 = 2^3$ codewords.

If G is a generator matrix of an (n, k) code C, then any set of k columns of G that are independent is called an *information set* of C. If a certain set of k columns of one generator matrix is independent, then that set of columns of any generator matrix is independent. Any (n, k) code with $k \neq n$ and fewer than $n - k$ zero columns has more than one information set. It is a fact that the information sets constructed from any generator matrix G' of C will be the same as those constructed from G.

Another way to describe a code is by parity check equations. In C_1, as the first three positions are information positions, we can express the redundancy positions in terms of these. So we let $(a_1, a_2, a_3, a_4, a_5)$ be any vector in C_1 and suppose that we know the information positions a_1, a_2, and a_3. Then the redundancy positions can be computed in terms of these as follows.

$$a_4 = a_1 + a_3$$
$$a_5 = a_1 + a_2 + a_3.$$

Any codeword $(a_1, a_2, \ldots, a_5)$ in C_1 satisfies these equations. They are the parity check equations for C_1. We can use these to write down all vectors in C_1. So, for example, if $a_1 = a_2 = 1$ and $a_3 = 0$, then $a_4 = 1 + 0 = 1$,

$a_5 = 1 + 1 + 0 = 0$, and $(1, 1, 0, 1, 0)$ is in C_1. This is the sum of rows 1 and 2 of G_1.

A set of equations that give the redundancy positions in terms of the information positions are called *parity check equations*. We can express all such equations in terms of the parity check matrix. In order to do this, we use the inner product of two vectors. This is the same inner product we used in Hamming decoding.

If $\mathbf{u} = (u_1, \ldots, u_n)$ and $\mathbf{v} = (v_1, \ldots, v_n)$ are two vectors in V over $GF(p)$, for p a prime, then the *inner product* of $\mathbf{u}$ and $\mathbf{v}$ is $\mathbf{u} \cdot \mathbf{v} = \sum_{i=1}^{n} u_i v_i \pmod{p}$. The inner product is linear in both variables, $(\alpha_1 u_1 + \alpha_2 u_2) \cdot (\beta_1 v_1 + \beta_2 v_2) = \alpha_1 \beta_1 u_1 \cdot v_1 + \alpha_1 \beta_2 u_1 \cdot v_2 + \alpha_2 \beta_1 u_2 \cdot v_1 + \alpha_2 \beta_2 u_2 \cdot v_2$. Clearly $\mathbf{u} \cdot \mathbf{v} = \mathbf{v} \cdot \mathbf{u}$.

If $\mathbf{u} \cdot \mathbf{v} = 0$, we say that $\mathbf{u}$ and $\mathbf{v}$ are *orthogonal* to each other. For binary vectors this means that they have an even number of 1's in common. Let

$$H_1 = \begin{pmatrix} 1 & 0 & 1 & 1 & 0 \\ 1 & 1 & 1 & 0 & 1 \end{pmatrix}.$$

Note that a vector $(a_1, a_2, a_3, a_4, a_5)$ is orthogonal to the first row of H_1 if $a_1 + a_3 + a_4 = 0$, which is the same as our first parity check equation $a_4 = a_1 + a_3$. Similarly being orthogonal to the second row of H_1 is the same as satisfying the second parity check equation. Hence we can now say that C_1 is the set of all 5-tuples that are orthogonal to each row of the parity check matrix H_1. This is exactly the same as saying that the vectors in C_1 satisfy the parity check equations given above.

If C is a code, we let $C^{\perp} = \{\mathbf{u} \in V | \mathbf{u} \cdot \mathbf{w} = \mathbf{0}$ for all $\mathbf{w} \in C\}$. It is known that if C is k-dimensional, then $C^{\perp}$ is $(n - k)$-dimensional. $C^{\perp}$ is called the *dual* or *orthogonal code* of C.

We say that an (n, k) code C is specified by a *parity check matrix* H if every vector in C is orthogonal to the rows of a matrix H of rank $n - k$ with n columns. In this situation we are describing C as being everything orthogonal to $C^{\perp}$. A way of saying this is that $\mathbf{w}$ is in C if and only if $\mathbf{w}H^T = 0$. A code can be completely described by giving a generator matrix or alternatively by giving a parity check matrix, and the two descriptions are equivalent.

It follows that a code C is given by a generator matrix G and a parity check matrix H iff $C^{\perp}$ is given by the generator matrix H and the parity check matrix G.

Encoding is the process of adding redundancy digits to the information digits. We have given here two ways of encoding any code, one by taking linear combinations of the rows of a generator matrix and the other by parity check equations. There are other ways for special families of codes like cyclic codes. The encoding process in general is not difficult. The difficult problem is decoding.

Since an (n, k) code can be encoded in many ways, it is not necessarily true that the first k positions are an information set. However, some k positions are, and C is equivalent to a code whose first k positions are information positions. Two binary codes are said to be *equivalent* to each other if one can be obtained from the other by a permutation of the coordinate indices of any generator matrix.

For example, the two codes below are equivalent since the second can be obtained from the first by the coordinate permutation $(1, 4)(2, 5)(3, 6)$; that is, we interchange columns 1 and 4, columns 2 and 5, and columns 3 and 6.

1	2	3	4	5	6	1	2	3	4	5	6
1	0	0	0	1	1	0	1	1	1	0	0
0	1	0	1	0	1	1	0	1	0	1	0
0	0	1	1	1	0	1	1	0	0	0	1

It is not always obvious from given generator matrices that two codes are equivalent or are even the same code.

Two codes over $GF(q)$ are *equivalent* if one can be obtained from the other by a coordinate permutation followed by multiplying some (or no) columns of a generator matrix by a nonzero element of $GF(q)$. Equivalent codes have exactly the same error-correcting properties. If one can be decoded, so can the other; just permute first and then decode. So they are not essentially different.

We say that a generator matrix G of an (n, k) code C is in *standard form* if $G = (I, A)$, where I is the $k \times k$ identity matrix and A is a $k \times (n - k)$ matrix. Generator matrices of the Hamming $(7, 4)$ code and C_1 were given in standard form. Any (n, k) code is equivalent to an (n, k) code with a generator matrix in standard form [see the lemma in the Appendix]. The advantage of this form is given by the following theorem.

Theorem 1. If an (n, k) code C has a generator matrix $G = (I, A)$ in standard form, then a parity check matrix of C is $H = (-A^t, I)$ where A^t is the transpose of A and is an $(n - k) x k$ matrix and I is the $(n - k) x (n - k)$ identity matrix.

Proof. It can be seen by direct computation that the rows of G and H are orthogonal to each other. We just check this for the first rows, so let $A = (a_{ij})$. Then the first row of G, $\mathbf{g}_1 = (1, 0, \ldots, 0, a_{11}, a_{12}, \ldots, a_{1(n-k)})$, and the first row of H, $\mathbf{h}_1 = (-a_{11}, -a_{21}, \ldots, -a_{k1}, 1, 0, \ldots, 0)$, so that $\mathbf{g}_1 \cdot \mathbf{h}_1 = -a_{11} + a_{11} = 0$. Clearly G has rank k and H has rank $(n - k)$.

$$\text{Q.E.D.}$$

This theorem makes it very easy to write down H, given G, and conversely. Notice that the G and H given for C_1 satisfy Theorem 1. We consider now C_2, a $(4, 2)$ ternary code with generator matrix

$$G_2 = \begin{pmatrix} 1 & 0 & 1 & 1 \\ 0 & 1 & 2 & 1 \end{pmatrix}.$$

The elements 0, 1, and 2 are in $GF(3)$, the field of three elements, and we add them mod 3. Then we can immediately compute

$$H_2 = \begin{pmatrix} 2 & 1 & 1 & 0 \\ 2 & 2 & 0 & 1 \end{pmatrix}.$$

Clearly the rank of H_2 is correct and we can check by hand that the rows of G_2 and H_2 are orthogonal to each other.

1.3 WEIGHT, MINIMUM WEIGHT, AND MAXIMUM-LIKELIHOOD DECODING

A very important concept in coding is the *weight* of a vector. By definition this is the number of nonzero components it has and is denoted by $wt(\mathbf{u})$. Thus the weight of any nonzero vector in the last example, C_2, is 3. The all-one binary vector of length n, call it $\mathbf{h} = (1, 1, \ldots, 1)$, has weight n. We call the binary code generated by $\mathbf{h}$ the *repetition code*. If C is the $(n, 1)$ repetition code, then $C^\perp$, an $(n, n - 1)$ code, consists of all even weight vectors of length n. We can write down a generator matrix E_n of this space.

$$E_n = \begin{pmatrix} 1 & 1 & 0 & 0 & \cdots & 0 \\ 1 & 0 & 1 & 0 & \cdots & 0 \\ & \vdots & & & & \\ 1 & 0 & 0 & 0 & \cdots & 1 \end{pmatrix}.$$

Another important concept, as we see from the next theorem, is the *minimum weight* of a code, denoted by d. This is the weight of the nonzero vector of smallest weight in the code. So for C_2 it is 3; for any of the even weight codes E_n it is 2.

Let us recall the generator matrix of the Hamming $(7, 4)$ code and see if we can find d.

$$G = \begin{pmatrix} 1 & 0 & 0 & 0 & 0 & 1 & 1 \\ 0 & 1 & 0 & 0 & 1 & 0 & 1 \\ 0 & 0 & 1 & 0 & 1 & 1 & 0 \\ 0 & 0 & 0 & 1 & 1 & 1 & 1 \end{pmatrix}.$$

We could determine d by listing all the codewords. Another way to do this, which might be useful with larger codes, is to compute the weights of combinations of rows of G. The weight of each of the first three rows of G is 3 and of the fourth is 4, so that $d \leq 3$. But the weight of a combination of two rows is ≥ 3 (why?) and of three or more rows is ≥ 3 (why?). This is enough to tell us that $d = 3$.

An (n, k) code with minimum weight d is often called an (n, k, d) *code*. Thus the Hamming code is a $(7, 4, 3)$ code.

The *weight distribution* of a code is the number of vectors of any weight in the code. This is often described by the list of numbers A_i where A_i is the number of vectors of weight i in the code. A_0 is always 1. Consider the weight distribution of the Hamming code. Again we could find this by listing all the codewords. But note that we already know that $A_0 = 1$ and $d = 3$. Since the sum of the rows of G is $\mathbf{h}$, $A_7 = 1$ and whenever $\mathbf{v}$ is in the code so is $\mathbf{h} + \mathbf{v}$. Hence the only other possible nonzero weights are 3 and 4 and they must occur equally often so that the weight distribution is $A_0 = A_7 = 1$, $A_3 = A_4 = 7$. The A_i that are 0 are usually not listed.

We define the *distance* between two vectors $\mathbf{u}$ and $\mathbf{v}$ to be the number of positions in which they differ and denote it by $d(\mathbf{u}, \mathbf{v})$. Thus the distance between the first two rows $\mathbf{g}_1$ and $\mathbf{g}_2$ of G is 4. The distance between two vectors in C_2, for example, is $d((1, 0, 1, 1), (0, 1, 2, 1)) = 3$. It is easy to see that

$$d(\mathbf{u}, \mathbf{v}) = wt(\mathbf{u} - \mathbf{v}).$$

Note that for binary codes $\mathbf{u} - \mathbf{v} = \mathbf{u} + \mathbf{v}$. The distance function is a metric. This means that, for any $\mathbf{u}$, $\mathbf{v}$, and $\mathbf{w}$ in a space V, we have the following three conditions.

(i) $d(\mathbf{u}, \mathbf{u}) = \mathbf{0}$.
(ii) $d(\mathbf{u}, \mathbf{v}) = d(\mathbf{v}, \mathbf{u})$.
(iii) $d(\mathbf{u}, \mathbf{w}) \leq d(\mathbf{u}, \mathbf{v}) + d(\mathbf{v}, \mathbf{w})$.

The first two conditions are very easy to verify. The third, known as the triangle inequality, is left for Problem 21.

We again consider the important decoding problem. If we receive a vector $\mathbf{v}$, which might have been distorted in transmission, we are faced with the problem of deciding which vector $\mathbf{u}$ was sent. One thing we could try to do is list all the codewords and compute the distance between $\mathbf{v}$ and each vector in the code. Then the most likely transmitted $\mathbf{u}$ is that vector that has the smallest distance from $\mathbf{v}$. The method of decoding a received vector to the closest code vector is called *maximum-likelihood decoding*.

Another way of stating this decoding method is in terms of error vectors. If **u** is transmitted and **v** is received, then the *error vector* **e** is defined to be **v** − **u**. Thus if **u** = (1, 0, 0, 1) and **v** = (0, 0, 0, 1) is received, then **e** = (1, 0, 0, 0) shows an error in the first position. Thus maximum-likelihood decoding can be rephrased as follows. If **v** is received, decode **v** to **u** where **e** is the vector of smallest weight with **v** = **e** + **u** for some **u** in the code.

The next theorem shows that d is a very simple measure of the "goodness" of a code. In order to do this, we define a *sphere of radius r* about a vector **u**, denoted by $S_r(\mathbf{u})$ as follows.

$$S_r(\mathbf{u}) = \{\mathbf{v} \in V \mid d(\mathbf{u}, \mathbf{v}) \leq r\}.$$

In other words, $S_r(\mathbf{u})$ is the set of all vectors in the space whose distance from **u** is less than or equal to r, the usual definition of a sphere.

Let $[x]$ denote the greatest integer less than or equal to x, that is, $[\frac{3}{2}] = [1] = 1$.

Theorem 2. If d is the minimum weight of a code C, then C can correct $t = [(d - 1)/2]$ or fewer errors, and conversely.

Proof. We prove that spheres of radius $t = [(d - 1)/2]$ about codewords are disjoint. Suppose not. Let **u** and **w** be distinct vectors in C and assume that $S_t(\mathbf{u}) \cap S_t(\mathbf{w})$ is nonempty. Suppose $\mathbf{v} \in S_t(\mathbf{u}) \cap S_t(\mathbf{w})$ (Figure 1.3). Then $d(\mathbf{u}, \mathbf{w}) \leq d(\mathbf{u}, \mathbf{v}) + d(\mathbf{v}, \mathbf{w})$ by the triangle inequality and this is $\leq 2t$ since the points are in the spheres. Now $2t \leq d - 1$ so that $d(\mathbf{u}, \mathbf{w}) \leq d - 1$. But $d(\mathbf{u}, \mathbf{w}) = wt(\mathbf{u} - \mathbf{w})$, which must be $\geq d$ since **u** − **w** is a nonzero vector in C. This contradiction shows that the spheres of radius t about codewords are disjoint (Figure 1.4).

This means that if t or fewer errors occur, the received vector **v** is in a sphere of radius t about a unique, closest codeword **u**. We decode **v** to **u**.   Q.E.D.

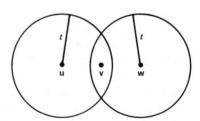

Figure 1.3 $\mathbf{v} \in S_t(\mathbf{u}) \cap S_t(\mathbf{w})$.

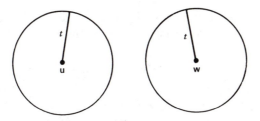

Figure 1.4 Disjoint spheres about codewords.

Note that Theorem 2 holds for nonlinear codes also if we substitute minimum distance for minimum weight in the theorem's statement. There is no distinction between the two concepts for linear codes.

Thus, given n and k, we want a code with a d as large as possible since such a code can intrinsically correct more errors. Such codes are hard to find.

Recall that we determined that $d = 3$ for the Hamming $(7, 4)$ code so, by Theorem 2, it can correct $[(3 - 1)/2] = 1$ error. We also knew this since we have an elegant algorithm, Hamming decoding, for correcting single errors. Theorem 2 does not give such an algorithm. The decoding method we could use is to list all the codewords, compare the received word to the listed codewords, and decode to the closest codeword. As we saw in Section 1.1, there are good codes with too many codewords to list by hand. Some of these could be listed in a computer and then the comparisons would be done by computer. However, there are usually more efficient ways to decode. Also, some practical codes are too large for this table lookup method to be at all feasible. A main concern of coding theory is devising efficient decoding algorithms. In some practical situations codes are used that do not have the highest possible d but that can be decoded easily.

If $[(d - 1)/2]$ or fewer errors have occurred, the received vector $\mathbf{v}$ will be in a sphere of radius $[(d - 1)/2]$ about a unique codeword. If more errors have occurred, there could be several codewords at a smallest distance from $\mathbf{v}$. If we need to decode every received vector, we could choose any one of these and decode $\mathbf{v}$ to it. This is called *complete decoding*. We may have to do this when no feedback is available, as with data stored on magnetic tape or when communicating with a satellite. Another decoding technique is to decode only those received messages that have $[(d - 1)/2]$ or fewer errors and detect the others. This is called *incomplete decoding*. Perhaps retransmission can be requested if feedback is available. What is done depends on the practical situation.

If $\mathbf{u}$ and $\mathbf{v}$ are binary vectors, we let $\mathbf{u} * \mathbf{v}$ denote the number of 1's $\mathbf{u}$ and $\mathbf{v}$ have in common. The following is a very useful fact.

$$wt(\mathbf{u} + \mathbf{v}) = wt(\mathbf{u}) + wt(\mathbf{v}) - 2(\mathbf{u} * \mathbf{v}).$$

We call a code C *self-orthogonal* if $C \subset C^{\perp}$. C_2 is a self-orthogonal code. All weights in a binary self-orthogonal code are even as every vector must be orthogonal to itself. If we add an overall parity check to all the vectors in the Hamming $(7, 4)$ code, we obtain an $(8, 4)$ code called the extended Hamming code, which has the following generator matrix.

$$\begin{pmatrix} 1 & 0 & 0 & 0 & 0 & 1 & 1 & 1 \\ 0 & 1 & 0 & 0 & 1 & 0 & 1 & 1 \\ 0 & 0 & 1 & 0 & 1 & 1 & 0 & 1 \\ 0 & 0 & 0 & 1 & 1 & 1 & 1 & 0 \end{pmatrix}.$$

This code is self-orthogonal as we can see from the following theorem.

Theorem 3. If the rows of a generator matrix G for a binary (n, k) code C have even weight and are orthogonal to each other, then C is self-orthogonal, and conversely.

If the rows of a generator matrix G for a ternary (n, k) code C' have weights divisible by 3 and are orthogonal to each other, then C' is self-orthogonal, and conversely.

Proof. We want to show that every vector in C is orthogonal to itself and that any two vectors in C are orthogonal to each other. Note first that each row of G is orthogonal to itself since it has even weight. Any two rows are orthogonal to each other by assumption. Let $\mathbf{u}$ and $\mathbf{v}$ be any two (possibly equal) vectors in C. Then each is a linear combination of the rows of G and $\mathbf{u} \cdot \mathbf{v} = 0$ by the linearity of the inner product. The proof for C' is similar.

Theorem 4. If the rows of a generator matrix G for a binary (n, k) code C have weights divisible by 4 and are orthogonal to each other, then C is self-orthogonal and all weights in C are divisible by 4.

Proof. By Theorem 3, C is self-orthogonal. The only thing to show is that all weights in C are divisible by 4. We know this for the rows of G by assumption. If $\mathbf{g}_1$ and $\mathbf{g}_2$ are rows of G, then $wt(\mathbf{g}_1 + \mathbf{g}_2) = wt(\mathbf{g}_1) + wt(\mathbf{g}_2) - 2(\mathbf{g}_1 * \mathbf{g}_2)$. Since $\mathbf{g}_1 * \mathbf{g}_2$ is even because $\mathbf{g}_1$ and $\mathbf{g}_2$ are orthogonal to each other, $wt(\mathbf{g}_1 + \mathbf{g}_2)$ is divisible by 4. The theorem now holds by finite induction on the number of rows in the expression of a vector as a linear combination of rows of G.

Please note that the codes described as $C_1, C_2, \ldots$ are listed in the index.

PROBLEMS

1. Which types of errors can the overall parity check code detect?

2. If **x** is in the Hamming code and is transmitted with no errors, which numbers in binary do $\mathbf{x} \cdot \mathbf{a}$, $\mathbf{x} \cdot \mathbf{b}$, and $\mathbf{x} \cdot \mathbf{c}$ form?

3. Using Hamming decoding, decode the message $(0, 1, 1, 1, 0, 0, 1)$.

4. We have a B.S.C. with $q = .90$ and $p = .10$. We have messages consisting of three digits encoded by repeating them twice and decoded by majority count. What is the probability of receiving the message correctly without any coding? With the coding described? (Look at all the errors this code can correct.)

5. Answer Problem 4 if $q = .99$ and $p = .01$. Compare your answer to Problem 4.

6. If C is the $(3, 1)$ binary code whose only nonzero vector is **h**, compute P_{err} for any symbol error probability p. Evaluate P_{err} for $p = .01$. How many errors can C detect?

7. Answer Problem 6 if C is the $(5, 1)$ binary code whose only nonzero vector is **h**.

8. How many codewords does an (n, k) ternary code have?

9. How many codewords does an (n, k) code over $GF(q)$ have?

10. List all the codewords in C_1.

11. Give at least three information sets for C_1.

12. Give generator and parity check matrices for the code in Section 1.1 that detects single errors, that is, the code that has four information digits that are repeated.

13. Give generator and parity check matrices for the binary code consisting of all even weight vectors of length 8.

14. Give parity check equations for the $(6, 3)$ binary code C_3 with generator matrix G.

$$G = \begin{pmatrix} 1 & 0 & 0 & 0 & 1 & 1 \\ 0 & 1 & 1 & 0 & 0 & 1 \\ 0 & 0 & 1 & 1 & 1 & 0 \end{pmatrix}.$$

What is the matrix H corresponding to these equations?

15. Give a parity check matrix for the $(7, 4)$ Hamming code.

16. Why does Hamming decoding work?

17. Show that in a binary code either all the vectors have even weight or
half have even weight and half have odd weight.

18. Show that in a binary self-orthogonal code, either all the vectors have
weight divisible by 4 or half have even weight, not divisible by 4, and
half have weight divisible by 4.

19. Show that in a binary (n, k) code with no column of 0's, the set of all
codewords that are 0 in a fixed column is an $(n, k - 1)$ code.

20. If C is an (n, k) binary code with a generator matrix that has no
column of 0's, show that the sum of all the weights of codewords in C
is $n \cdot 2^{k-1}$.

21. Verify the triangle inequality, that is, $d(\mathbf{u}, \mathbf{w}) \le d(\mathbf{u}, \mathbf{v}) + d(\mathbf{v}, \mathbf{w})$ for
all $\mathbf{u}$, $\mathbf{v}$, and $\mathbf{w}$ in V.

22. Find the weight distribution of C_2.

23. If C is a ternary self-orthogonal code, show that $A_i = 0$ unless 3
divides i.

24. Is it possible to find eight binary vectors of length 6 so that $d(\mathbf{u}, \mathbf{v}) \ge 3$
for any two of them?

25. Is it possible to find nine binary vectors of length 6 so that $d(\mathbf{u}, \mathbf{v}) \ge 3$
for any two of them?

26. Find the weight distribution of the extended Hamming $(8, 4)$ code.

2

Useful Background

2.1 SYNDROME DECODING

We have seen one decoding method that is applicable to every code. This is the complete code listing method described after Theorem 2. We also saw Hamming decoding, which is designed for only one code, the Hamming $(7, 4)$ code. Hamming decoding is a more efficient way of decoding the Hamming code than the complete listing since it requires the computation of three inner products whereas the listing method entails 16 comparisons. The storage requirements are also different as the listing method requires storing 16 codewords while Hamming decoding needs only the vectors $\mathbf{a}$, $\mathbf{b}$, and $\mathbf{c}$. In general, decoding schemes designed for specific codes are more efficient than decoding schemes that can be used for any code. Syndrome decoding is a decoding scheme that can be used for any code but it is often more efficient than the complete listing method. If we devise a decoding scheme for a specific code or for a family of codes, a scheme that looks efficient, it is a good idea to compare it with syndrome decoding.

We have until now regarded a code C as a vector subspace of a space of n-tuples V. However, it can be easily seen that V is an abelian group under addition and that C is a subgroup. For syndrome decoding and other coding purposes, the *cosets* of a code are needed. If C is an (n, k) code over $GF(q)$ and $\mathbf{a}$ is in V, the *coset* of C, determined by $\mathbf{a}$ and denoted by $\mathbf{a} + C$, is $\{\mathbf{a} + \mathbf{c} | \mathbf{c} \in C\}$. This is the coset of C that contains $\mathbf{a}$. There is some coset of C containing any $\mathbf{v} \in V$; for example, $\mathbf{v} + C$ contains $\mathbf{v}$. If $\mathbf{a}$ is in C, $\mathbf{a} + C$ is just C. A coset can be represented by any element in it in the sense that if $\mathbf{b}$ is in $\mathbf{a} + C$, then $\mathbf{a} + C = \mathbf{b} + C$ since $\mathbf{b} = \mathbf{a} + \mathbf{c}$ for some $\mathbf{c}$ in C. The proofs of the following facts about cosets are left for Problem 1.

   (i) Every coset of C has the same number of elements as C does.

   (ii) Any two cosets are either disjoint or identical.

(iii) V is the union of all the cosets of C.

(iv) C has q^{n-k} cosets. In particular, a binary (n, k) code has 2^{n-k} cosets.

Consider a received vector $\mathbf{y}$ and express it as $\mathbf{x} + \mathbf{e}$, where $\mathbf{x}$ is a codeword and $\mathbf{e}$ is an error vector. Then $\mathbf{y}$ is in some coset of C and this coset contains all expressions $\mathbf{e} = \mathbf{y} - \mathbf{x}$ where $\mathbf{x}$ is in C. If we choose a vector $\mathbf{e}$ of smallest weight in this coset and decode $\mathbf{y}$ to $\mathbf{x} = \mathbf{y} - \mathbf{e}$, then $\mathbf{x}$ will be a vector in C closest to $\mathbf{y}$. There can be several vectors of smallest weight in this coset and any one of them can be chosen. We call a vector of smallest weight in a coset a *coset leader*. We can restate maximum-likelihood decoding in these terms. Given a received vector $\mathbf{y}$, pick a coset leader $\mathbf{e}$ in $\mathbf{y} + C$. Decode $\mathbf{y}$ to $\mathbf{x} = \mathbf{y} - \mathbf{e}$. This can be clarified by use of the standard array. The *standard array* of a code is defined to be a table of vectors whose rows are the cosets of C arranged as follows. The first row is C itself with the zero vector in the first column. The first entry of any other row (i.e., any other coset) contains a coset leader and the remainder of the row is constructed by adding this leader to the codewords in the first row to obtain the other vectors in the coset. Each element in the coset is placed in the column of the codeword it came from.

We illustrate this with the standard array for a binary code C whose generator matrix is

$$G = \begin{pmatrix} 1 & 0 & 1 & 0 \\ 0 & 1 & 1 & 1 \end{pmatrix}.$$

Hence H can be taken to be the parity check matrix,

$$H = \begin{pmatrix} 1 & 1 & 1 & 0 \\ 0 & 1 & 0 & 1 \end{pmatrix}.$$

The first row consists of the codewords with the zero vector first (Table 2.1). The other codewords are listed in any order. Then we choose a coset leader for the first coset. If $(1, 0, 0, 0)$ is not in the code, this would be a good choice. This is then added to the codewords to get the entire row. We can continue choosing vectors of weight 1 as coset leaders if they have not appeared in any previous coset. This is enough for C, but for other codes

Table 2.1   Standard Array for C

		Coset Leaders			
Codewords	+	0 0 0 0	1 0 1 0	0 1 1 1	1 1 0 1
Other Cosets		1 0 0 0	0 0 1 0	1 1 1 1	0 1 0 1
		0 1 0 0	1 1 1 0	0 0 1 1	1 0 0 1
		0 0 0 1	1 0 1 1	0 1 1 0	1 1 0 0

we could have leaders of weight 2, 3, and so on. The standard array can be used for decoding as follows. Locate the received vector $\mathbf{y}$ in the standard array. Decode $\mathbf{y}$ to the codeword $\mathbf{x}$ at the top of the column. We see that $\mathbf{e}$, the coset leader, is the error vector. Since we have decoded $\mathbf{y}$ to a closest vector $\mathbf{x}$, this is maximum-likelihood decoding.

If C is a binary code of length 100, then the standard array would consist of 2^{100} entries, which we would have to store and search through to locate a received y. The use of the syndromes eliminates many of these entries.

Let H be a parity check matrix of an (n, k) code C with rows $\mathbf{h}_1, \ldots, \mathbf{h}_{n-k}$. If $\mathbf{y}$ is any vector in V, the *syndrome* of $\mathbf{y}$ is defined to be the column vector

$$\text{syn}(\mathbf{y}) = \begin{pmatrix} \mathbf{y} \cdot \mathbf{h}_1 \\ \vdots \\ \mathbf{y} \cdot \mathbf{h}_{n-k} \end{pmatrix} = \mathbf{y} H^T$$

of height $n - k$.

Theorem 5. Every vector in a fixed coset has the same syndrome. Vectors in different cosets have different syndromes. All possible q^{n-k} syndromes occur as syndromes of some vectors.

Proof. If $\mathbf{a} + C$ is a coset of C, two elements in $\mathbf{a} + C$ can be written as $\mathbf{a} + \mathbf{c}_1$ and $\mathbf{a} + \mathbf{c}_2$ with $\mathbf{c}_1$ and $\mathbf{c}_2$ in C. Then $(\mathbf{a} + \mathbf{c}_1 \cdot \mathbf{h}_i) = (\mathbf{a} \cdot \mathbf{h}_i) = (\mathbf{a} + \mathbf{c}_2 \cdot \mathbf{h}_i)$, for each row $\mathbf{h}_i$ of H so that vectors in the same coset have the same syndrome. Suppose $\mathbf{a} + \mathbf{c}_1$ and $\mathbf{b} + \mathbf{c}_2$ are in distinct cosets and they have the same syndrome. Then $(\mathbf{a}, \mathbf{h}_i) = (\mathbf{b}, \mathbf{h}_i)$ for all i where $1 \leq i \leq n - k$ so that $\mathbf{a} - \mathbf{b}$ is orthogonal to all rows of H and hence is in C. But this would mean that $\mathbf{a}$ and $\mathbf{b}$ are in the same coset. This contradiction shows distinct cosets have distinct syndromes. Since there are q^{n-k} distinct cosets, there are q^{n-k} distinct syndromes. These are all possible vectors with $n - k$ components from $GF(q)$.   Q.E.D.

We give now the four syndromes of C preceded by their coset leaders:

$$(0,0,0,0) \quad \begin{pmatrix} 0 \\ 0 \end{pmatrix}$$

$$(1,0,0,0) \quad \begin{pmatrix} 1 \\ 0 \end{pmatrix}$$

$$(0,1,0,0) \quad \begin{pmatrix} 1 \\ 1 \end{pmatrix}$$

$$(0,0,0,1) \quad \begin{pmatrix} 0 \\ 1 \end{pmatrix}.$$

Note that the syndrome of $(1, 0, 0, 0)$ is the first column of H, that of $(0, 1, 0, 0)$ the second column, and that of $(0, 0, 0, 1)$ the fourth column of H.

Theorem 6.   If C is a binary code and $\mathbf{e}$ is any vector, the syndrome of $\mathbf{e}$ is the sum of those columns of H where $\mathbf{e}$ has nonzero components.

Proof.   This is immediate from the definition of syndrome.   Q.E.D.

If there is a single error, the syndrome will be that column of H corresponding to the error.

We are now ready to define *syndrome decoding*. We choose a set of coset leaders of an (n, k) code C and list them with their syndromes. Since all the vectors in a coset have the same syndrome, this list contains all possible q^{n-k} syndromes. In practice, we do not have to write down a standard array. The code itself has the zero vector as its syndrome and we can use the zero vector as coset leader. We can then choose vectors of weight 1 as coset leaders. We compute their syndromes. Whenever we get a new syndrome, we have a new coset leader. When we finish with vectors of weight 1 and there are more coset leaders, we go on to see if vectors of weight 2 can be coset leaders. Thus each time we get a new syndrome, we put it in the list with the coset leader of weight i that gave rise to it. After we complete the vectors of weight i, we continue with vectors of weight $i + 1$ until we reach our q^{n-k} syndromes. To decode a received vector $\mathbf{y}$, compute syn($\mathbf{y}$); locate this in the syndrome list. Subtract the coset leader $\mathbf{e}$ corresponding to this syndrome from $\mathbf{y}$. Decode $\mathbf{y}$ as $\mathbf{y} - \mathbf{e} = \mathbf{x}$.

Theorem 7.   Syndrome decoding is a maximum-likelihood decoding scheme.

Notice how our storage requirements have dropped from the ones needed for, say, a binary $(100, 60)$ code. For syndrome decoding, we store 2^{40} coset leaders and their syndromes. This is quite a saving over 2^{60} items. It is also easier to search through 2^{40} syndromes rather than through 2^{60} vectors. If we need a complete decoding algorithm, we can decode each received vector as described. If our code has minimum weight d and $t = [(d - 1)/2]$, an alternative incomplete decoding scheme would be to decode all vectors whose coset leaders have weight t or less, and detect otherwise. For example, if we have a code with minimum weight 5, then we can be confident about correcting all errors of weights 1 and 2 and we might be able to correct some errors of weight 3. If our need for reliability is very great and we are able to retransmit, we could ask for all other messages to be retransmitted. If we can tolerate some errors of weight 3 or more, which are after all very unlikely, or if retransmission is impractical, we can use the complete decoding algorithm.

We can define the *weight* of a *coset* to be the weight of its coset leader, which is the smallest weight of any vector in the coset. The code itself has coset weight 0. We define the *coset weight distribution* of a code to be the set of numbers $\{a_i\}$ where a_i is the number of cosets of weight i.

We can compute the probability P of correctly decoding a message using syndrome decoding in terms of the a_i since a message is decoded correctly whenever the coset leader is the actual error vector. Thus for an (n, k) binary code transmitted over a B.S.C.,

$$P = \sum_{i=0}^{n} a_i q^{n-i} p^i.$$

It is useful to know the binomial coefficients. For $n \geq r > 0$ the number of subsets of size r of a set of size n is the *binomial coefficient* $\binom{n}{r}$, pronounced n choose r, and equals $n!/((n - r)!r!)$. The number of binary vectors of length n and weight r is $\binom{n}{r}$. Binomial coefficients can also be used to calculate the probability of correctly receiving a message such as in Problem 1.4.

2.2   PERFECT CODES, HAMMING CODES, SPHERE-PACKING BOUND

In Theorem 2 we showed that spheres of radius $t = [(d - 1)/2]$ about codewords in a code of minimum weight d are disjoint. It is possible that there could be vectors in V that are not contained in any of these spheres. As we shall see, this is what usually happens. For any specific code this is easy to determine. Consider C_3 (in Problem 1.14) a binary $(6, 3, 3)$ code; let us count the number of vectors in a sphere of radius $t = [(3 - 1)/2] = 1$ about codewords. The sphere about the zero vector contains this vector and the six vectors of weight 1 for a total of seven vectors. Note that a sphere about any other codeword c has the same number of vectors as the sphere about the zero vector since each vector in this sphere can be obtained by adding c to a vector in the zero sphere. Since there are $2^3 = 8$ vectors in C, there are eight spheres so that there are $7 \cdot 8$ vectors in V in these spheres. Since there are $2^6 = 64$ vectors in V, there are eight vectors outside these spheres (which vectors are they?).

A code C of minimum weight d is called *perfect* if all the vectors in V are contained in the spheres of radius $t = [(d - 1)/2]$ about the codewords. In this case the spheres are said to cover the space.

A perfect code can correct all patterns of t or fewer errors and no pattern of more than t errors. For their n and k, they are the best codes. They are also mathematically interesting structures so people have spent much time looking for them. Before giving the results of this search, we identify the perfect codes we know and describe new ones.

The binary Hamming $(7, 4, 3)$ code is perfect. This is immediate since 2^3 (the number of vectors in a sphere of radius 1 about a codeword) times 2^4 (the number of codewords) equals 2^7, the total number of vectors in V. Two other codes that are known to be perfect are the binary Golay $(23, 12, 7)$ code and the ternary Golay $(11, 6, 5)$ code (see Problems 18 and 19). The *trivial perfect codes* are the whole space or a binary repetition code of odd length.

We have already seen several ways of showing that the $(7, 4, 3)$ Hamming code is single-error-correcting. One way is by observing that the columns of its parity check matrix are distinct; in fact they are all the nonzero binary triples. If we regard these columns as numbers in binary and list them by their numerical values, the resulting syndrome decoding scheme with this parity check matrix yields Hamming decoding.

We can use this observation to construct an infinite family of binary, single-error-correcting codes. These are known as the general Hamming codes. For each r there is a *general* binary *Hamming code*, denoted $Ham(r, 2)$, whose parity check matrix has as columns all nonzero binary r-tuples. We can order the columns by the numerical values of the r-tuples thought of as binary representations of integers. Any other ordering would give an equivalent code. Note that the parity check matrix of $Ham(3, 2)$ is given by the vectors $\mathbf{a}$, $\mathbf{b}$, and $\mathbf{c}$ in Section 1.1. Clearly each $Ham(r, 2)$ is a single-error-correcting code as the vectors of weight 1 have distinct syndromes, the columns of its parity check matrix. It can be easily shown to be a binary $(2^r - 1, 2^r - 1 - r, 3)$ code.

There is an entirely analogous definition of a general Hamming code over $GF(q)$; here we take one of the $q - 1$ nonzero multiples of a nonzero vector for a column of a parity check matrix of $Ham(r, q)$. For example, one parity check matrix for $Ham(3, 3)$ is

$$H = \begin{pmatrix} 1 & 0 & 0 & 1 & 1 & 1 & 1 & 0 & 0 & 1 & 1 & 1 & 1 \\ 0 & 1 & 0 & 1 & 2 & 0 & 0 & 1 & 1 & 1 & 1 & 2 & 2 \\ 0 & 0 & 1 & 0 & 0 & 1 & 2 & 1 & 2 & 1 & 2 & 1 & 2 \end{pmatrix}.$$

Theorem 8. The general Hamming $((q^r - 1)/(q - 1) = n, n - r, 3)$ codes over $GF(q)$ are perfect single-error-correcting codes.

Proof. Each is a single-error-correcting code because every vector of weight 1 is in a distinct coset. They are perfect because $(n(q - 1) + 1)(q^{n-r}) = q^n$ where $n(q - 1) + 1$ is the number of vectors in a sphere of radius 1 about a codeword and q^{n-r} is the number of spheres. Q.E.D.

Note that once we know the Hamming codes are single-error-correcting codes, we know that they are perfect and hence $d = 3$.

If we were to look for perfect codes, where would we look? Since all the vectors in the space must be contained in spheres about codewords, the values n, k, and d have to satisfy certain constraints. It is not reasonable to look for a perfect code of any length n. The first thing to do is to find these constraints. To do this, we again count the number of vectors in a sphere, multiply by the number of spheres, and set this equal to the number of vectors in the space. This proves Theorem 9.

Theorem 9. In order for a perfect t-error-correcting binary (n, k) code to exist, the numbers n, k, and t must satisfy the following equation.

$$\left(\binom{n}{0} + \binom{n}{1} + \cdots + \binom{n}{t}\right)2^k = 2^n.$$

In order for a perfect t-error-correcting (n, k) code over $GF(q)$ to exist, the numbers n, k, and t must satisfy the following equation.

$$\left(\binom{n}{0} + (q - 1)\binom{n}{1} + \cdots + (q - 1)^t\binom{n}{t}\right)q^k = q^n.$$

Consider now for which parameters a binary perfect code could exist. If $t = 1$, we have $(1 + n)2^k = 2^n$ so that $n = 2^{n-k} - 1$. Letting $r = n - k$, we have the parameters $n = 2^r - 1$, $k = 2^r - 1 - r$, and of course $d = 3$, which are satisfied by $\text{Ham}(r, 2)$. So for this family of possible parameters, we have perfect codes with these parameters. If $t = 2$, we have $\left(1 + n + \binom{n}{2}\right)2^k = 2^n$ so that $1 + n + \binom{n}{2} = 2^{n-k}$. The first n for which $1 + n + \binom{n}{2}$ is a power of 2 is $n = 5$. A perfect code with these parameters is the $(5, 1, 5)$ trivial code. The second n for which $1 + n + \binom{n}{2}$ is a power of 2 is $n = 90$ and it can be shown [chap. 9] that there is no perfect code of length 90. If $t = 3$, a sphere contains $1 + n + \binom{n}{2} + \binom{n}{3}$ points and this is a power of 2 for $n = 23$. It is believed that Marcel Golay noticed this and then proceeded with the difficult demonstration that a binary $(23, 12, 7)$

code exists. The same thing presumably happened when he noticed that $1 + 2n + 4\binom{n}{2}$ is a power of 3 for $n = 11$ and constructed the perfect Golay ternary $(11, 6, 5)$ code. He demonstrated all this and more in a one-page paper [35].

If we have any (n, k, d) code C, then either C is perfect or there are vectors outside the spheres of radius t about the codewords. This proves the next theorem.

Theorem 10 (The Sphere-Packing Bound). If C is an (n, k, d) code over $GF(q)$, then

$$\left(\binom{n}{0} + (q-1)\binom{n}{1} + \cdots + (q-1)^t\binom{n}{t}\right)q^k \le q^n.$$

Hence given n and k, this equation bounds t and so bounds d.

It is an interesting fact that no new multiple-error-correcting perfect codes are possible. This may be easier to believe in light of the somewhat surprising fact that the existence of a perfect code is connected to the existence of integral roots of the Lloyd polynomial [12]. The entire situation is described in Theorem 11 even though it is too difficult to prove here.

Theorem 11. The only nontrivial multiple-error-correcting perfect codes are equivalent to either the binary $(23, 12, 7)$ code or the ternary $(11, 6, 5)$ code. The only nontrivial single-error-correcting perfect codes have the parameters of the Hamming codes.

The fact that the only multiple-error-correcting perfect codes and the only nontrivial single-error-correcting perfect codes have the parameters of the Golay codes and Hamming codes, respectively, was proven by Tietäväinen [29] after much work on these problems by van Lint. The fact that codes with the Golay parameters are equivalent to the Golay codes was proven by Pless [21].

2.3 THE PACKING RADIUS, THE COVERING RADIUS, M.D.S. CODES, AND SOME BOUNDS

We define the *packing radius* t to be the largest among the numbers s where the spheres of radius s about codewords are disjoint.

Theorem 12.   The packing radius t has the following properties.

  (i) If C has minimum weight d, $t = [(d - 1)/2]$.

  (ii) t is the largest among the numbers s so that each vector of weight $\leq s$ is a unique coset leader.

Proof.   Let $t' = [(d - 1)/2]$. We know that spheres of radius t' about codewords are disjoint by Theorem 2. We want to show now that spheres of any larger radius are not. It is enough to show that spheres of radius $t' + 1$ are not disjoint. Let $\mathbf{u}$ be a vector in C of weight d. Suppose first that d is even and let $\mathbf{x}$ be a vector with $d/2$ nonzero components agreeing with some $d/2$ nonzero components in $\mathbf{u}$. Then $\mathbf{x} \in S_{(t'+1)}(\mathbf{u}) \cap S_{(t'+1)}(\mathbf{0})$ since $t' + 1 = d/2$. If d is odd, let $\mathbf{x}$ have $(d + 1)/2$ nonzero components in common with $\mathbf{u}$. Then $d(\mathbf{x}, \mathbf{u}) = (d - 1)/2 = t'$ and $d(\mathbf{x}, \mathbf{0}) = (d + 1)/2 = t' + 1$ so that $\mathbf{x} \in S_{(t'+1)}(\mathbf{u}) \cap S_{(t'+1)}(\mathbf{0})$. Hence $t = t'$.

Problem 20 shows that any vector of weight $\leq t$ is a unique coset leader. When d is even, it is enough to show that there are two vectors of weight $t + 1$ in the same coset. This is the content of Problem 21. When d is odd and $\mathbf{u}$ is a vector in C of weight d, let $\mathbf{x}$ be a vector of weight $t + 1$, which agrees with $\mathbf{u}$ on $t + 1$ nonzero components. Then $\mathbf{y} = \mathbf{u} - \mathbf{x}$ is in the same coset as $-\mathbf{x}$ and has weight t so that $-\mathbf{x}$ is not a coset leader.   Q.E.D.

We define the *covering radius r* to be the smallest number s so that spheres of radius s about codewords cover V.

Theorem 13.   The covering radius has the following properties.

  (i) r is the weight of the coset of largest weight.

  (ii) r is the smallest among the numbers s so that every syndrome is a combination of s or fewer columns of any parity check matrix.

Proof.   Suppose $\mathbf{x}$ is a coset leader of weight greater than r. Then $d(\mathbf{c}, \mathbf{x}) = wt(\mathbf{x} - \mathbf{c})$ is greater than r for all $\mathbf{c}$ in the code. Thus $\mathbf{x}$ cannot be in any sphere of radius r about a codeword. Conversely let a be the weight of the coset leader of greatest weight. We show that spheres of radius a about codewords cover the space since then r must be less than or equal to a. If these spheres do not cover the space, then there is a vector $\mathbf{y}$ whose distance from all codewords is greater than a. But $\mathbf{y}$ must be in some coset with coset leader $\mathbf{x}$. Hence $\mathbf{y} = \mathbf{x} + \mathbf{c}$ for some $\mathbf{c}$ in the code. Now $d(\mathbf{y}, \mathbf{c}) = d(\mathbf{x} + \mathbf{c}, \mathbf{c}) = wt(\mathbf{x})$, which does not exceed a by assumption.

To prove (ii) we note that the syndrome corresponding to a coset leader of weight i is a combination of i columns of any parity check matrix. Hence (ii) follows from (i).   Q.E.D.

If $t = r$, the code is perfect. As we saw, there are only two (up to equivalence) multiple-error-correcting perfect codes.

If $t + 1 = r$, the code is called *quasi-perfect*. With a quasi-perfect code we can correct all errors of weight t or less and some of weight $t + 1$. So these are very practical codes and we can recover from our despair at the paucity of perfect codes as there are many quasi-perfect codes.

The following theorem is quite useful.

Theorem 14.   If $\mathbf{u}$ is a vector in C of weight s, then there is a dependence relation among s columns of any parity check matrix of C and conversely any dependence relation among s columns of a parity check matrix of C yields a vector of weight s in C.

Proof.   Let H be a parity check matrix of C. Since $\mathbf{u}$ is orthogonal to each row of H, the s components in $\mathbf{u}$ that are nonzero are the coefficients of the dependence relation of the s columns of H corresponding to the s nonzero components. The converse holds by the same reasoning.   Q.E.D.

Using this theorem, we can obtain some information about the minimum weight in C by looking at the columns of a parity check matrix H. For example, H has no zero columns if and only if C has no vectors of weight 1. For a binary code the columns of H are all distinct iff no two add to zero, so any dependence must include at least three columns; thus $d \geq 3$. We have seen this fact before in syndrome decoding. If C is over $GF(q)$, then $d \geq 3$ means that no two columns of H are multiples of each other. This provides another proof that the Hamming codes have minimum weight 3.

Corollary 1. C has minimum weight d iff d is the largest number so that every $d - 1$ columns of any parity check matrix H of C are independent.

Corollary 2.   If C has minimum weight d, then C can detect all errors of weight $\leq d - 1$.

Proof.   Let H be a parity check matrix of C. By Corollary 1, every $d - 1$ columns of H are independent. Let a received vector $\mathbf{y} = \mathbf{c} + \mathbf{e}$ where $\mathbf{c}$ is in C and $\mathbf{e}$ is an error vector of smallest weight. If this weight is $\leq d - 1$, then syn($\mathbf{y}$) = syn($\mathbf{e}$) $\neq 0$ and we have detected an error of weight $\leq d - 1$.

Q.E.D.

Corollary 3. If C has minimum weight $2(t + 1)$, we can simultaneously correct all errors of weight t or less and detect all errors of weight $t + 1$.

Proof. A syndrome decoding scheme will correct any error of weight t or less. As a vector of weight $t + 1$ cannot be in a sphere of radius t about a codeword, any error of weight $t + 1$ will be detected. Although some errors of weight greater than $t + 1$ may be detected, we cannot be sure of this as some might wind up in one of our spheres.   Q.E.D.

Corollary 4. $n - k \geq d - 1$ (Singleton bound).

Proof. This holds because the rank of H is $n - k$.   Q.E.D.

An (n, k, d) code having the largest possible minimum weight $d = n - k + 1$ is called a *maximum distance separable* code or an *M.D.S. code*. These codes are related to many interesting combinatorial constructions [15].

The $(4, 2, 3)$ ternary code C_1 is an M.D.S. code.

Theorem 15. If C is an (n, k, d) code, then every $(n - d + 1)$ coordinate positions contain an information set. Furthermore, d is the largest number with this property.

Proof. Let G be a generator matrix for C and let S be a set of $(n - d + 1)$ coordinate positions. Suppose that S does not contain an information set. Consider the matrix A whose columns are those columns of G labeled by the numbers in S. A is a $kx(n - d + 1)$ matrix whose rank is less than k by the assumption (since the row rank of A equals its column rank) that no k columns are independent. Hence there is a dependence relation among the rows of A, which we denote by $\mathbf{a}_1, \ldots, \mathbf{a}_k$. There are scalars $\alpha_1, \ldots, \alpha_k$ not all zero so that $\alpha_1 \mathbf{a}_1 + \cdots + \alpha_k \mathbf{a}_k = 0$. Let $\mathbf{g}_1, \ldots, \mathbf{g}_k$ be the rows of G and consider the vector $\mathbf{x} = \alpha_1 \mathbf{g}_1 + \alpha_2 \mathbf{g}_2 + \cdots + \alpha_k \mathbf{g}_k$. Notice that $\mathbf{x}$ is in C and has 0's in all the positions in S so that $wt(\mathbf{x}) \leq n - (n - d + 1) = d - 1$. This contradiction proves the first statement of the theorem. If $\mathbf{u}$ is a vector in C of weight d, then the $n - d$ positions where $\mathbf{u}$ is 0 cannot contain an information set since the rank of the submatrix of G with these positions as columns is less than k.   Q.E.D.

Corollary 1.   Every k positions in an M.D.S. code is an information set.

Corollary 2.   The dual of an M.D.S. code C is again an M.D.S. code.

Proof.   By Corollary 1, every k positions of C is an information set. Regarding a generator matrix of C as a parity check matrix of $C^\perp$, Corollary 1 to Theorem 14 tells us that $C^\perp$ has minimum weight $k + 1$. For $C^\perp$ to be an M.D.S. code we need to know that $n - (n - k) = k = (k + 1) - 1$.   Q.E.D.

We have already seen some bounds, the sphere-packing bound and the Singleton bound, both of which can be viewed as bounding d given n and k. The next bound is somewhat different. Here we construct a code C with minimum weight d and with fewer than or equal to m redundancy positions, that is, $m \geq n - k$. We obtain a C with as large an n as possible so that these properties hold. Let us consider binary codes first. We start with d and m and attempt to construct a parity check matrix H for C. The columns of H are binary m-tuples chosen so that no $d - 1$ columns are dependent. This is enough, by the corollary to Theorem 14, to insure that C has minimum weight d. Our method is to choose as many m-tuples as we can so that no $d - 1$ are dependent. The number of these m-tuples is then n. We choose any nonzero m-tuple as the first column. The second m-tuple can be any one ($\neq 0$) distinct from the first. Suppose that we have chosen a set S of i m-tuples so that no $d - 1$ are dependent. Then we can choose another m-tuple if one is available. So we count the number of unqualified m-tuples. These are all the m-tuples that are linear combinations of $d - 2$-tuples in S and their number is $\binom{i}{1} + \binom{i}{2} + \cdots + \binom{i}{d-2} = s$. We can choose another m-tuple if a nonzero one is available, which will be the case if $s < 2^m - 1$ since $d - 1$ columns are dependent iff one of these columns is a linear combination of the remaining $d - 2$ columns. Hence if $i = n - 1$, we will be able to choose an nth m-tuple. The matrix H will then be the parity check matrix of a code of length n with minimum weight at least d and with dimension at least $k = n - m$. This last holds since the rank of H is less than or equal to m as it has m rows. This proves the following theorem for the binary case. The proof for the general case is analogous.

Theorem 16   (Varshamov-Gilbert Bound).   There exists a binary code of length n, minimum distance d or more, and dimension $k \geq n - m$, whenever

$$\binom{n-1}{1} + \binom{n-1}{2} + \cdots + \binom{n-1}{d-2} < 2^m - 1.$$

There exists a code over $GF(q)$ of length n, minimum distance d or more, and dimension $k \geq n - m$, whenever

$$(q - 1)\binom{n - 1}{1} + (q - 1)^2\binom{n - 1}{2} + \cdots + (q - 1)^{d-2}\binom{n - 1}{d - 2} < q^m - 1.$$

This is an optimistic theorem as it says that for any minimum weight d and redundancy m there is a code of length n that can correct $[(d - 1)/2]$ errors and has dimension greater than or equal to $n - m$. It is similar to Shannon's theorem in this sense. It is also similar in that the procedure implicit in the proof for finding such a code is not usable in practice.

One of the fundamental problems in coding theory can be viewed as constructing the largest number of vectors of length n whose mutual distance is d or more. Naturally this problem has been studied for both linear and nonlinear codes and this largest number for binary codes is denoted by $A(n, d)$. We have actually been looking at this inadvertently for some values of n and d. In fact, Problems 24 and 25 in Chapter 1 (if done correctly) show that $A(6, 3) = 8$. The code achieving this bound just consists of 8 vectors and need not be linear but in fact there is a linear $(6, 3, 3)$ code, C_3. The Varshamov–Gilbert theorem for linear codes gives us the following bound on $A(n, d)$.

Corollary. If k is the largest integer so that $2^k < 2^n / \sum_{i=0}^{d-2}\binom{n - 1}{i}$ then $A(n, d) \geq 2^k$.

In order to give you a feeling for the values of $A(n, d)$ we give the following table. This table is Table 9.1 from the recent book [33] by Conway and Sloane.

Some of the codes in the table are linear and some are not. We can detect some nonlinear ones at a glance, for example $A(9, 4) = 20$ and as 20 is not a power of 2, these 20 vectors are not in any linear code. If the entry is a power of 2 it does not mean that there must be a linear code realizing that $A(n, d)$. We will see an example of this in 10.3. Where the value of $A(n, d)$ is not known, bounds are given. Thus $72 \leq A(11, 4) \leq 79$.

Table 2.2 lists only even values of d, however odd values of d can also be found from the following fact.

Fact. If d is odd, $A(n - 1, d - 1) = A(n, d)$.

Proof. Suppose we have a set S of M vectors of length $n - 1$ whose minimum distance is $d - 1$. If two vectors are distance $d - 1$ apart, then

Table 2.2 $A(n,d)$ for $n \leq 24$ and $d \leq 10$

n	$d = 4$	$d = 6$	$d = 8$	$d = 10$
6	4	2	1	1
7	8	2	1	1
8	16	2	2	1
9	20	4	2	1
10	40	6	2	2
11	72–79	12	2	2
12	144–158	24	4	2
13	256	32	4	2
14	512	64	8	2
15	1024	128	16	4
16	2048	256	32	4
17	2720–3276	256–340	36–37	6
18	5248–6552	512–680	64–74	10
19	10496–13104	1024–1288	128–144	20
20	20480–26208	2048–2372	256–279	40
21	36864–43690	2560–4096	512	40–48
22	73728–87380	4096–6942	1024	48–88
23	147456–173784	8192–13774	2048	64–150
24	294912–344636	16384–24106	4096	128–280

Source: Conway and Sloane [33, Table 9.1].

one must have odd weight and the other even weight since $d - 1$ is odd. Add an overall parity check to the vectors in S. Then two vectors which were distance $d - 1$ apart will be at distance d from each other. Hence we have a set of M vectors of length n whose minimum distance is d showing that $A(n - 1, d - 1) \leq A(n, d)$.

Suppose now that we have a set of M vectors of length n and minimum distance d. Find two vectors x and y which are distance d apart. Find a coordinate in which x and y differ and delete this coordinate. Then we get a set of M vectors of length $n - 1$ and minimum distance $d - 1$. Hence $A(n, d) \leq A(n - 1, d - 1)$.   Q.E.D.

2.4 SELF-DUAL CODES, THE GOLAY CODES

As we noted before, if C is an (n, k) code, the dual code $C^{\perp}$ is an $(n, n - k)$ code. From this and the fact that $C^{\perp \perp} \supseteq C$, it follows that $C^{\perp \perp} = C$. We defined a code to be self-orthogonal if it is contained in its dual code. An example of a binary self-orthogonal $(7, 3)$ code is C_4 given by the following generator matrix.

$$G = \begin{pmatrix} 0 & 0 & 0 & 1 & 1 & 1 & 1 \\ 0 & 1 & 1 & 0 & 0 & 1 & 1 \\ 1 & 0 & 1 & 0 & 1 & 0 & 1 \end{pmatrix}.$$

Theorem 3 tells us that C_4 is self-orthogonal. Indeed, the weight distribution of C_4 is $A_4 = 7$, $A_0 = 1$. Then $C_4^{\perp}$ is a $(7, 4)$ code and it is easy to see that $C_4^{\perp}$ is the code generated by C_4 and $\mathbf{h}$ (the all-one vector).

Theorem 17. If C is a binary $(n, (n - 1)/2)$ self-orthogonal code, for odd n, then $C^{\perp}$ is the $(n, (n + 1)/2)$ code generated by C and $\mathbf{h}$.

Proof. We know that $C^{\perp}$ is an $(n, (n + 1)/2)$ code and it contains C by assumption. Since all weights in C are even, $\mathbf{h}$ is in $C^{\perp}$.   Q.E.D.

A code C is called *self-dual* if $C = C^{\perp}$. In this case n must be even and C must be an $(n, n/2)$ code. An example of a binary self-dual code is C_5, which is the $(8, 4)$ code whose generator matrix G is formed from a parity check matrix of C_4 by adding an overall parity check.

$$G = \begin{pmatrix} 1 & 1 & 1 & 1 & 1 & 1 & 1 & 1 \\ 0 & 0 & 0 & 1 & 1 & 1 & 1 & 0 \\ 0 & 1 & 1 & 0 & 0 & 1 & 1 & 0 \\ 1 & 0 & 1 & 0 & 1 & 0 & 1 & 0 \end{pmatrix}.$$

Again we see that C_5 is self-orthogonal, hence self-dual. So G is also a parity check matrix of C_5.

We have already seen a ternary self-dual code, namely C_2.

Theorem 18. If C is a self-dual code with generator matrix $(I|A)$, then C also has $(-A'|I)$ as a generator matrix.

Proof. This is because any parity check matrix of C is a generator matrix of $C^{\perp} = C$.   Q.E.D.

If n is even, a self-dual $(n, n/2)$ binary code exists. This can be seen because it is possible to construct one (see Problem 25). However, this is not so for ternary self-dual codes. We state the following theorem without proof [21].

Theorem 19. A self-dual $(n, n/2)$ ternary code exists iff n is divisible by 4.

A binary self-dual code C is called *doubly even* if $A_i = 0$ unless i is divisible by 4. By Theorem 4 we see that the extended Hamming $(8, 4)$ code is doubly even.

We state the following theorem without proof [7].

Theorem 20. A doubly even $(n, n/2)$ code exists iff n is divisible by 8.

As an application of these ideas, we define the Golay codes. We give the binary $(24, 12)$ Golay code by a generator matrix $G = (I|A)$ where I is the 12×12 identity matrix and A is the 12×12 matrix given below. The blanks denote 0's.

$$
A = \begin{pmatrix}
 & 1 & 1 & 1 & 1 & 1 & 1 & 1 & 1 & 1 & 1 & 1 \\
1 & 1 & 1 &   & 1 & 1 & 1 &   &   &   & 1 &   \\
1 & 1 &   & 1 & 1 & 1 &   &   &   & 1 &   & 1 \\
1 &   & 1 & 1 & 1 &   &   &   & 1 &   & 1 & 1 \\
1 & 1 & 1 & 1 &   &   &   & 1 &   & 1 & 1 &   \\
1 & 1 & 1 &   &   &   & 1 &   & 1 & 1 &   & 1 \\
1 & 1 &   &   &   & 1 &   & 1 & 1 &   & 1 & 1 \\
1 &   &   &   & 1 &   & 1 & 1 &   & 1 & 1 & 1 \\
1 &   &   & 1 &   & 1 & 1 &   & 1 & 1 & 1 &   \\
1 &   & 1 &   & 1 & 1 &   & 1 & 1 & 1 &   &   \\
1 & 1 &   & 1 & 1 &   & 1 & 1 & 1 &   &   &   \\
1 &   &   & 1 & 1 &   & 1 & 1 & 1 &   &   & 1
\end{pmatrix}.
$$

The construction of A will be more natural after we study finite fields. By Theorem 4, we know that C is doubly even so that the weight of any nonzero vector is divisible by 4.

We would like to find the minimum weight d of C. At first glance this looks quite difficult. We cannot list the 2^{12} vectors in C by hand and count their weights. Note that $A^t = A$ so that $G' = (A|I)$ is also a generator matrix for C. We look at G again and compute the weights of the rows of G. The first row has weight 12 and all the others have weight 8. Since C is doubly even, either $d = 4$ or $d = 8$. We now look at weights of sums of two rows of G. If the first row is one of the vectors, the sum has weight 8. We see this instantly since any row of A other than the first, has six 1's in the last 11 positions and a 1 in the first position. To find the sum of any other two rows we need only look at the second row of G and take its sum with each of the remaining ten rows (why?). These vectors are also seen to have weight 8. Now a nice thing happens. We do not have to form the combinations of the rows in G three at a time because we can show that such a combination cannot have weight 4. Suppose not. Then there is an $\mathbf{x}$ in C of the form $\mathbf{x} = (\mathbf{y}, \mathbf{z})$ where $\mathbf{y}$ and $\mathbf{z}$ are of length 12 and $wt(\mathbf{y}) = 3$, $wt(\mathbf{z}) = 1$. But G' is also a basis of C and a vector such as $\mathbf{x}$ would have to be a row of G' but no row of G' has weight 4. No combination of four vectors of G can have weight 4 (why?). We do not have to consider combinations of five or more vectors as they would necessarily have weight 8 or higher. Hence $d = 8$ and C is a triple-error-correcting code.

We obtain the Golay (23, 12) code by removing a column of G. Although it is not obvious, no matter which column of G we remove, we get an equivalent code. This is not true for all codes. The Golay code has minimum weight 7 and is a triple-error-correcting code.

If C is an (n, k) binary code with odd weight vectors, then the code we obtain by adding an overall parity check is an $(n + 1, k)$ code called the *extended C*. This process is called *extending C*.

Note that the extended C has only even weight vectors.

If C is an (n, k) code for n even, then the code we obtain by removing a column of a generator matrix of C is called a *punctured C*. This process is called *puncturing C*. Note that for a given C, it is possible that puncturing at different columns give inequivalent codes. The punctured code has length $n - 1$ and dimension k or $k - 1$. If C has minimum weight d, the punctured code usually has minimum weight $d - 1$, but could conceivably have minimum weight d.

The binary extended Hamming code is a $(2^r, 2^r - 1 - r, 4)$ code. The dual of this code, called a first order Reed–Muller code (see 10.4), is an important $(2^r, r + 1)$ code.

If C is an (n, k, d) code, a *shortened code C'* of C is the set of all codewords in C which are 0 in a fixed position with that position deleted. If the deleted position had ones in it, C' is an $(n - 1, k - 1, d')$ code with $d' \geq d$. Note that C_4 is a shortened code of C_5. A shortened code of the $(2^r, 2^r - 1 - r, 4)$ extended Hamming code and the $(2^r - 1, r + 1)$ punctured first-order Reed–Muller code are duals of each other.

We obtained the Golay (23, 12) code C' by puncturing the Golay (24, 12) code C. Alternatively we could have started with a definition of C' and obtained C as its extension.

Golay also discovered a ternary (12, 6) Golay C with a generator matrix $G = (I|A)$ where A is as follows.

$$A = \begin{pmatrix} 0 & 1 & 1 & 1 & 1 & 1 \\ 1 & 0 & 1 & 2 & 2 & 1 \\ 1 & 1 & 0 & 1 & 2 & 2 \\ 1 & 2 & 1 & 0 & 1 & 2 \\ 1 & 2 & 2 & 1 & 0 & 1 \\ 1 & 1 & 2 & 2 & 1 & 0 \end{pmatrix}.$$

By Theorem 3, C is self-orthogonal, hence self-dual. The fact that $d = 6$ is left for Problem 27.

PROBLEMS

1. Prove the four numbered facts about cosets given in Section 2.1.

2. How many errors can C_2 (the code constructed after Theorem 1 in Chapter 1) correct?

3. Construct a standard array for the code C_3 (Problem 1.14). For each coset give its syndrome.

4. Using the constructions of Problem 3, decode the received vectors $y_1 = (0, 1, 1, 0, 1, 1)$ and $y_2 = (0, 0, 0, 1, 0, 0)$ for C_3.

5. Find a pattern of 2 errors in C_3 which your standard array decoding scheme will correct and find a pattern of 2 errors which it will not correct.

6. Compute the coset weight distribution of C_3.

7. Calculate the probability of correctly decoding a message in C_3 using syndrome decoding if $q = .9$ and $p = .1$. What is the probability of receiving a message correctly (for the same p and q) if no coding is used?

8. If C is the $(3, 1)$ repetition code, compute P_{err} for any symbol error probability p. Evaluate P_{err} for $p = .01$. How many errors can this code detect?

9. Answer problem 8 if C is the $(5, 1)$ repetition code.

10. What can you say about the coset weight distribution of a $(20, 12)$ double-error-correcting binary code?

11. Show that a binary code can correct all single errors iff any parity check matrix has distinct nonzero columns.

12. The code Ham$(4, 2)$ has the following parity check matrix H.

$$H = \begin{pmatrix} 0 & 0 & 0 & 0 & 0 & 0 & 0 & 1 & 1 & 1 & 1 & 1 & 1 & 1 & 1 \\ 0 & 0 & 0 & 1 & 1 & 1 & 1 & 0 & 0 & 0 & 0 & 1 & 1 & 1 & 1 \\ 0 & 1 & 1 & 0 & 0 & 1 & 1 & 0 & 0 & 1 & 1 & 0 & 0 & 1 & 1 \\ 1 & 0 & 1 & 0 & 1 & 0 & 1 & 0 & 1 & 0 & 1 & 0 & 1 & 0 & 1 \end{pmatrix}.$$

Decode the vectors $y_1 = (1,1,1,0,1,1,1,0,0,0,0,0,0,0,0)$ and $y_2 = (1,1,0,0,1,1,0,0,1,1,0,0,1,1,1)$ for Ham(4, 2).

13. Is there a $(12, 7, 5)$ binary code?

14. Construct a standard array for the ternary Hamming $(4, 2, 3)$ code. Here $q = 3$ and $r = 2$.

15. Using the parity check matrix H given below, devise a decoding scheme for the extended Hamming $(8, 4)$ code that is analogous to Hamming decoding. Correct as many errors as you can and detect as many errors as you can detect (but cannot correct).

$$H = \begin{pmatrix} 1 & 1 & 1 & 1 & 1 & 1 & 1 & 1 \\ 0 & 0 & 0 & 1 & 1 & 1 & 1 & 0 \\ 0 & 1 & 1 & 0 & 0 & 1 & 1 & 0 \\ 1 & 0 & 1 & 0 & 1 & 0 & 1 & 0 \end{pmatrix}.$$

16. Devise a decoding scheme for Ham(3, 3).

17. Find the coset weight distribution of the Hamming single-error-correcting code of length $2^r - 1$.

18. Prove that any binary $(23, 12, 7)$ code is perfect.

19. Prove that any ternary $(11, 6, 5)$ code is perfect.

20. If C has minimum weight d, prove that any vector of weight $t = [(d - 1)/2]$ or less is a unique coset leader.

21. If d is the minimum weight of a code C, $t = [(d - 1)/2]$, and d is even, show that there are two vectors of weight $t + 1$ in some coset of C.

22. Show that the only binary M.D.S. codes are the whole space, E_n, or its dual the repetition code.

23. Show that every two columns of any generator matrix of C_4 are distinct.

24. The $(23, 12)$ Golay code C is the dual of a self-orthogonal $(23, 11)$ code. If the weight distribution of $C^\perp$ is $A_0 = 1$, $A_8 = 506$, $A_{12} = 1288$, and $A_{16} = 253$, what is the weight distribution of C?

25. Give a generator matrix of a $(10, 5)$ binary self-dual code.

26. Find a code C such that at least two of its punctured codes are not equivalent.

27. Show that the ternary $(12, 6)$ Golay code has minimum weight 6.

28. If C is an (n, k) binary linear code, show that its extended code C' is also a linear code. If H is a parity check matrix of C, construct a parity check matrix of C'.

29. Describe a generator matrix of the first-order Reed–Muller $(2^r, r + 1)$ code.

30. Show that the $(2^r - 1, 2^r - 1 - r, 3)$ Hamming code and a shortened code of the $(2^r, r + 1)$ first-order Reed–Muller code are duals of each other.

3

A Double-Error-Correcting B.C.H. Code and a Finite Field of 16 Elements

3.1 THE PROBLEM

We have seen the efficient decoding scheme for the Hamming $(7,4)$ code and we have constructed an infinite family of single-error-correcting codes H_r. The binary rth Hamming code is a $(2^r - 1, 2^r - 1 - r, 3)$ code and can be decoded by Hamming decoding, that is, by choosing a parity check matrix so that the syndrome of any received vector gives the position in error in binary. Inspired by Hamming decoding, much effort has gone into constructing double-error-correcting codes with decoding similar to Hamming decoding. The jump from single-error-correcting to double-error-correcting was quite difficult and consumed a decade's worth of effort with a result that is considerably more complex [2, 5]. In order to see the problems involved, we make that attempt now.

How might we try to construct binary double-error-correcting codes of length $n = 2^r - 1$? If we want decoding analogous to Hamming decoding, we would start with the construction of a parity check matrix H. As we would need more redundancy than a parity check matrix of $\mathrm{Ham}(r, 2)$ has, we could begin by doubling the number of rows of this matrix. We start with $r = 4$ and a parity check matrix with eight rows. Keeping $\mathrm{Ham}(4, 2)$ in mind, we choose the first four rows to be the numbers 1 through 15 in binary.

$$
H = \begin{pmatrix}
0 & 0 & & 1 \\
0 & 0 & & 1 \\
0 & 1 & \cdots & 1 \\
1 & 0 & & 1 \\
f(1) & f(2) & & f(15)
\end{pmatrix},
$$

where $f(1), f(2), \ldots, f(15)$ represent the binary 4-tuples under the numbers $1, 2, \ldots, 15$, respectively. These remain to be chosen. If we have two errors in columns i and j, then the syndrome of the received vector is

$$\begin{pmatrix} i + j \\ f(i) + f(j) \end{pmatrix},$$

the sum of columns i and j of H. Let $y_1 = i + j$ and $y_2 = f(i) + f(j)$. We want to choose f so that we can solve for i and j given y_1 and y_2. In order to do this, we need to be able to do arithmetic with binary 4-tuples so that we can solve equations. It would be very useful to be able to add, subtract, multiply, and divide 4-tuples, in other words, to make the 4-tuples into a field with 16 elements.

A *field F* is, by definition, a set of elements with two operations $+$ and $\cdot$ satisfying the following properties.

(i) F is closed under $+$ and $\cdot$, that is, $\alpha + \beta$ and $\alpha \cdot \beta$ are in F whenever α and β are in F.

For all α, β, and γ in F, the following laws hold.

(ii) *Commutative laws.* $\alpha + \beta = \beta + \alpha$ and $\alpha\beta = \beta\alpha$.

(iii) *Associative laws.* $\alpha + (\beta + \gamma) = (\alpha + \beta) + \gamma$ and
$$\alpha(\beta\gamma) = (\alpha\beta)\gamma.$$

(iv) *Distributive law.* $\alpha(\beta + \gamma) = \alpha\beta + \alpha\gamma$.

Furthermore, there are identity elements 0 and 1 for addition and multiplication, respectively.

(v) $\alpha + 0 = 0 + \alpha = \alpha$ and $\alpha \cdot 1 = 1 \cdot \alpha = \alpha$.

There are inverses also.

(vi) For any α in F, there is an element $(-\alpha)$ in F so that $\alpha + (-\alpha) = (-\alpha) + \alpha = 0$. For any $\alpha \neq 0$ in F there is an element (α^{-1}) in F so that $\alpha(\alpha^{-1}) = (\alpha^{-1})\alpha = 1$.

We can regard F as having the four operations $+$, $-$, $\cdot$, and $\div$ where $-$ and $\div$ are given by (vi) with the understanding that $\alpha - \beta = \alpha + (-\beta)$ and $\alpha \div \beta = \alpha(\beta^{-1})$ for $\beta \neq 0$. The rational numbers and the real numbers are examples of fields with an infinite number of elements. We are interested here only in finite fields, that is fields that have a finite number of elements. If p is a prime, the integers with the operations $+, -, \times, \div$ performed modulo p constitute a field. The elements in this field may be written as $\{0, 1, 2, \ldots, p - 1\}$. We have already seen the field of two elements $\{0, 1\}$ with $1 + 1 = 0$ and the field of three elements $\{0, 1, 2\}$ with $1 + 2 = 0$.

An element $\alpha \neq 0$ is called a *divisor of zero* if $\alpha\beta = 0$ for some $\beta \neq 0$. It is an easy exercise (Problem 2) to show that a field has no divisors of zero.

Before constructing the field of 16 elements, we need more tools.

3.2 POLYNOMIALS

By definition, a *polynomial* $f(x)$ is an expression of the form $f(x) = \alpha_0 + \alpha_1 x + \cdots + \alpha_n x^n$ where the α_i are elements in some field F. We call the elements of F scalars. The *degree* of $f(x)$ is the largest n such that $\alpha_n \neq 0$. A polynomial of degree n is called *monic* if $\alpha_n = 1$. Polynomials can be added, subtracted, multiplied, and divided in the usual fashion.

We illustrate this with the following binary polynomials.

$$x^4 + x^3 + x + 1 = (x^3 + x^2 + 1) + (x^4 + x^2 + x)$$
$$(x^2 + x + 1)(x^2 + 1) = x^4 + x^3 + x + 1.$$

If we wish to divide $x^5 + x^3 + x^2 + 1 = a(x)$ by $x^4 + x^3 + 1 = b(x)$, we write the following.

$$
\begin{array}{r}
x + 1 \\
x^4 + x^3 + 1 \overline{\big)\, x^5 + x^3 + x^2 + 1} \\
\underline{x^5 + x^4 + x } \\
x^4 + x^3 + x^2 + x + 1 \\
\underline{x^4 + x^3 + 1} \\
x^2 + x
\end{array}
$$

Hence $(x^5 + x^3 + x^2 + 1) = (x^4 + x^3 + 1)(x + 1) + (x^2 + x)$ or $a(x) = b(x)s(x) + r(x)$ where $s(x) = x + 1$ and $r(x) = x^2 + x$.

A polynomial is said to be *irreducible* if it has no divisors except scalar multiples of itself and scalars. As we shall see, monic irreducible polynomials act like prime numbers.

Recall the division algorithm for integers. If a and b are two positive integers, then there are unique integers s and r so that $a = bs + r$ where $0 \leq r < b$.

The *Division algorithm* for polynomials is as follows. We consider polynomials with coefficients in a field F. If $a(x)$ and $b(x) \neq 0$ are polynomials, then there are unique polynomials $s(x)$ and $r(x)$ so that $a(x) = b(x)s(x) + r(x)$ where the degree of $r(x)$ is less than the degree of $b(x)$. An instance of this is given by the last example.

The greatest common divisor of two positive integers a and b, denoted by g.c.d.(a, b), is that positive integer c that divides both a and b and is such that if d divides a and b, then d must divide c.

If $a(x)$ and $b(x)$ are polynomials over a field F, then the *greatest common divisor* of $a(x)$ and $b(x)$, denoted by g.c.d.$(a(x), b(x))$, is that monic polynomial $c(x)$ that divides both $a(x)$ and $b(x)$ and is such that if $d(x)$ divides $a(x)$ and $b(x)$, then $d(x)$ must divide $c(x)$.

The *least common multiple* of $a(x)$ and $b(x)$, denoted by l.c.m.$(a(x), b(x))$, is the multiple of both of smallest degree.

Another algorithm that is valid for both integers and polynomials is the Euclidean algorithm. For integers this says that given two integers a and b, there are integers c and d so that $ac + bd =$ g.c.d.(a, b).

The *Euclidean algorithm* for polynomials over a field F is as follows. Given $a(x)$ and $b(x)$, there are polynomials $c(x)$ and $d(x)$ so that $a(x)c(x) + b(x)d(x) =$ g.c.d.$(a(x), b(x))$.

We illustrate the Euclidean algorithm with the binary polynomials $a(x)$, $b(x)$, $s(x)$, and $r(x)$ in our previous example. We had $a(x) = b(x)s(x) + r(x)$. Similarly we can compute $x^4 + x^3 + 1 = (x^2 + x)x^2 + 1$, or in other words, $b(x) = r(x)s_1(x) + r_1(x)$ where $s_1(x) = x^2$ and $r_1(x) = 1$. Continuing, we have $r(x) = r_1(x)s_2(x)$ where $s_2(x) = x^2 + x$. Our series of equations is as follows.

    (i) $a(x) = b(x)s(x) + r(x)$.

    (ii) $b(x) = r(x)s_1(x) + r_1(x)$.

    (iii) $r(x) = r_1(x)s_2(x)$.

Note that any common divisor of $a(x)$ and $b(x)$ divides $r(x)$ by (i), hence $r_1(x)$ by (ii). But by (iii), $r_1(x)$ divides $r(x)$ and so divides $b(x)$ and $a(x)$ by (ii) and (i). So the greatest common divisor of our $a(x)$ and $b(x)$ is $r_1(x) = 1$.

There is a general procedure analogous to this for finding the greatest common divisor of any two polynomials. The process consists of dividing appropriate polynomials until a remainder of 0 results. The previous remainder is the greatest common divisor. Of course, the number of steps in the process varies, but it must terminate since the degree of each new remainder is strictly less than the degree of the dividend (the older remainder).

This process, which finds the greatest common divisor of polynomials $a(x)$ and $b(x)$, can be reversed to find the polynomials $c(x)$ and $d(x)$ in the Euclidean algorithm with $a(x)c(x) + b(x)d(x) = \text{g.c.d.}(a(x), b(x))$. We illustrate this with our example.

$$r_1(x) = b(x) - r(x)s_1(x) \qquad \text{by (ii)}$$
$$= b(x) + (b(x)s(x) - a(x))s_1(x) \qquad \text{by (i)}$$
$$= b(x)(1 + s(x)s_1(x)) + a(x)(-s_1(x))$$

so that $c(x) = -s_1(x) = s_1(x)$ since in binary $-$ is $+$, and $d(x) = 1 + s(x)s_1(x)$. Replacing these by the actual polynomials, we have

$$1 = (x^5 + x^3 + x^2 + 1)x^2 + (x^4 + x^3 + 1)(x^3 + x^2 + 1),$$

which can be checked by hand. As with the process for finding the greatest common divisor, this method can be made into a rigorous proof of the Euclidean algorithm.

If a prime p divides ab, then either p divides a or p divides b. We now show that if an irreducible monic polynomial $f(x)$ divides $g(x)h(x)$, then either $f(x)$ divides $g(x)$ or $f(x)$ divides $h(x)$. If $f(x)$ does not divide $g(x)$, then $\text{g.c.d.}(f(x), g(x)) = 1$ and by the Euclidean algorithm we have $1 = c(x)f(x) + d(x)g(x)$. Multiplying by $h(x)$, we have $h(x) = c(x)f(x)h(x) + d(x)g(x)h(x)$ and, since $f(x)$ divides the right side, it must divide $h(x)$, the left side.

It is known that every natural number can be expressed as a product of prime powers. The analogous theorem is true for monic irreducible polynomials. The proof of this theorem is Problem 9.

Theorem 21. Every monic polynomial over a field F can be expressed uniquely as a product of irreducible monic polynomials over F.

If $f(x)$ is a polynomial over a field F, $\alpha \in F$, and $f(\alpha) = 0$, then α is called a *root* of $f(x)$.

Theorem 22. If $f(x)$ is a polynomial over a field F, then α is a root of $f(x)$ iff $f(x) = g(x)(x - \alpha)$.

Proof. Clearly if $f(x) = g(x)(x - \alpha)$, then $f(\alpha) = 0$. For any α, by the division algorithm, we can write $f(x) = (x - \alpha)b(x) + r(x)$ where the degree of $r(x)$ is less than 1. Hence $r(x)$ is a constant that must be 0 since $r(\alpha) = 0$.   Q.E.D.

Corollary. A polynomial over a field F of degree n has at most n distinct roots.

Just as we can consider integers modulo an integer, we can consider *polynomials modulo some polynomial* $f(x)$. As usual, our polynomials are all over the same field. We say that $a(x)$ is *congruent* to $b(x)$ modulo $f(x)$, denoted by $a(x) \equiv b(x)$ (modulo $f(x)$), iff there is a $c(x)$ with $a(x) = c(x)f(x) + b(x)$. If $a(x)$ is given and we consider all $b(x)$ so that $a(x) \equiv b(x)$ (modulo $f(x)$), then there is a unique polynomial $c(x)$ of degree less than $f(x)$ so that $a(x) \equiv c(x)$ (modulo $f(x)$) (Problem 11). The congruence relation satisfies the following properties whose proofs are left to the Problems.

Suppose that $a(x) \equiv c(x)$ (modulo $f(x)$) and $b(x) \equiv d(x)$ (modulo $f(x)$); then we have the following.

(i) $a(x) \pm b(x) \equiv c(x) \pm d(x)$ (modulo $f(x)$).

(ii) $a(x)b(x) \equiv c(x)d(x)$ (modulo $f(x)$).

3.3 A FINITE FIELD OF 16 ELEMENTS

We return to the problem of making a field out of the 16 binary 4-tuples. It seems natural to let 0000 be 0 (using the usual addition) and 0001 be 1. We let the 4-tuples correspond to polynomials of degree less than 4 with coefficients in the field of two elements. Then it is reasonable to let 0010 correspond to x, 0100 correspond to x^2, and 1000 correspond to x^3. We can already add 4-tuples so let us keep that, and we can multiply some 4-tuples together by our choice of x and its powers. Let us now list the 16 4-tuples and see what we have and what we are missing. We first list the 4-tuple, then its corresponding polynomial next to it.

0000						1000	x^3					
0001						1001	x^3				$+$	1
0010		x				1010	x^3			$+$ x		
0011		x	$+$	1		1011	x^3			$+$ x	$+$	1
0100	x^2					1100	x^3	$+$	x^2			
0101	x^2		$+$	1		1101	x^3	$+$	x^2		$+$	1
0110	x^2	$+$	x			1110	x^3	$+$	x^2 $+$ x			
0111	x^2	$+$	x	$+$	1	1111	x^3	$+$	x^2 $+$ x	$+$	1

We can add any two 4-tuples and multiply some together. For example, $(x + 1)x^2 = x^3 + x^2$, so $0011 \cdot 0100 = 1100$ but what is $(x^2 + 1)x^2 = x^4 + x^2$? Our trouble here is that we do not know which 4-tuple x^4 is. Aside from these difficulties, we have to check that each nonzero element has a multiplicative inverse. We cannot do this. However, there is a way out. We can take our polynomials modulo a polynomial $f(x)$, which we can choose to be $x^4 + x^3 + 1$, of degree 4. As $f(x) \equiv 0$ (modulo $f(x)$), $x^4 = -x^3 - 1 = x^3 + 1$ over the binary field so whenever we see an x^4 we replace it with $x^3 + 1$. Then $(x^2 + 1)x^2 = x^4 + x^2 = x^3 + 1 + x^2 = x^3 + x^2 + 1$. We can also multiply $x^2 + 1$ by x^3. This is $(x^2 + 1)x^3 = x^5 + x^3 = x^4 + x + x^3 = x^3 + 1 + x + x^3 = x + 1$. We see that we can now multiply any two 4-tuples, but do we have inverses? The answer is yes if $f(x)$ is irreducible. We can see this by using the Euclidean algorithm. If $a(x)$ is a polynomial of degree less than 4 and $f(x)$ is an irreducible polynomial of degree 4, then g.c.d.$(a(x), f(x)) = 1$ and thus there are polynomials $c(x)$ and $d(x)$ so that $a(x)c(x) + f(x)d(x) = 1$. Hence $a(x)c(x) \equiv 1$ (modulo $f(x)$) and we know that there is a unique polynomial $c'(x)$ (which may be $c(x)$ if its degree is less than 4) of degree less than 4 so that $a(x)c'(x) \equiv 1$ (modulo $f(x)$) (see Problem 11). Then $c'(x)$ is the inverse of $a(x)$.

The polynomial $f(x) = x^4 + x^3 + 1$ is irreducible over the field of two elements. This can be seen if we try to factor $f(x)$. If it factors, there would have to be either a factor of degree 1 or a factor of degree 2. By Theorem 22, $f(x)$ has a factor of degree 1 iff it has a root in the binary field. As $f(0) = f(1) = 1$, f has no factor of degree 1. By Problem 7, we know all the irreducible, binary polynomials of degree 2 and we can compute that none of them is a factor of $f(x)$ because $(x^2 + x + 1)^2$ does not equal $f(x)$.

We can now compute the inverse of any of our 4-tuples. For example, if we want the inverse of $x^3 + 1$, we could consider the equation $(x^3 + 1)(\alpha_3 x^3 + \alpha_2 x^2 + \alpha_1 x + \alpha_0) = 1$ and solve the four equations we get by equating the coefficients of the various powers of x on each side of the equation for α_3, α_2, α_1, and α_0. There is an easier way in this case.

We have constructed a field of 16 elements, which we denote by $GF(16)$. We rewrite its table now to make it easier to find multiplicative inverses and to multiply two elements in general. We let α be a root of $f(x) = x^4 + x^3 + 1$ in $GF(16)$ so that $\alpha^4 = \alpha^3 + 1$ and we compute the powers of α and α^i. We see that $\alpha^5 = \alpha^3 + \alpha + 1$, $\alpha^6 = \alpha^4 + \alpha^2 + \alpha = \alpha^3 + \alpha^2 + \alpha + 1$. The new table (Table 3.1) of $GF(16)$ has three columns, the first giving the 4-tuple, the second giving the powers of α arranged in increasing order, and the third giving α^i as a polynomial in α of degree ≤ 3. Note that $\alpha^{15} = 1$.

If we wish to compute the inverse of $\alpha^3 + 1$, we note that $\alpha^3 + 1 = \alpha^4$ and $\alpha^4 \cdot \alpha^{11} = \alpha^{15} = 1$ so that $(\alpha^3 + 1)^{-1} = \alpha^{11} = \alpha^3 + \alpha^2 + 1$. The second column is useful for multiplying and dividing, the third for adding. We

Table 3.1   *GF*(16) Where α Is a Root of the Irreducible
Polynomial $f(x) = x^4 + x^3 + 1$

1	2	3						
0000	0							0
0001	1							1
0010	α					α		
0100	α^2			α^2				
1000	α^3	α^3						
1001	α^4	α^3					$+$	1
1011	α^5	α^3			$+$	α	$+$	1
1111	α^6	α^3	$+$	α^2	$+$	α	$+$	1
0111	α^7			α^2	$+$	α	$+$	1
1110	α^8	α^3	$+$	α^2	$+$	α		
0101	α^9			α^2			$+$	1
1010	α^{10}	α^3			$+$	α		
1101	α^{11}	α^3	$+$	α^2			$+$	1
0011	α^{12}					α	$+$	1
0110	α^{13}			α^2	$+$	α		
1100	α^{14}	α^3	$+$	α^2				

switch from one column to another whenever it is useful to do so. This table should be used when doing arithmetic in *GF*(16). Another useful fact is that $(a(x))^2 = a(x^2)$ for any polynomial $a(x)$ over the binary field. Thus $(x + 1)^2 = x^2 + 1$ and $(x + 1)^4 = x^4 + 1$.

This construction of *GF*(16) is quite general as we shall see in the next chapter. It is possible to construct any finite field by means of an irreducible polynomial over a smaller field, and it is also possible to express all nonzero field elements as the powers of one element.

3.4 THE DOUBLE-ERROR-CORRECTING BOSE-CHAUDHURI-HOCQUENGHEM (B.C.H.) CODE

Our aim is to construct a double-error-correcting code of length 15 that we can decode efficiently. As suggested at the beginning of Section 3.1, we start with a parity check matrix H with 8 rows of the following form.

$$H = \begin{pmatrix} 1 & 2 & \cdots & 15 \\ f(1) & f(2) & \cdots & f(15) \end{pmatrix}.$$

The numbers $1, 2, \ldots, 15$ are the 4-tuples representing these numbers in binary. $f(1), \ldots, f(15)$ are the 4-tuples under $1, \ldots, 15$, and f remains to be chosen so that we can decode double errors. Recall that if $\mathbf{y}$ is a received vector with two errors in columns i and j, then the syndrome of $\mathbf{y}$,

$$\text{syn}(\mathbf{y}) = \begin{pmatrix} i + j \\ f(i) + f(j) \end{pmatrix} = \begin{pmatrix} y_1 \\ y_3 \end{pmatrix}.$$

So given y_1 and y_3, we want to solve $y_1 = i + j$ and $y_3 = f(i) + f(j)$ for i and j.

Let us consider some choices of f. The first obvious choice is to let f be the identity so that $f(i) = i$ for all i. Then $y_1 = y_3 = i + j$ and we cannot solve for i and j. We might try powers next. What if $f(i) = i^2$ for all i. Then $y_1 = i + j$ and $y_3 = i^2 + j^2$. But we are over the binary field and $i^2 + j^2 = (i + j)^2$ so that $y_3 = (i + j)^2 = y_1^2$ and we cannot solve for i and j. Well, how about $f(i) = i^3$? Then $y_1 = i + j$ and $y_3 = i^3 + j^3 = (i + j)(i^2 + ij + j^2)$ so that $y_3/y_1 = i^2 + ij + j^2 = y_1^2 + ij$. Noticing that $i + j = y_1$, and $ij = y_3/y_1 - y_1^2 = y_3/y_1 + y_1^2$, we see that i and j are roots of the equation $(x + i)(x + j) = x^2 + (i + j)x + ij = x^2 + y_1 x + (y_3/y_1 + y_1^2)$. This looks good! We know the coefficients of this quadratic equation and we can try to find its roots.

We constructed a field whose elements are the 16 4-tuples so that we could do arithmetic. Since our multiplication is easiest using powers of α, it is more convenient to rearrange the columns of H to correspond to these powers. With the choice of f to be $f(i) = i^3$, H' has the following form.

$$H' = \begin{pmatrix} 1\alpha\alpha^2 & \cdots & \alpha^{14} \\ 1\alpha^3\alpha^6 & \cdots & \alpha^{12} \end{pmatrix}.$$

If $\mathbf{y} = \mathbf{c} + \mathbf{e}$ where $\mathbf{c}$ is in the code and $\mathbf{e}$ is the error vector, then $\mathbf{y}(\alpha) = \mathbf{e}(\alpha)$ so that $y_1 = \mathbf{y}(\alpha)$. Similarly $y_3 = \mathbf{y}(\alpha^3)$. If we let $y_2 = \mathbf{y}(\alpha^2)$, then $y_2 = y_1^2$.

Suppose we have a received $\mathbf{y}$ with two errors in the third and seventh columns. Then

$$\text{syn}(\mathbf{y}) = \begin{pmatrix} \alpha^2 + \alpha^6 \\ \alpha^6 + \alpha^3 \end{pmatrix} = \begin{pmatrix} \alpha^5 \\ \alpha^7 \end{pmatrix}.$$

So we want to factor the equation $x^2 + \alpha^5 x + (\alpha^7/\alpha^5 + \alpha^{10}) = x^2 + \alpha^5 x + \alpha^8$ in $GF(16)$. In order to do this, notice that $(x + \alpha^i)(x + \alpha^j) = x^2 + (\alpha^i + \alpha^j)x + \alpha^{i+j}$. We want to find a pair i and j so that $i + j \equiv 8$ (modulo 15) and $\alpha^i + \alpha^j = \alpha^5$. It turns out that $i = 2$ and $j = 6$ works. In other cases we might have to consider $i + j = 23$ just as in high school factoring.

If no errors have occurred, then

$$\text{syn}(\mathbf{y}) = \begin{pmatrix} 0 \\ 0 \end{pmatrix}.$$

If one error has occurred, then

$$\text{syn}(\mathbf{y}) = \begin{pmatrix} \alpha^i \\ \alpha^{3i} \end{pmatrix}$$

and the error is in the $(i + 1)$st position. If two errors have occurred, then

$$\text{syn}(\mathbf{y}) = \begin{pmatrix} \alpha^i + \alpha^j \\ \alpha^{3i} + \alpha^{3j} \end{pmatrix} = \begin{pmatrix} y_1 \\ y_3 \end{pmatrix}$$

where α^i and α^j are the roots of $x^2 + y_1 x + (y_3/y_1 + y_2)$ in $GF(16)$. The errors are then in positions $i + 1$ and $j + 1$.

We are now ready to state our decoding algorithm. If $\mathbf{y}$ is received, compute $\text{syn}(\mathbf{y}) = \begin{pmatrix} y_1 \\ y_3 \end{pmatrix}$.

(i) If $\text{syn}(\mathbf{y}) = \begin{pmatrix} 0 \\ 0 \end{pmatrix}$, we say no errors have occurred.

(ii) If $\text{syn}(\mathbf{y}) = \begin{pmatrix} \alpha^i \\ \alpha^{3i} \end{pmatrix}$, $\alpha \neq 0$, then we say that there is a single error in the $(i + 1)$st position.

(iii) If $\text{syn}(\mathbf{y}) = \begin{pmatrix} y_1 \\ y_3 \end{pmatrix}$ and $y_3 \neq y_1^3$, we consider the equation $x^2 + y_1 x + (y_3/y_1 + y_2)$. If it has roots α^i and α^j, we say that there are two errors in the $(i + 1)$st and $(j + 1)$st positions.

(iv) If $\text{syn}(\mathbf{y})$ does not fall under cases (i), (ii), or (iii) above, we say we have detected more than two errors.

Instead of the polynomial above, let's consider the polynomial $(y_3/y_1 + y_2)x^2 + y_1 x + 1$. Then the inverses of the roots of this polynomial give the error locations. This is a more complicated polynomial but has the advantage that, after $\text{syn}(\mathbf{y})$ is computed, its degree equals the number of errors which have occurred.

Note that a quadratic equation over $GF(16)$ need not factor in $GF(16)$ so that case (iv) is possible.

We can write H' as a binary matrix, which we do below. We can use either form of H' for our syndrome calculations.

$$H' = \begin{pmatrix}
0 & 0 & 0 & 1 & 1 & 1 & 1 & 0 & 1 & 0 & 1 & 1 & 0 & 0 & 1 \\
0 & 0 & 1 & 0 & 0 & 0 & 1 & 1 & 1 & 1 & 0 & 1 & 0 & 1 & 1 \\
0 & 1 & 0 & 0 & 0 & 1 & 1 & 1 & 1 & 0 & 1 & 0 & 1 & 1 & 0 \\
1 & 0 & 0 & 0 & 1 & 1 & 1 & 1 & 0 & 1 & 0 & 1 & 1 & 0 & 0 \\
0 & 1 & 1 & 0 & 0 & 0 & 1 & 1 & 0 & 0 & 0 & 1 & 1 & 0 & 0 \\
0 & 0 & 1 & 1 & 0 & 0 & 0 & 1 & 1 & 0 & 0 & 0 & 1 & 1 & 0 \\
0 & 0 & 1 & 0 & 1 & 0 & 0 & 1 & 0 & 1 & 0 & 0 & 1 & 0 & 1 \\
1 & 0 & 1 & 1 & 1 & 1 & 0 & 1 & 1 & 1 & 1 & 0 & 1 & 1 & 1
\end{pmatrix}.$$

PROBLEMS

1. Show that $\alpha \cdot 0 = 0 \cdot \alpha = 0$ for all elements α in a field.

2. Show that a field does not have any divisors of zero.

3. Give multiplication and addition tables for the field of five elements.

4. Find the greatest common divisor of the following pairs of binary polynomials.

   (a) $x + 1$ and $x^3 + 1$.

   (b) $x + 1$ and $x^4 + 1$.

   (c) $x^3 + x + 1$ and $x^6 + x^5 + x^4 + x^3 + x^2 + x + 1$.

   (d) $x^7 + 1$ and $x^3 + x + 1$.

   (e) $x^4 + x^3 + x^2 + 1$ and $x^6 + x^5 + x^4 + x^3 + x^2 + x + 1$.

5. If $a(x) = x^5 + x^3 + x^2 + 1$ and $b(x) = x^4 + x^3 + 1$ are binary polynomials, find $s(x)$ and $r(x)$ in the division algorithm.

6. If $a = 126$ and $b = 60$, find g.c.d.(a, b) and express it as a linear combination of a and b.

7. List all binary, irreducible polynomials of degrees less than or equal to 5.

8. List all monic irreducible polynomials over the field of three elements of degrees less than or equal to 3.

9. Show that every monic polynomial can be expressed uniquely as a product of irreducible monic polynomials.

10. Find a polynomial that is reducible over one field and irreducible over another field.

11. Show that for each polynomial $a(x)$ there is a unique polynomial $c(x)$ of degree less than the degree of $f(x)$ such that $a(x) \equiv c(x)$ (modulo $f(x)$).

12. (a) If a, b, c, d, and f are integers such that $a \equiv c$ (modulo f) and $b \equiv d$ (modulo f), show that

   (1) $a \pm b \equiv c \pm d$ (modulo f) and

   (2) $ab \equiv cd$ (modulo f).

   (b) Prove the addition and multiplication properties of congruence given in Section 3.2.

13. Perform the following computations in $GF(16)$.

   (a) $1001 \cdot 1011 + 0101 \div 1100$.

   (b) $(1111)^{1/2} + 1101$.

   (c) $(1110)^{1/2}$.

14. If $a(x)$ is a binary polynomial, prove that $(a(x))^2 = a(x^2)$.

15. Using the double-error-correcting B.C.H. code, find the position(s) in error of vectors $\mathbf{x}$ and $\mathbf{y}$ whose syndromes are $\text{syn}(\mathbf{x}) = \begin{pmatrix} \alpha^{11} \\ \alpha^{14} \end{pmatrix}$ and $\text{syn}(\mathbf{y}) = \begin{pmatrix} \alpha^6 \\ \alpha^3 \end{pmatrix}$.

16. Using the double-error-correcting B.C.H. code, decode the following received vectors.

   (a) $\mathbf{x} = (0, 1, 0, 0, 0, 0, 0, 1, 0, 0, 0, 0, 0, 0, 0)$.

   (b) $\mathbf{y} = (1, 1, 1, 0, 1, 1, 1, 1, 1, 1, 1, 1, 1, 1, 1)$.

   (c) $\mathbf{z} = (1, 1, 0, 1, 1, 1, 1, 0, 1, 0, 1, 1, 0, 0, 1)$.

17. Find a quadratic equation over $GF(16)$ that cannot be factored.

18. Show that the binary code with parity check matrix H' is a $(15, 7, 5)$ code.

4

Finite Fields

4.1 GROUPS

As we saw in Chapter 3, finite fields are very useful tools for constructing multiple-error-correcting codes. A knowledge of finite fields is useful in order to understand the important class of cyclic codes. First we spend a short time discussing groups, as a few group theoretic concepts are needed in the theory of finite fields.

A *group* G is a set of elements and an operation, call it $*$, with the following properties.

(i) G is closed under $*$, that is, if g and h are in G, so is $g * h$.

(ii) The operation $*$ is associative.

(iii) G has an identity e so that $e * g = g * e = g$ for all g in G.

(iv) Every element g in G has an inverse, denoted by g^{-1}, so that $g * g^{-1} = g^{-1} * g = e$.

It can be shown that the identity is unique and that each element in G has a unique inverse.

A group G is called *abelian* if $g * h = h * g$ for all g and h in G. We are concerned only with abelian groups.

We have already seen many examples of groups. A code C is an abelian group where $*$ is the operation $+$. The identity element is the zero vector. If C is a binary code, then every vector is its own inverse. The definition of a field can be rephrased in terms of groups. In this way a field F is a set of elements with two operations $+$ (plus) and $\cdot$ (times) such that F is an abelian group under $+$ and the nonzero elements in F constitute an abelian group under $\cdot$ and the distributive law holds.

It is convenient in the following to regard the group operation as $\cdot$ rather than $*$. In this notation $(g * \cdots * g)$, with r, g's, would be written g^r. The results written in this way are also valid for groups written with $+$ to stand for the operation and for that situation g^r should be replaced by rg and g^{-1} by $-g$.

The *order* of a *group* is the number of elements in it, and we consider only finite groups. The *order* of an *element* g in a group G is the smallest positive number r so that $g^r = e$. Notice that an element of order r has r distinct powers $g, g^2, \ldots, g^{r-1}, g^r = e$.

A *subgroup H* of a group G is a subset of G that is also a group with the same operation as G.

Theorem 23 (Lagrange).   The order of a subgroup H of G divides the order of G.

Proof. We can define the cosets of H exactly as we defined cosets of a code and we can show that the cosets of H satisfy the same properties. Each coset of H has the same number of elements as H does, the cosets are all disjoint, and their union is all of G. This proves the theorem.

Corollary.   The order of any element g in G divides the order of G.

Proof.   The set of elements $\{ g^i | i \leq r \}$ constitutes a subgroup H of G.

If C is a binary (n, k) code in a space V of n-tuples, then V is an abelian group under $+$ and C is a subgroup. The order of V is 2^n and the order of C is 2^k, which divides 2^n. C has 2^{n-k} cosets.

A group G is called *cyclic* if it consists of an element g and its powers. The element g is called the generator of G. A cyclic group can have more than one generator. Any element g in G generates a cyclic subgroup H of G consisting of the powers of g.

Theorem 24.   If an element g has order r, then $g^s = e$ iff s is a multiple of r.

Proof.   If s is not a multiple of r, then by the division algorithm, $s = ar + b$ with $0 < b < r$. Then $g^s = g^{ar+b} = (g^r)^a g^b = g^b = e$, which contradicts the fact that r is the order of g. Clearly $g^s = (g^r)^a = e$.

Theorem 25.   If g is an element of order r, then g^s has order $r/\text{g.c.d.}(s, r)$.

The proof is left to Problem 2.

Theorem 26. If g and h are in an abelian group, g has order r, h has order s, and g.c.d.$(r, s) = 1$, then gh has order rs.

The proof is left to Problem 3.

Let us suppose that we have a finite field F. Then it has a multiplicative identity that we call 1. Consider the additive cyclic group generated by 1. Since the elements of F form a group under $+$, this is a subgroup of F and so 1 has some finite order n. This is the smallest number so that

$$\underbrace{1 + 1 + \cdots + 1}_{n \text{ times}} = 0.$$

Clearly n must be a prime p since if $n = ab = 0$, then either a or b is 0. As we have seen, in the binary field $1 + 1 = 0$ and in the field of three elements $1 + 1 + 1 = 0$.

Let $GF(p)$ denote the integers mod p. We can consider $GF(p)$ as consisting of the numbers $\{0, 1, \ldots, p - 1\}$ with the usual operations performed mod p. For example, if $p = 7$, $GF(7) = \{0, 1, 2, 3, 4, 5, 6\}$ and $3 \cdot 4 = 12 \equiv 5$ (modulo 7).

Theorem 27. If p is a prime, then the integers mod p, $GF(p)$, constitute a field. Every finite field F contains a subfield that is $GF(p)$, up to relabeling, for some prime p and $p \cdot \alpha = 0$ for every α in F.

Proof. We have seen that any finite field F contains the integers mod p for some p. We need only show that these elements constitute a field. Clearly the elements in $GF(p)$ form an abelian group under $+$. To see that they form an abelian group under $\cdot$, we need only show that every element has a multiplicative inverse. But this follows from the Euclidean algorithm for integers. If $a < p$, then g.c.d.$(a, p) = 1$ so that there are a, b, and c with $ab + pc = 1$. Hence $ab \equiv 1 \pmod{p}$ and there is an integer b' between 1 and $p - 1$ so that $b' \equiv b \pmod{p}$ and $ab' \equiv 1 \pmod{p}$. Then b' is the inverse of a.

Notice that $p\alpha = (p \cdot 1)\alpha = 0$, proving the last statement. Q.E.D.

If F contains the prime field $GF(p)$, then p is called the *characteristic* of F.

The following theorem is useful for computing in fields of characteristic p.

Theorem 28. In a field F of characteristic p, $(x \pm y)^p = x^p \pm y^p$ for any x and y (variables or elements in F).

Proof. The proof consists of expanding $(x + y)^p$ by the binomial theorem. Thus $(x + y)^p = x^p + \binom{p}{1}x^{p-1}y + \binom{p}{2}x^{p-2}y^2 + \cdots + y^p$. For $(x - y)^p$ we replace y by $-y$ in this expansion. Every term, except the first and last, is multiplied by some binomial coefficient $\binom{p}{i}$ for $i \geq 1$. Each of these can be seen to have p as a factor when multiplied out. Hence in F they are all 0 and the theorem holds.   Q.E.D.

Corollary. $(x \pm y)^{p^m} = x^{p^m} \pm y^{p^m}$.

Proof. If $m = 1$, this is the theorem. Notice that $(x + y)^{p^2} = ((x + y)^p)^p$ $= (x^p + y^p)^p = (x^{p^2} + y^{p^2})$. The corollary follows by repeating this $m - 1$ times.

The *order* of a *finite field* is the number of elements in it. Every finite field F is denoted by $GF(n)$ where n is the order of F. The letters GF stand for Galois field(s) named after their discoverer Evariste Galois (1811–1832), who died in a duel at the age of 20. We have already seen the Galois field $GF(16)$ of 16 elements, which has characteristic 2. As we shall see, every finite field has p^r elements for some prime p and we can validly call it $GF(p^r)$ since there is only one field of p^r elements up to relabeling.

4.2 THE STRUCTURE OF A FINITE FIELD

We constructed $GF(16) = GF(2^4)$ as the set of congruence classes of a polynomial of degree 4 that is irreducible over $GF(2)$. This is quite general.

If F is a field, $F[x]$ is, by definition, the set of all polynomials in x with coefficients in F with the usual addition, subtraction, and multiplication of polynomials. Clearly, $F[x]$ is a ring.

For any monic polynomial $f(x)$ of nonzero degree we let $F[x]/(f(x))$ denote the set of congruence classes of polynomials in $F[x]$ modulo $f(x)$. This is called the *ring of polynomials modulo $f(x)$*. It is a ring consisting of all polynomials whose degree is less than the degree of $f(x)$ with polynomial addition and subtraction and multiplication modulo $f(x)$.

Theorem 29. $F[x]/(f(x))$ is a field iff $f(x)$ is irreducible.

Let $f(x)$ be an irreducible polynomial of degree m over $GF(p)$. Then $F' = GF(p)[x]/(f(x))$ is a field with p^m elements. We can also regard F' as the set of polynomials in α, with the usual operations, for α a root of $f(x)$.

Proof. The only fact we have to verify to show that $F[x]/(f(x))$ is a group under times is that these polynomials have multiplicative inverses. This follows as before by the Euclidean algorithm for polynomials since $f(x)$ is irreducible.

The elements in F' can be considered as all polynomials of degree less than m with coefficients in $GF(p)$ and there are p^m such polynomials. They can also be considered as all m-tuples over $GF(p)$ and in both representations they have the usual addition and multiplication modulo $f(x)$. This is exactly analogous to the situation for $GF(16)$. Using only the additive structure, the m-tuples are the vector space of dimension m consisting of all m-tuples over $GF(p)$. This vector space has p^m elements.

When constructing $GF(16)$ we saw that we could regard that field as arising from $GF(2)$ by adjoining a root α of $x^4 + x^3 + 1$ so that $\alpha^4 + \alpha^3 + 1 = 0$. Similarly we can regard F' as being obtained from $GF(p)$ by adjoining a root of our irreducible polynomial $f(x)$. The field elements can be regarded as either polynomials modulo $f(x)$ or as polynomials in α.   Q.E.D.

Theorem 29 is a very useful theorem for constructing a finite field F. We noticed that the multiplicative group of $GF(16)$ is cyclic. This holds in general. We say that α is a *primitive* element of F if every nonzero element in F is a power of α. The order of an element in a finite field is its multiplicative order. A primitive element in a field of q elements has order $q - 1$. It is not always the case that a root of an irreducible polynomial is a primitive element. We see examples of this in $GF(16)$ in Section 4.3. An irreducible polynomial having a primitive element as a root is called a *primitive polynomial.* Once a primitive polynomial over $GF(p)$ is found of degree m, the table for F can be constructed as $GF(16)$ was constructed. Unfortunately there is no easy way to tell whether any given irreducible polynomial is primitive. That there are such is guaranteed by the next theorem.

Theorem 30. Every finite field has a primitive element.

Proof. Suppose F has q elements and let α be the element in F of greatest order, which we call r. Then $r \leq q - 1$, because the powers $\alpha, \alpha^2, \ldots, \alpha^r$ must be distinct and nonzero. Let β be some other element in F of order s. We show that s must divide r. Let $r = \prod p_i^{a_i}$ and $s = \prod p_i^{b_i}$ be the prime power decompositions of r and s. Let $a = \prod p_i^{a_i}$ if $a_i < b_i$ and let $b = \prod p_i^{b_i}$ if $b_i \leq a_i$. Then g.c.d.$(r/a, s/b) = 1$ and $rs/ab = $ l.c.m.(r, s). By Theorem 25, α^a has order r/a and β^b has order s/b. Hence by Theorem 26, $\alpha^a \beta^b$ has order $rs/ab = $ l.c.m.(r, s) and so is $\geq r$. But by the choice of α this must equal r so that s divides r. Hence every element is a root of the equation $x^r - 1 = 0$. As this polynomial has at most r distinct roots, by Theorem 22, $r = q - 1$. Q.E.D.

Corollary. Every element in a field F of order q satisfies the equation $x^q = x$. Every nonzero element in F satisfies the equation $x^{q-1} = 1$.

Theorem 30 says that the multiplicative group of a finite field is cyclic. The following corollary for integers is quite useful.

Corollary. Every integer x such that g.c.d.$(x, p) = 1$ satisfies the equation $x^{p-1} \equiv 1$ (modulo p).

Proof. This follows from the theorem when $F = GF(p)$.

Theorem 31. Every finite field F has p^m elements for some prime p.

Proof. Every F contains a prime subfield that is $GF(p)$ up to relabeling. The elements in F form a vector space over $GF(p)$. Let α be the primitive element that we know is in F by the last theorem. Let m be the smallest positive integer such that α^m is a linear combination, with coefficients in $GF(p)$, of smaller powers of α. Say $\alpha^m = \sum_{i=0}^{m-1} a_i \alpha^i$ for a_i in $GF(p)$. Such an m must exist since F is a finite field. As $\alpha^{m+1} = \alpha(\alpha^m) = \alpha(\sum_{i=0}^{m-1} a_i \alpha^i) = \sum_{i=0}^{m-2} a_i \alpha^{i+1} + a_{m-1}\alpha^m$, we can express α^{m+1} as a linear combination of $1, \alpha, \ldots, \alpha^{m-1}$. Clearly by continuing in this fashion we can express all powers of α, that is all nonzero elements in F, as linear combinations of $1, \alpha, \ldots, \alpha^{m-1}$. Hence F is an m-dimensional vector space over $GF(p)$, which has $1, \alpha, \ldots, \alpha^{m-1}$ as a basis. Thus F has p^m elements. Q.E.D.

A finite field F is said to be *isomorphic* to a finite field F' if the order of F equals the order of F' and there is a mapping φ from F to F' so that:

  (i) φ preserves addition: $\varphi(\alpha + \beta) = \varphi(\alpha) + \varphi(\beta)$.
 (ii) φ preserves multiplication: $\varphi(\alpha\beta) = \varphi(\alpha)\varphi(\beta)$.
(iii) φ is onto, that is any β in F' equals $\varphi(\alpha)$ for some α in F. Since our fields are finite, φ is onto iff φ is one-one, that is $\varphi(\alpha) = 0$ implies $\alpha = 0$ (Problem 7).

Furthermore, φ is called an *isomorphism*. An isomorphism amounts to a relabeling of the elements of the field that preserves $+$ and $\cdot$. This implies that $\varphi(0) = 0$ and $\varphi(1) = 1$.

Theorem 32. If a field of $q = p^m$ elements exists, then it is unique up to isomorphism. We call this field $GF(p^m)$.

Proof. We know that any finite field F must have $q = p^m$ elements and that every nonzero element of F satisfies $x^{q-1} = 1$. By Problem 13, this equation has $q - 1$ distinct roots. Hence the field elements are precisely the $q - 1$ roots of the equation $x^{q-1} = 1$ and the element 0.

Let α be a primitive element in F and let $m(x)$ be the monic polynomial of lowest degree with coefficients in $GF(p)$ of which α is a root. This is the minimal polynomial of α described in Section 4.3. We want to show that all roots of $m(x)$ satisfy $x^{q-1} - 1 = 0$. By the division algorithm, $x^{q-1} - 1 = m(x)a(x) + r(x)$ where the degree of $r(x)$ is less than the degree of $m(x)$. Since $\alpha^{q-1} - 1 = 0$ and $m(\alpha) = 0$, $r(\alpha) = 0$, and since $m(x)$ has the lowest degree with this property, $r(x)$ is identically 0. Hence all roots of $m(x)$ satisfy the equation $x^{q-1} - 1 = 0$. Let F' be another field of q elements and let β be a primitive element in F'. All nonzero elements in F' satisfy $x^{q-1} - 1 = 0$. Since $m(x)$ divides $x^{q-1} - 1$, some power of β, β^i say, must be a root of $m(x)$. Then the mapping $\varphi(\alpha) = \beta^i$ can be verified to be an isomorphism between F and F'. This verification is similar to the ones required in Problems 14 and 15.   Q.E.D.

Although we do not show it here, it can be shown that for any positive integer m, there is an irreducible polynomial over $GF(p)$ of degree m [2].

Theorem 33. For any prime p and positive integer m, there is a unique (up to isomorphism) field of p^m elements, $GF(p^m)$.

Proof. We know that such a field is unique if it exists. The existence of the irreducible polynomial of degree m over $GF(p)$ allows us to construct $GF(p^m)$ by Theorem 29.

An isomorphism φ sending a field F onto itself is called an *automorphism*.

Theorem 34. If F is a finite field of characteristic p, then the mapping φ defined by $\varphi(\alpha) = \alpha^p$ is an automorphism of F.

Proof. Clearly φ preserves multiplication. The fact that φ preserves addition follows from Theorem 28. It is easy to show that φ is one-one since $\varphi(\alpha) = 0$ implies $\alpha = 0$.

Notice that Theorem 34 says that every element in a finite field of characteristic p has a pth root. In a finite field of characteristic 2, every element has a square root and every element is a square.

4.3 MINIMAL POLYNOMIALS

We have noticed by now that some fields are contained in other fields and we investigate this phenomenon more thoroughly in this section.

A field F' is called *a subfield* of a field F if F' is contained in F and has the same operations F has. We have already seen that any finite field contains $GF(p)$ for some prime p.

We call $m(x)$ the *minimal polynomial* of an element α in $GF(p^r)$ if $m(x)$ is the monic polynomial of smallest degree with coefficients in $GF(p)$ that has α as a root. Such a polynomial exists since α satisfies the equation $x^{p^r} = x$. The next theorem gives several useful facts about minimal polynomials.

Theorem 35. Let $m(x)$ be the minimal polynomial of an element α in a finite field $GF(p^r)$. Then the following facts hold.

 (i) $m(x)$ is irreducible.
 (ii) If α is a root of a polynomial $f(x)$ with coefficients in $GF(p)$, then $m(x)$ divides $f(x)$.
 (iii) $m(x)$ divides $x^{p^r} - x$.
 (iv) If $m(x)$ is primitive, then its degree is r. In any case the degree of $m(x)$ is $\leq r$.

Proof.

 (i) If $m(x)$ is reducible, then $m(x) = a(x)b(x)$ and as $m(\alpha) = 0$, either $a(\alpha)$ or $b(\alpha)$ is 0 contradicting the fact that $m(x)$ is the polynomial of smallest degree with α as a root.
 (ii) By the division algorithm, we have $f(x) = a(x)m(x) + r(x)$ where the degree of $r(x)$ is less than the degree of $m(x)$. Since $f(\alpha) = m(\alpha) = 0$, $r(\alpha) = 0$ and since the degree of $r(x)$ is less than the degree of $m(x)$, $r(x)$ is identically 0.
 (iii) This follows from (ii) since any element in $GF(p^r)$ is a root of the equation $x^{p^r} = x$.
 (iv) Since α is in $GF(p^r)$ and $GF(p^r)$ is an r-dimensional vector space over $GF(p)$, the set of vectors $1, \alpha, \ldots, \alpha^r$ must be linearly depen-

dent and so satisfy an equation of degree less than or equal to r. If $m(x)$ is primitive α generates all of $GF(p^r)$ and so $m(x)$ must have degree r.

Consider $GF(2^4)$. We compute the minimal polynomial of each of its elements. In Section 3.3 we constructed $GF(16)$ using the primitive, irreducible polynomial $f(x) = x^4 + x^3 + 1$, which has a root α. Clearly $f(x)$ is the minimal polynomial of α. Now $f(x)$ has four roots and we can determine all of them. Since $\alpha^4 + \alpha^3 + 1 = 0$, $\alpha^8 + \alpha^6 + 1 = (\alpha^4 + \alpha^3 + 1)^2 = 0$ so that α^2 is a root of $f(x)$. Similarly $\alpha^4 = (\alpha^2)^2$ and $\alpha^8 = (\alpha^4)^2$ are roots of $f(x)$ and $f(x)$ is the minimal polynomial of each of these four elements. Do we know any other minimal polynomials? Well, 0 and 1 must satisfy $x^2 = x$ so the minimal polynomial of 1 is $x + 1$. We know all irreducible, binary polynomials of degree 4 and $x^4 + x + 1 = g(x)$ is one. Since $g(x)$ can be used to construct a field of 16 elements, $g(x)$ must have roots in $GF(16)$. We could find them by just testing which powers of α satisfy $g(x)$, but there is an easier way.

If $f(x)$ is a polynomial of degree m, the *reciprocal polynomial of* $f(x)$ is defined to be $x^m f(x^{-1})$. If $f(x) = a_n x^n + a_{n-1} x^{n-1} + \cdots + a_0$, its reciprocal polynomial equals $a_0 x^n + a_1 x^{n-1} + \cdots + a_n$, that is, the coefficients are written in reverse order.

Theorem 36. If α is a root of $f(x)$, α^{-1} is a root of $g(x)$, the reciprocal polynomial of $f(x)$. Also, $f(x)$ is irreducible iff its reciprocal polynomial is irreducible and $f(x)$ is primitive iff its reciprocal polynomial is primitive.

Proof. Since $f(\alpha) = 0$, $g(\alpha^{-1}) = \alpha^{-m} f(\alpha) = 0$. Problem 11 asks for the proof of the irreducibility criterion. The second statement holds since α and α^{-1} have the same order.

Returning to our example of $GF(16)$, the reciprocal polynomial of $f(x)$ is $x^4 f(x^{-1}) = x^4(x^{-4} + x^{-3} + 1) = x^4 + x + 1 = g(x)$ and, by the last theorem, $g(x)$ has roots $\alpha^{-1} = \alpha^{14}$, $\alpha^{-2} = \alpha^{13}$, $\alpha^{-4} = \alpha^{11}$, and $\alpha^{-8} = \alpha^7$. Since $g(x)$ is primitive, $g(x)$ is clearly the minimal polynomial of these elements. We have now located minimal polynomials for nine nonzero elements in $GF(16)$ and we are missing them for the six elements α^3, α^5, α^6, α^9, α^{10}, and α^{12}. By Problem 3.7, we know all binary irreducible polynomials and $x^4 + x^3 + x^2 + x + 1$ is one. Note that this polynomial equals its reciprocal polynomial. Again it can be used to construct $GF(16)$ and so its roots are in $GF(16)$. It can be verified that these are α^3, α^6, α^{12}, and α^9 and that $x^4 + x^3 + x^2 + x + 1$ is their minimal polynomial. This leaves α^5 and α^{10} and it can be seen that they satisfy the equation $x^2 + x + 1 = 0$

and that this is their minimal polynomial. We tabulate this information below.

Elements in $GF(16)$	Minimal Polynomials
$\alpha, \alpha^2, \alpha^4, \alpha^8$	$x^4 + x^3 + 1$
$\alpha^7, \alpha^{14}, \alpha^{13}, \alpha^{11}$	$x^4 + x + 1$
α^5, α^{10}	$x^2 + x + 1$
$\alpha^3, \alpha^6, \alpha^{12}, \alpha^9$	$x^4 + x^3 + x^2 + x + 1$
$\alpha^{15} = 1$	$x + 1$
0	x

Each of these minimal polynomials must divide $x^{16} - x$ and, computing the sums of their degrees, we get $4 \cdot 3 + 1 \cdot 2 + 2 \cdot 1 = 16$. Hence $x^{16} + x$ must equal $(x^4 + x^3 + 1)(x^4 + x + 1)(x^4 + x^3 + x^2 + x + 1)(x^2 + x + 1)(x + 1)x$. Notice that 0 and 1 constitute $GF(2)$ and that 0, 1, α^5, and α^{10} are the elements of $GF(4)$. The subfields contained in $GF(16)$, the way in which $x^{16} + x$ factors, and the form of the roots of the minimal polynomials can all be explained by general theorems.

Lemma. $GF(p^s) \subseteq GF(p^r)$ iff $x^{p^s-1} - 1$ divides $x^{p^r-1} - 1$.

Proof. This is so since all nonzero elements of $GF(p^s)$ are roots of the equation $x^{p^s-1} = 1$ and all the nonzero elements of $GF(p^r)$ are roots of the equation $x^{p^r-1} = 1$.

Lemma. If x is a variable or an integer, $x^m - 1$ divides $(x^n - 1)$ iff m divides n.

Proof. If we divide $x^n - 1$ by $x^m - 1$, we get the following.

$$x^n - 1 = (x^m - 1)(x^{n-m} + x^{n-2m} + x^{n-3m} + \cdots + x^{n-km})$$
$$+ (x^{n-km} - 1)$$

where km is the largest multiple of m that is less than n. From this we see that $x^m - 1$ divides $x^n - 1$ iff $n = km$.

Theorem 37. $GF(p^s) \subseteq GF(p^r)$ iff s divides r and an element α in $GF(p^r)$ is in $GF(p^s)$ iff $\alpha^{p^s} = \alpha$.

Proof. The two lemmas give us the following equivalences. $GF(p^s) \subseteq GF(p^r)$ if $x^{p^s-1} - 1$ divides $x^{p^r-1} - 1$ iff $p^s - 1$ divides $p^r - 1$ iff s

divides r. The second part of the theorem holds since the elements in $GF(p^s)$ are roots of the equation $x^{p^s} = x$.

Theorem 38. $x^{p^r} - x$ is the product of all monic polynomials irreducible over $GF(p)$ whose degrees divide r.

Proof. Suppose that $f(x)$ is an irreducible polynomial of degree m where m divides r. Then $f(x)$ can be used to construct $GF(p^m)$ and either $GF(p^m)$ is $GF(p^r)$ if $m = r$ or $GF(p^m)$ is contained in $GF(p^r)$ if $m \neq r$ by Theorem 37. If α is a root of $f(x)$, then $\alpha^{p^r} = \alpha$, which implies that $f(x)$ divides $x^{p^r} - x$. Conversely suppose that $f(x)$ is an irreducible polynomial of degree m that divides $x^{p^r} - x$. We can construct $GF(p^m)$ using $f(x)$, and $GF(p^m)$ must be contained in $GF(p^r)$ since all the roots of $f(x)$ satisfy the equation $x^{p^r} = 1$. Hence by Theorem 37, m divides r. Note that each factor occurs exactly once by Problems 12 and 13. Q.E.D.

We still have one observation about $GF(16)$ to investigate, namely the structure of the roots. Recall that Problem 3.14 says that $a(x^2) = (a(x))^2$ whenever $a(x)$ is a binary polynomial. This explains why, if β is a root of a binary polynomial, then β^2 is a root also. In the table giving the elements in $GF(16)$ and their minimal polynomials, the elements are ordered $\beta, \beta^2, (\beta^2)^2 = \beta^4, \ldots$.

Theorem 39. If $f(x)$ is a polynomial with coefficients in $GF(p^r)$, then $f(x^{p^r}) = (f(x))^{p^r}$.

Proof. We write $f(x)$ as $\alpha_0 + \alpha_1 x + \cdots + \alpha_m x^m$. Then $f(x^{p^r}) = \alpha_0 + \alpha_1 x^{p^r} + \cdots + \alpha_m (x^{p^r})^m = (\alpha_0 + \alpha_1 x + \cdots + \alpha_m x^m)^{p^r}$ since $(x + y)^{p^r} = x^{p^r} + y^{p^r}$. Q.E.D.

Theorem 40. Let $f(x)$ be a polynomial over $GF(p)$ and let α be a root of $f(x)$ of order n in the multiplicative group of some field F. Let r be the smallest integer so that $p^{r+1} \equiv 1$ (modulo n). Then $\alpha, \alpha^p, \alpha^{p^2}, \ldots, \alpha^{p^r}$ are all distinct roots of $f(x)$.

Proof. Clearly $\alpha, \alpha^p, \alpha^{p^2}, \ldots, \alpha^{p^r}$ are all roots of $f(x)$. If $\alpha^{p^i} = \alpha^{p^j}$ for some i and j with, say, $i > j$, then $\alpha^{p^i - p^j} = 1$. Thus $p^i - p^j$ is a multiple of n. This is so iff $p^i \equiv p^j$ (modulo n) iff $p^{i-j} \equiv 1$ (modulo n) iff $i - j$ is a multiple of $r + 1$. Q.E.D.

We examine this theorem for some elements in $GF(16)$. The polynomial $x^4 + x^3 + 1$ has roots $\alpha, \alpha^2, \alpha^4 = \alpha^{2^2}, \alpha^8 = \alpha^{2^3}$, and $\alpha^{2^4} = \alpha$. The order of

α is 15 and 4 is the smallest integer so that $2^4 \equiv 1$ (modulo 15). The polynomial $x^2 + x + 1$ has roots $\beta = \alpha^5$ and $\beta^2 = \alpha^{10}$. Note that β has order 3 and $2^2 \equiv 1$ (modulo 3). Consider now the set of numbers that appear as powers of α for the different irreducible polynomials in the table of minimal polynomials of $GF(16)$. Notice that all the elements of a set can be computed from any element by multiplying by 2, then multiplying the previous result by 2, and so on writing all results modulo 15. We list these sets and their corresponding polynomials.

Minimal Polynomials	Powers of α
$x^4 + x + 1$	$(1, 2, 4, 8)$
$x^4 + x^3 + 1$	$(7, 14, 13, 11)$
$x^4 + x^3 + x^2 + x + 1$	$(3, 6, 12, 9)$
$x^2 + x + 1$	$(5, 10)$
$x + 1$	(0)

Consider any s so that $0 \leq s < p^m - 1$ and let r be the smallest number with the property that $p^{r+1}s \equiv s \pmod{p^m - 1}$. The *cyclotomic coset* containing s consists of $\{s, ps, p^2s, \ldots, p^rs\}$ where each p^is is reduced $\bmod(p^m - 1)$. If g.c.d.$(s, p^m - 1) = 1$, then $r = m - 1$, but if g.c.d.$(s, p^m - 1) \neq 1$, then r varies with s. The sets in the example above are all the cyclotomic cosets for $2^4 - 1 = 15$. Even though they are not cosets of a group, the cyclotomic cosets partition the integers $\bmod(p^m - 1)$, that is, each integer $\bmod(p^m - 1)$ is in exactly one cyclotomic coset (Problem 19). If u is any element in its cyclotomic coset, we denote the coset by C_u.

Theorem 41. Let α be an element in $GF(p^m)$ and let $m(x)$ be its minimal polynomial. Let β be a primitive element in $GF(p^m)$ and let $\alpha = \beta^t$. If u is the smallest element in the cyclotomic coset containing t, then $m(x) = \prod_{i \in C_u}(x - \beta^i)$.

Proof. If α is primitive, its order is $p^m - 1$ and without loss of generality, we can let $t = 1$. Let $m_1(x) = \prod_{i \in C_1}(x - \alpha^i)$. In Theorem 40 n is $p^m - 1$ and r is $m - 1$ so that $\alpha, \alpha^p, \ldots, \alpha^{p^r}$ are all distinct roots of $m(x)$, which implies that $m_1(x)$ divides $m(x)$. Now $m_1(x) = x^{r+1} - (\alpha + \alpha^p + \alpha^{p^2} + \cdots + \alpha^{p^r})x^r + \cdots + (-1)^{r+1}(\alpha^{1+p+\cdots+p^r})$ and each coefficient γ of $m_1(x)$ has the property that $\gamma^p = \gamma$, by Theorem 28, so that all the coefficients of $m_1(x)$ are in $GF(p)$ by Theorem 37. Hence $m(x) = m_1(x)$.

If α is not primitive, then the order of α is $n = (p^m - 1)/s$ for some s. Let u be the smallest element in the cyclotomic coset that contains s and define $m_1(x) = \prod_{i \in C_u}(x - \beta^i)$. Now $p^{r+1}s \equiv s \pmod{p^m - 1}$ iff $p^{r+1} \equiv 1 \pmod{n}$ (Problem 20) so that, by Theorem 40, $\alpha = \beta^s$, $\alpha^p = \beta^{ps}, \ldots, \alpha^{p^r} = \beta^{p^r s}$ are all distinct roots of $m(x)$ so that $m_1(x)$ divides $m(x)$. As in the previous situation, it can be shown that all the coefficients of $m_1(x)$ are in $GF(p)$ so that $m(x) = m_1(x)$.   Q.E.D.

Note that this theorem shows that the degree of $m(x)$ is the size of a certain cyclotomic coset.

Let us refer to our example of $GF(16)$. The minimal polynomial of the primitive element α is $(x - \alpha)(x - \alpha^2)(x - \alpha^4)(x - \alpha^8) = x^4 + x^3 + 1$, and the minimal polynomial of the primitive element α^7 is $(x - \alpha^7) \times (x - \alpha^{14})(x - \alpha^{13})(x - \alpha^{11}) = x^4 + x + 1$. The element α^3 is not primitive even though its minimal polynomial has degree 4. The order of α^3 in $GF(16)$ is $5 = \frac{15}{3}$ ($n = 5$, $s = r = 3$) and its minimal polynomial is $(x - \alpha^3)(x - \alpha^6)(x - \alpha^{12})(x - \alpha^9) = x^4 + x^3 + x^2 + x + 1$. This polynomial is not a primitive polynomial. Lastly the element α^5 is also not primitive. Its order in $GF(16)$ is $3 = (2^4 - 1)/5$ ($n = 3$, $s = 5$, $r = 1$) and its minimal polynomial, $(x - \alpha^5)(x - \alpha^{10})$, has degree 2.

The cyclotomic cosets have the nice property that they give us much information about a finite field without much work. So, for example, let us compute the cyclotomic cosets when $p^m = 2^6$ and see what information we get about $GF(2^6)$. These cosets are

$$C_0 = \{0\}, \quad C_1 = \{1, 2, 4, 8, 16, 32\}, \quad C_3 = \{3, 6, 12, 24, 48, 33\},$$

$$C_5 = \{5, 10, 20, 40, 17, 34\}, \quad C_7 = \{7, 14, 28, 56, 49, 35\},$$

$$C_9 = \{9, 18, 36\}, \quad C_{11} = \{11, 22, 44, 25, 50, 37\},$$

$$C_{13} = \{13, 26, 52, 41, 19, 38\}, \quad C_{15} = \{15, 30, 60, 57, 51, 39\},$$

$$C_{21} = \{21, 42\}, \quad C_{23} = \{23, 46, 29, 58, 53, 43\}, \quad C_{27} = \{27, 54, 45\},$$

$$C_{31} = \{31, 62, 61, 59, 55, 47\}.$$

From this routine computation we can tell that $x^{63} + 1$ is the product of nine irreducible polynomials of degree 6, two irreducible polynomials of degree 3, one irreducible polynomial of degree 2, and one of degree 1. The polynomial of degree 1 is $x + 1$ and its roots together with 0 constitute the subfield $GF(2)$. The polynomial of degree 2 is $x^2 + x + 1$ and its roots together with 0 and 1 form $GF(4)$. Note that we have two copies of $GF(8)$ in $GF(64)$ corresponding to the two polynomials $x^3 + x^2 + 1$ and $x^3 + x + 1$. The ones of degree 6 are considerably more difficult to find. But this simple computation tells us that there are exactly nine irreducible binary polynomials of degree 6.

4.4 FACTORING $x^n - 1$

Factoring $x^n - 1$ is important for constructing cyclic codes. When $n = p^m - 1$, we have some knowledge of the factors. Consider the binary polynomials $x^3 - 1$ and $x^7 - 1$. First we factor $x^4 - x = x^{2^2} + x = x(x + 1) \times (x^2 + x + 1)$, the product of all irreducible polynomials whose degrees divide 2. Then $x^3 - 1 = x^3 + 1 = (x + 1)(x^2 + x + 1)$. Similarly $x^8 - x = x^{2^3} + x = x(x + 1)(x^3 + x^2 + 1)(x^3 + x + 1)$, the product of all irreducible polynomials whose degrees divide 3. Then $x^7 - 1 = (x + 1)(x^3 + x^2 + 1)(x^3 + x + 1)$. We have already seen the factorization of $x^{16} - x$, and we give the factorization of $x^{32} - x$.

$$x^{32} - x = x(x + 1)(x^5 + x^2 + 1)(x^5 + x^3 + 1)(x^5 + x^4 + x^3 + x^2 + 1)$$
$$\times (x^5 + x^3 + x^2 + x + 1)(x^5 + x^4 + x^2 + x + 1)$$
$$\times (x^5 + x^4 + x^3 + x + 1).$$

What about $x^n - 1$ when $n \neq p^m - 1$? Let us consider the binary polynomials $x^5 - 1$ and $x^{23} - 1$. We can use some of the same type of reasoning we have used before. If α is a root of $x^5 - 1$, so are $\alpha^2, \alpha^4, \alpha^8 = \alpha^3$, and $\alpha^6 = \alpha$. Thus $x^5 - 1$ has one factor of degree 4 and so must be $(x + 1)(x^4 + x^3 + x^2 + x + 1)$. We discuss this more fully.

We suppose for the rest of this section that g.c.d.$(n, p) = 1$ so that p has an inverse modulo n. When p is 2 this means that n is odd. In factoring $x^n - 1$ over $GF(p)$ it is useful to extend the definition of cyclotomic cosets to integers n where n is not necessarily of the form $p^m - 1$. If $0 \leq s < n$, let r be the smallest number such that $p^{r+1}s \equiv s$ (modulo n). Such a number must exist since p has an inverse modulo n. As before, the *cyclotomic coset* containing s consists of $\{s, ps, p^2s, \ldots, p^rs\}$ where each p^is is reduced modulo n.

Given n and p, it is known that there is a smallest m so that n divides $p^m - 1$. By the second lemma to Theorem 37, this happens iff $x^n - 1$ divides $x^{p^m-1} - 1$ so that $GF(p^m)$ is the smallest field of characteristic p that contains all the roots of $x^n - 1$. Since g.c.d.$(n, p) = 1$, $x^n - 1$ has n distinct roots by (Problem 13) in $GF(p^m)$. The roots of $x^n - 1$ are a subgroup of the multiplicative group of $GF(p^m)$ and since any subgroup of a cyclic group is cyclic (Problem 1), they are all powers of a single root, which is called a *primitive n^{th} root of unity*. The following theorem is analogous to Theorem 41.

Theorem 42. Let α be a root of $x^n = 1$ in the smallest finite field F of characteristic p that contains α and let $m(x)$ be its minimal polynomial. Let β be a primitive n^{th} root of unity in F and let $\alpha = \beta^s$. If u is the smallest element in the cyclotomic coset of n containing s, then $m(x) = \prod_{i \in C_u}(x - \beta^i)$.

The proof is analogous to that of Theorem 41 and we omit it.

Again this shows that the degree of $m(x)$ is the size of a cyclotomic coset.

This theorem is useful in that we need only know n and p and by computing cyclotomic cosets of n, an easy thing to do, we can find both m and the number of factors of $x^n - 1$. This is illustrated by the next example.

If we compute the cyclotomic cosets for $n = 23$ and $p = 2$ we get $C_0 = \{0\}$, $C_1 = \{1, 2, 4, 8, 16, 9, 18, 13, 3, 6, 12\}$, and $C_5 = \{5, 10, 20, 17, 11, 22, 21, 19, 15, 7, 14\}$ so $x^{23} - 1$ has two factors of degree 11 and one of degree $1, (x - 1)$. Each of degree 11 is a minimum polynomial of a primitive 23rd root of unity that is contained in $GF(2^{11})$ as $2^{11} - 1 = 2047 = 23 \cdot 89$. The factors of degree 11 are not easy to find. In general, factoring $x^n - 1$ is difficult to do and tables of irreducible polynomials [19] have been computed to help with this problem because of the application to cyclic codes.

PROBLEMS

1. Prove that every subgroup of a cyclic group is cyclic.

2. Prove Theorem 25.

3. Prove Theorem 26.

4. Prove that an element in a group has a unique inverse.

5. Give all generators of the cyclic group of order 15.

6. Construct tables analogous to the table for $GF(16)$ in Section 3.3 for the following fields:

   (a) $GF(4)$.

   (b) $GF(8)$.

   (c) $GF(9)$.

7. Let φ be a mapping from one finite set into another finite set of the same size. Prove that φ is onto iff φ is one-one.

8. Which elements of $GF(16)$ are primitive?

9. How many primitive elements does each of the fields in Problem 6 contain?

10. Show that $x^4 + x^3 + x^2 + x + 1$ is irreducible over $GF(2)$ but not primitive.

11. Prove that a polynomial is irreducible iff its reciprocal polynomial is irreducible.

12. Suppose $x^n - 1$ has a root α in some field $F = GF(2^m)$. Then $\alpha^n = 1$ so that $x^n - 1 = x^n - \alpha^n = (x - \alpha)(x^{n-1} + \alpha x^{n-2} + \cdots + \alpha^{n-1})$. If n is odd, deduce that α is not a repeated root.

13. If $x^n - 1$ factors in $GF(p^m)$ and g.c.d.$(n, p) = 1$, show that $x^n - 1$ has distinct roots.

14. Construct two copies of $GF(8)$ using the two irreducible polynomials of degree 3. Explicitly give the isomorphism between the fields you have constructed.

15. Explicitly give the isomorphism between the two copies of $GF(16)$ obtained from the two irreducible primitive polynomials of degree 4.

16. If $p \neq 2$, show that exactly half the nonzero elements in $GF(p)$ are squares.

17. Show that any irreducible polynomial, of degree > 2, that equals its reciprocal polynomial cannot be primitive.

18. Identify all subfields of the following fields.

   (a) $GF(2^5)$,

   (b) $GF(2^{12})$,

   (c) $GF(3^4)$.

19. Let $S = \{s | 0 \le s < p^m - 1\}$. Show that every element in S is in exactly one cyclotomic coset.

20. Show that $p^{r+1}s \equiv s \pmod{p^m - 1}$ iff $p^{r+1} \equiv 1 \pmod{n}$, for $n = (p^m - 1)/s$, assuming that s divides $(p^m - 1)$.

21. Let α be a primitive element in each of the following finite fields.

   (a) $GF(4)$.

   (b) $GF(8)$.

   (c) $GF(9)$.

   For each of these fields, find the minimal polynomials of all powers of α. By using cyclotomic cosets, indicate which powers of α are the roots of each polynomial. This is what was done for $GF(16)$ in Section 4.3.

22. Show that Ham(2, 4) is an M.D.S. code.

23. Find a generator matrix of a $(5, 3, 3)$ M.D.S. code over $GF(4)$.

24. Compute the cyclotomic cosets for $2^5 - 1$. In the factorization of $x^{31} - 1$ given in Section 4.4, identify reciprocal polynomials. Give the minimal polynomial for each element of $GF(2^5)$.

25. Find the irreducible factors of $x^n - 1$ over $GF(2)$ for $n = 9$ and 13.

26. What are the degrees of the irreducible factors of $x^{17} - 1$ over $GF(2)$? What is the smallest field of characteristic 2 in which $x^{17} - 1$ factors into linear factors?

27. How many polynomials of the form $x^2 + \alpha x + \beta$ with $\beta \ne 0$ are there over $GF(4)$? How many polynomials of the form $(x + \gamma)(x + \delta)$ with $\gamma, \delta \ne 0$ are there over $GF(4)$?

28. How many monic irreducible polynomials of degree 2 are there over $GF(4)$? Write them all.

5

Cyclic Codes

5.1 THE ORIGIN AND DEFINITION OF CYCLIC CODES

Cyclic codes are an important class of codes for many reasons. One is that they can be efficiently encoded by means of shift registers. There are also decoding schemes utilizing shift registers. Many important codes such as the Golay codes, the Hamming codes, and the B.C.H. codes can be represented as cyclic codes. Furthermore, much is known theoretically about cyclic codes, which enhances their practical applications.

We start with a device called a (linear) shift register. This is commonly used to encode cyclic codes. As we shall see, the encoding process is efficient because no storage is required as the code words are generated by shifting and adding. There are two basic building blocks for shift registers. One is the storage element, which can be a flip-flop, in which a field element is stored, and which has one input and one output. This is represented as follows: $\leftarrow \square \leftarrow$. The arrows indicate the input and output. For illustration purposes we consider shift registers only for $GF(2)$. The other building block is the binary adder, which has two inputs and one output, which is the binary sum of the inputs. This is represented as follows with the arrows representing the inputs and output:

We give an example of a shift register, Figure 5.1, with four storage elements and two binary adders. There are others with the same number of storage elements and adders attached differently.

At time zero, four binary elements are placed in a_0, a_1, a_2, and a_3. After one time interval a_0 is output, a_1 is shifted into a_0, a_2 into a_1, a_3 into a_2, and the new element is entered into a_3. In our example this element is the sum $a_0 + a_2 + a_3$. We suppose that the digits 1101 are

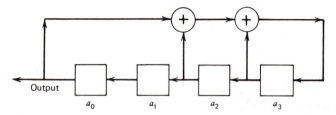

Figure 5.1   A shift register.

placed in a_0, a_1, a_2, and a_3 and follow the outputs and inputs for seven time intervals.

If this process is continued, the vector $(1, 1, 0, 1, 0, 0, 0)$ will be repeated. This shift register will repeat any vector of length 7 that it has generated from four initial entries in a_0, a_1, a_2, and a_3. We see later that this has to be so. We can regard the initial four positions as information positions and the whole process as encoding these information positions to obtain a length 7 codeword. It is not hard to check that the code generated is actually a linear code. This code has the property that whenever $(a_0, a_1, a_2, a_3, a_4, a_5, a_6)$ is a codeword so is $(a_6, a_0, a_1, a_2, a_3, a_4, a_5)$, that is, whenever a vector is in the code so are all of its cyclic shifts. We can see this because we know that each vector will be repeated, as in Table 5.1, and the last seven digits to come out of the shift register after any number of shifts form a vector of the code. Every 7-tuple of successive digits in Table 5.1 is a codeword; hence so is $(a_6, a_0, a_1, a_2, a_3, a_4, a_5)$. When

Table 5.1   A Repeated Vector

			Outputs				a_0	a_1	a_2	a_3	Time
							1	1	0	1	t_0
						1	1	0	1	0	t_1
					1	1	0	1	0	0	t_2
				1	1	0	1	0	0	0	t_3
			1	1	0	1	0	0	0	1	t_4
		1	1	0	1	0	0	0	1	1	t_5
	1	1	0	1	0	0	0	1	1	0	t_6
1	1	0	1	0	0	0	1	1	0	1	t_7

$\vdots$

1	1	0	1	0	0	0	1	1	0	1	0	0	0	Time
a_0	a_1	a_2	a_3	a_4	a_5	a_6	a_0	a_1	a_2	a_3	a_4	a_5	a_6	t_{10}

discussing cyclic codes we number n coordinate positions with $0, 1, \ldots, n - 1$.

An (n, k) code C is called *cyclic* if whenever $x = (a_0, a_1, \ldots, a_{n-1})$ is in C, so is its first cyclic shift $y = (a_{n-1}, a_0, \ldots, a_{n-2})$. Notice that this means that $(a_{n-2}, a_{n-1}, a_0, \ldots, a_{n-3})$, the first cyclic shift of y, and all the other cyclic shifts of x are also in C.

When considering cyclic codes it is useful to let a vector $(a_0, a_1, \ldots, a_{n-1})$ correspond to a polynomial $a_0 + a_1x + a_2x^2 + \cdots + a_{n-1}x^{n-1}$. Then $(a_{n-1}, a_0, \ldots, a_{n-2})$ corresponds to $a_{n-1} + a_0x + a_1x^2 + \cdots + a_{n-2}x^{n-1}$. Note that this polynomial equals the polynomial

$$\left(a_0 + a_1x + \cdots + a_{n-1}x^{n-1} \right) x \ \left(\text{modulo} \ \left(x^n - 1 \right) \right).$$

For cyclic codes we are really interested in $R_n = F[x]/(x^n - 1)$, which consists of congruence classes of polynomials in $F[x]$ modulo $(x^n - 1)$. As before, we think of these classes as polynomials of degree less than n. Polynomials are added and subtracted in R_n as in $F[x]$ but multiplication is modulo $(x^n - 1)$. Explicitly, if we have two polynomials $a(x)$ and $b(x)$, their product in $F[x]$ is $a(x)b(x) = c(x)(x^n - 1) + r(x)$ with the degree of $r(x)$ less than the degree of $x^n - 1$ by the division algorithm. We regard $r(x)$ as the product of $a(x)$ and $b(x)$ when we consider R_n to be all polynomials in $F[x]$ of degree less than n with multiplication modulo $(x^n - 1)$. Both $F[x]$ and R_n are examples of the algebraic structure defined next.

A *commutative ring R with unit* is a set with two operations, + (plus) and · (times), with the following properties.

(i) R is closed under + and ·.

(ii) R is an abelian group under +.

(iii) The associative law for multiplication holds. $a(bc) = (ab)c$ for all a, b, and c in R.

(iv) Multiplication is commutative, $ab = ba$ for all a and b in R.

(v) R has an identity 1 for multiplication. $a \cdot 1 = 1 \cdot a = a$ for all a in R.

(vi) The distributive law holds. $a(b + c) = ab + ac$ for all a, b, and c in R.

Note that R need not be a field as a nonzero element need not have a multiplicative inverse. The integers with + and · are an example of a commutative ring with unit.

The concept we find really useful is that of an ideal. An *ideal* I in a commutative ring R is a set of elements in R satisfying the following two conditions.

(i) If a is in I, then ab is in I for all b in R.

(ii) If a and b are in I, then $a + b$ and $a - b$ are also in I.

The second condition means that I is a subgroup of the additive group of R.

Let V be the space of all n-tuples over $GF(q)$ with the coordinates labeled from 0 through $n - 1$, and let a vector $v = (a_0, a_1, \ldots, a_{n-1})$ correspond to a polynomial $a_0 + a_1 x + \cdots + a_{n-1} x^{n-1}$ in $R_n = F[x]/(x^n - 1)$ where $F = GF(q)$. The next theorem explains the usefulness of this correspondence.

Theorem 43. A set of elements S in R_n corresponds to a cyclic code C iff S is an ideal in R_n.

Proof. Suppose S is a set of elements in R_n that corresponds to a cyclic code. Then if $a_1(x)$ and $a_2(x)$ are in S, so are $a_1(x) \pm a_2(x)$ by the definition cᵒ a code. Recall that the cyclic shift corresponds to multiplication by x so that if $a(x)$ is in S, then $a(x)x$ is in S, as is $(a(x)x)x = a(x)x^2$, and so on. Consider $a(x)b(x)$ for $a(x)$ in S and $b(x) = b_0 + b_1 x + b_2 x^2 + \cdots + b_{n-1} x^{n-1}$, some polynomial in R_n. Then $a(x)b(x) = b_0 a(x) + b_1 a(x)x + \cdots + b_{n-1} a(x)x^{n-1}$ is again in S since each element in the sum is in S. Hence S is an ideal. If S is an ideal in R_n, then clearly the polynomials in S correspond to the vectors in a cyclic code.   Q.E.D.

Let V be the space of all binary 3-tuples. We simultaneously locate all binary cyclic codes in V and ideals in R_3 and indicate corresponding vectors.

Code	V	R_3
C_1	$(0, 0, 0)$	0
C_2	$(0, 0, 0)$	0
	$(1, 1, 1)$	$1 + x + x^2$
C_3	$(0, 0, 0)$	0
	$(1, 1, 0)$	$1 + x$
	$(0, 1, 1)$	$x + x^2$
	$(1, 0, 1)$	$1 + x^2$
C_4	all of V	all of R_3

From now on we refer to a cyclic code as either a code closed under the cyclic shift or an ideal in R_n.

5.2 HOW TO FIND CYCLIC CODES: THE GENERATOR POLYNOMIAL

If we look at our last example of C_3, we see that every vector in the code is a multiple of the polynomial $1 + x$. The vectors in the code are $x + x^2 = (1 + x)x$ and $1 + x^2 = (1 + x)^2$. It would be useful if this were true in general, and it is. The next idea is needed to express this.

An ideal I in R_n is called a *principal ideal* if every element in I is a multiple of a fixed polynomial $g(x)$. If I is principal, then $I = \{ c(x)g(x); c(x)$ in $R_n \}$. We denote this by $I = \langle g(x) \rangle$. Notice that $g(x)$ is not necessarily the only polynomial that generates I.

A ring is called a *principal ideal ring* ($P.I.R.$) if every ideal is principal. The integers are an example of a P.I.R. (Problem 4).

The next few theorems tell us how to find cyclic codes.

Theorem 44. If C is an ideal (i.e., a cyclic code of length n) in $R_n = F[x]/(x^n - 1)$, let $g(x)$ be the monic polynomial of smallest degree in C. Then $g(x)$ is uniquely determined and $C = \langle g(x) \rangle$.

Proof. We show in this theorem that R_n is a P.I.R. and that the monic generator of smallest degree of an ideal is unique even though an ideal can have other generators.

First we show that R_n is a P.I.R. Let $g(x)$ be the monic polynomial of smallest degree in C and let $a(x)$ be any other polynomial in C. By the division algorithm in $F[x]$, $a(x) = g(x)b(x) + r(x)$ where the degree of $r(x)$ is less than the degree of $g(x)$. By the definition of an ideal, $r(x)$ is in C. But this contradicts the choice of $g(x)$ unless $r(x)$ is identically zero so that $a(x) = g(x)b(x)$. Hence R_n is a P.I.R.

If $g(x)$ and $h(x)$ are monic polynomials of the same degree and both are in C, then $g(x) - h(x)$ is a polynomial in C of lower degree than either. This cannot happen if $g(x)$ has the smallest degree. Thus $g(x)$ is the unique monic polynomial of smallest degree in C and $C = \langle g(x) \rangle$. Q.E.D.

The following theorem tells us explicitly how to find this generator of a cyclic code. We consider C as consisting of representatives of degree less than n of the congruence classes of multiples of $g(x)$ modulo $(x^n - 1)$.

Theorem 45.   If C is an ideal in R_n, the unique monic generator, $g(x)$, of C of smallest degree divides $x^n - 1$ and conversely if a polynomial $g(x)$ in C divides $x^n - 1$, then $g(x)$ has the lowest degree in $\langle g(x) \rangle$.

Proof.   Suppose first that $g(x)$ is the monic polynomial of smallest degree in C. By the division algorithm in $F[x]$, $x^n - 1 = a(x)g(x) + r(x)$ where the degree of $r(x)$ is less than the degree of $g(x)$. Now $r(x) = -a(x)g(x)$ modulo $(x^n - 1)$ and so $r(x)$ is in $\langle g(x) \rangle$. This is a contradiction unless $r(x)$ is identically zero. Thus $g(x)$ divides $x^n - 1$.
   Conversely, suppose that $g(x)$ divides $x^n - 1$ and that $b(x)$ is in $\langle g(x) \rangle$ but has lower degree than $g(x)$. Then $b(x) = c(x)g(x) + (x^n - 1)d(x)$ in $F[x]$ because $b(x)$ is in C. However, since $g(x)$ divides $x^n - 1$, $g(x)$ divides $b(x)$, which is a contradiction.   Q.E.D.

   This says that, in order to construct a cyclic code, we need to factor $x^n - 1$. This is very useful even though it is often difficult to perform this factorization for large n. When considering binary cyclic codes, we assume that n is odd since in that case $x^n - 1$ has distinct factors (see Problem 5).
   The monic polynomial $g(x)$ of smallest degree in C is called the *generator polynomial* of C. By the previous theorems we know that $C = \langle g(x) \rangle$ and $g(x)$ divides $x^n - 1$. If we can factor $x^n - 1$ over $GF(q)$, we can construct all cyclic codes of length n over $GF(q)$. But it would be nice to know more about these codes. For instance, what is the dimension of a cyclic code with generator polynomial $g(x)$?

Theorem 46.   If the degree of $g(x)$ is $n - k$, then the dimension of $C = \langle g(x) \rangle$ is k. If $g(x) = g_0 + g_1 x + \cdots + g_{n-k} x^{n-k}$, then a generator matrix of C is the following.

$$
\begin{pmatrix}
g_0 & g_1 & g_2 & \cdots & g_{n-k} & 0 & 0 & \cdots & 0 \\
0 & g_0 & g_1 & \cdots & g_{n-k-1} & g_{n-k} & 0 & \cdots & 0 \\
0 & 0 & g_0 & \cdots & g_{n-k-2} & g_{n-k-1} & g_{n-k} & \cdots & 0 \\
\vdots & & & & & & & & \\
0 & 0 & 0 & \cdots & & & & & g_{n-k}
\end{pmatrix}.
$$

Proof.   The vectors $g(x), g(x)x, g(x)x^2, \ldots, g(x)x^{k-1}$ are linearly independent for if not then there would be field elements a_i, $0 \le i \le k - 1$, so that

$$
a_0 g(x) + a_1 g(x)x + \cdots + a_{k-1} g(x)x^{k-1}
$$
$$
= \left(a_0 + a_1 x + \cdots + a_{k-1} x^{k-1} \right) g(x) = 0.
$$

But this product has degree less than n so it cannot be 0 modulo $(x^n - 1)$ unless each a_i is 0. To see that these vectors span C, note that any $s(x)$ in C can be expressed as $c(x)g(x)$ where the degree of $c(x)$ is less than or equal to $k - 1$. Hence

$$c(x)g(x) = \left(c_0 + c_1 x + \cdots + c_{k-1}x^{k-1}\right)g(x)$$
$$= c_0 g(x) + c_1 g(x)x + \cdots + c_{k-1}g(x)x^{k-1}.$$

From this it follows that a generator matrix of C is the matrix whose first row is $g(x)$, whose second row is $g(x)x$, third row is $g(x)x^2, \ldots$ until $g(x)x^{k-1}$. This is the matrix portrayed above.

As an example, we construct binary cyclic codes for $n = 7$. The first thing to do is to factor $x^7 - 1$, which we know how to do. $x^7 - 1 = (1 + x)(1 + x + x^3)(1 + x^2 + x^3)$. This factorization gives us all cyclic codes of length 7. There are eight of them corresponding to the eight divisors of $x^7 - 1$ (see Problem 8). Consider $C = \langle g(x) \rangle$ where $g(x) = 1 + x + x^3$. Then C is four-dimensional and has the following generator matrix.

$$\begin{pmatrix} 1 & 1 & 0 & 1 & 0 & 0 & 0 \\ 0 & 1 & 1 & 0 & 1 & 0 & 0 \\ 0 & 0 & 1 & 1 & 0 & 1 & 0 \\ 0 & 0 & 0 & 1 & 1 & 0 & 1 \end{pmatrix}.$$

We recognize this as our shift register code example. But as yet we do not have an explanation of the connections in the shift register. These are given by the generator polynomial of the dual code, which is the topic of the next section.

5.3   THE GENERATOR POLYNOMIAL OF THE DUAL CODE

If we can factor $x^n - 1$ over $GF(q)$, then we know how many cyclic codes there are of length n over $GF(q)$. Furthermore, we know the dimension of the code from the degree of the factor. Also the factor gives a generator matrix explicitly. It would be nice if we could find a parity check matrix from the factors. We can actually do this by determining the generator polynomial of the dual code. This shows that the dual of a cyclic code is also cyclic although this can be seen directly from the definition of a cyclic code.

Suppose that $g(x)$ is the generator polynomial of a cyclic code C. We know that $g(x)$ divides $x^n - 1$ so that $x^n - 1 = g(x)h(x)$. If $g(x)$ has degree $n - k$, then C has dimension k and $h(x)$ has degree k. Since $h(x)$ divides $x^n - 1$, it is the generator polynomial of a cyclic code C' of dimension $n - k$. Now $C^\perp$ has dimension $n - k$ and it certainly would be convenient if $h(x)$ were the generator polynomial of $C^\perp$. There is no reason for this to be so. We have $g(x)h(x) = 0$ in R_n but it does not follow from this that the inner product of the two vectors $g(x)$ and $h(x)$ is 0. In fact it is not true in general that $h(x)$ is the generator of $C^\perp$ (it might be sometimes). What is surprising is that the generator polynomial of $C^\perp$ can be described in terms of $h(x)$. For this reason it is worth giving $h(x)$ a name.

If $x^n - 1 = g(x)h(x)$, and $g(x)$ is the generator polynomial of a cyclic code C, then $h(x)$ is called the *check polynomial* of C.

The relationship between polynomial multiplication being 0 in R_n and orthogonality of vectors is given in the next theorem.

Theorem 47. Suppose that $a(x) = (a_0, a_1, \ldots, a_{n-1})$ and $b(x) = (b_0, b_1, \ldots, b_{n-1})$. Then $a(x)b(x) = 0$ in R_n iff $a(x)$ is orthogonal to the vector $(b_{n-1}, \ldots, b_0)$ and every cyclic shift of this vector.

Proof. The proof is computational and for simplicity we give it for $n = 7$ although the general proof is similar. We can express the fact that $a(x) = (a_0, \ldots, a_6)$ is orthogonal to $(b_6, \ldots, b_0)$ and all its shifts by the following equations:

$$a_0 b_6 + a_1 b_5 + \cdots + a_6 b_0 = 0$$
$$a_0 b_0 + a_1 b_6 + \cdots + a_6 b_1 = 0$$
$$\vdots$$
$$a_0 b_5 + a_1 b_4 + \cdots + a_6 b_6 = 0.$$

We compute now

$$a(x)b(x) = \left(a_0 + a_1 x + \cdots + a_6 x^6\right)\left(b_0 + b_1 x + \cdots + b_6 x^6\right)$$

in R_7, which means that the product is taken modulo $x^7 - 1$. For the purposes of our proof, we write out the coefficients of the powers of x in the order x^6, $x^0 = 1, x, x^2, \ldots, x^5$. Then

$$\begin{aligned}
a(x)b(x) = &(a_0 b_6 + a_1 b_5 + \cdots + a_6 b_0)x^6 \\
&+ (a_0 b_0 + a_1 b_6 + \cdots + a_6 b_1) \\
&+ \cdots \\
&+ (a_0 b_5 + a_1 b_4 + \cdots + a_6 b_6)x^5.
\end{aligned}$$

The theorem follows since these coefficients equal the inner products above.   Q.E.D.

Theorem 48. If $g(x)h(x) = x^n - 1$ in $F[x]$ and $g(x)$ is the generator polynomial of a code C, then the reciprocal polynomial of $h(x)$ is the generator polynomial of $C^{\perp}$. Furthermore, if $h(x) = h_0 + h_1 x + \cdots + h_k x^k$, then the following is a parity check matrix H of C.

$$H = \begin{pmatrix} h_k & h_{k-1} & \cdots & h_0 & 0 & 0 & \cdots & 0 \\ 0 & h_k & \cdots & h_1 & h_0 & 0 & \cdots & 0 \\ & & \vdots & & & & & \\ 0 & 0 & h_k & \cdots & & & & h_0 \end{pmatrix}.$$

Hence $C^{\perp}$ is also cyclic.

Proof. In the last theorem let $a(x) = g(x)$ and $b(x) = h(x)$. Then the reciprocal polynomial of $h(x)$ is $x^k h(x^{-1}) = h_0 x^k + h_1 x^{k-1} + \cdots + h_k = h_k + h_{k-1}x + \cdots + h_0 x^k$. Theorem 47 shows that $g(x)$ is orthogonal to the reciprocal polynomial of $h(x)$ and all its cyclic shifts. Let G be the generator matrix of C given in Theorem 46. Then G consists of its first row r_1 and the first $k - 1$ cyclic shifts of r_1. Let A be the $n \times n$ matrix whose first k rows are the rows of G and whose succeeding $n - k$ rows are the remaining cyclic shifts of r_1. Let s_1 be the first row of H and let B be the $n \times n$ matrix consisting of s_1 and all of its cyclic shifts. Then r_1 is orthogonal to all the rows of B because $g(x)$ is orthogonal to the reciprocal polynomial of $h(x)$ and all its shifts. Since $(r_1, s_j) = (r_i, s_{l-1})$ where $l \equiv (j + i)$ (modulo n), all the rows of A are orthogonal to all the rows of B. Since the dimension of C is k and the dimension of the code with generator matrix H is $n - k$, by Problem 7, H is a parity check matrix of C and a generator matrix of $C^{\perp}$.   Q.E.D.

This is really very nice because after we factor $x^n - 1$ we can determine a generator polynomial for every cyclic code C and also generator and parity check matrices for C. Let us look again at our example of $x^7 - 1$ over $GF(2)$. This equals $(1 + x)(1 + x + x^3)(1 + x^2 + x^3)$. We constructed a generator matrix for the cyclic code C whose generator polynomial is $1 + x + x^3$. We now find a parity check matrix for C. The check polynomial $h(x)$ equals $(1 + x)(1 + x^2 + x^3) = 1 + x + x^2 + x^4$. Its reciprocal polynomial is $x^4(1 + x^{-1} + x^{-2} + x^{-4}) = 1 + x^2 + x^3 + x^4$.

Hence a parity check matrix for C is as follows.

$$H = \begin{pmatrix} 1 & 0 & 1 & 1 & 1 & 0 & 0 \\ 0 & 1 & 0 & 1 & 1 & 1 & 0 \\ 0 & 0 & 1 & 0 & 1 & 1 & 1 \end{pmatrix}.$$

It can be checked by direct computation that H is indeed a parity check matrix for C. In fact the connections for the shift register for C are governed by $1 + x^2 + x^3 + x^4$; that is, given the first four information positions of a vector v—v_0, v_1, v_2, and v_3—the fifth position of v, v_4, is the mod 2 sum of $v_0 + v_2 + v_3$. This expresses the fact that the first row of H is orthogonal to C. The sixth and seventh digits of v were similarly computed using the second and third rows of H. Since this procedure generates a cyclic code, it is not hard to show that the shift register we started with must repeat after every seven digits.

We can say more about cyclic codes from their generating polynomials.

Theorem 49. Let C_1 and C_2 be cyclic codes with generator polynomials $g_1(x)$ and $g_2(x)$. Then $C_1 \subseteq C_2$ iff $g_2(x)$ divides $g_1(x)$.

Proof. This follows since $C_1 \subseteq C_2$ iff $\langle g_1(x) \rangle \subseteq \langle g_2(x) \rangle$ iff $g_2(x)$ divides $g_1(x)$. Q.E.D.

Theorem 50. The binary cyclic code with generator polynomial $1 + x$ is the $(n - 1)$-dimensional code C consisting of all even weight vectors of length n. A binary cyclic code $C = \langle g(x) \rangle$ contains only even weight vectors iff $1 + x$ divides $g(x)$.

Proof. The cyclic code C with generator polynomial $1 + x$ has dimension $n - 1$. Then $C^\perp$ is the one-dimensional space with generator polynomial $1 + x + x^2 + \cdots + x^{n-1}$ since $(x^n - 1) = (1 + x)(1 + x + \cdots + x^{n-1})$ and $1 + x + \cdots + x^{n-1}$ is its own reciprocal polynomial. This is easily seen to be the code consisting of the zero vector and the all-one vector $\mathbf{h}$. Clearly a binary vector is orthogonal to $\mathbf{h}$ iff it has even weight.

A binary cyclic code C' with generator polynomial $g(x)$ contains only even weight vectors iff $C' \subseteq C$ iff $1 + x$ divides $g(x)$. Q.E.D.

Recall our last example of a binary length 7 code C with generator polynomial $1 + x + x^3$. We saw that this code contains odd weight vectors. However, the code with generator polynomial $(1 + x)(1 + x + x^3) = 1 + x^2 + x^3 + x^4$ has only even weight vectors and is contained in C.

Corollary. If a binary cyclic code with generator polynomial $g(x)$ is self-orthogonal, then $1 + x$ must divide $g(x)$.

Proof. In a binary self-orthogonal code, all weights are even. Clearly the converse need not hold. Q.E.D.

The following theorem is quite useful as it enables us to recognize whether a cyclic code is self-orthogonal or not from the factorization of $x^n - 1$.

Theorem 51. Let $x^n - 1 = g(x)h(x)$ over $GF(q)$. Then a cyclic code C with generator polynomial $g(x)$ is self-orthogonal iff the reciprocal polynomial of $h(x)$ divides $g(x)$.

Proof. A code C is self-orthogonal iff $C \subseteq C^\perp$ iff the generator polynomial of $C^\perp$ divides $g(x)$. Q.E.D.

Since $(x^7 + 1) = (1 + x)(1 + x + x^3)(1 + x^2 + x^3)$, the code with generator polynomial $1 + x^2 + x^3 + x^4 = (1 + x)(1 + x + x^3)$ is self-orthogonal since $x^3 h(x^{-1}) = 1 + x + x^3$, which divides $1 + x^2 + x^3 + x^4$.

5.4 IDEMPOTENTS AND MINIMAL IDEALS FOR BINARY CYCLIC CODES

In this section we consider only binary cyclic codes of odd length n. Then $x^n - 1$ has distinct factors. As we noted before, an ideal can have more than one generator. The generator polynomial has the nice property that its degree gives information about the dimension of the code, but to discover generator polynomials we must factor $x^n - 1$, and this can be quite difficult to do. There are other generators that can be found without factoring $x^n - 1$. These are called idempotent generators.

A generator $e(x)$ of an ideal in R_n is called an idempotent generator if it is an *idempotent*, that is, if $e^2(x) = e(x)$. This generator acts as a unit since, if $a(x)$ is in $\langle e(x) \rangle$, then $a(x) = b(x)e(x)$ and $a(x)e(x) = b(x)e^2(x) = b(x)e(x) = a(x)$. Conversely an idempotent that is a unit for an ideal I generates I (Problem 13).

How might we find these idempotent generators? Let us consider our old friend, $n = 7$. Suppose we have an idempotent $e(x) = \alpha_0 + \alpha_1 x + \cdots + \alpha_6 x^6$. Then $e(x)^2 = e(x)$ so that $e^2(x) = \alpha_0^2 + \alpha_1^2 x^2 + \cdots + \alpha_3^2 x^6 = e(x)$. Let S be the set of powers of x that occur with nonzero coefficients in $e(x)$. Then $e^2(x) = e(x)$ means that i is in S iff $2i$ (modulo 7) is in S. This can only occur if S is a union of cyclotomic cosets for $n = 7$. This is true in general, and the proof is essentially what we said above.

Lemma.   A binary polynomial $f(x)$ is an idempotent in R_n iff the set S of powers of x that occur with nonzero coefficients in $f(x)$ is a union of cyclotomic cosets for n.

Getting back to our example, we compute cyclotomic cosets for $n = 7$. $C_0 = \{0\}$, $C_1 = \{1, 2, 4\}$, $C_3 = \{3, 6, 5\}$. From this we can read off all eight idempotents. We list them below along with the generator polynomial for the code and the code's dimension. After the idempotent we write its relation to the generator polynomial.

Generator Polynomial	Dimension	Idempotent Generator
$g_1(x) = (1 + x + x^3)$ $\times (1 + x^2 + x^3)$	1	$e_1(x) = g_1(x)$ $= 1 + x + x^2 + x^3$ $+ x^4 + x^5 + x^6$
$g_2(x) = (1 + x)(1 + x + x^3)$	3	$e_2(x) = x^3 g_2(x)$ $= 1 + x^3 + x^5 + x^6$
$g_3(x) = (1 + x)(1 + x^2 + x^3)$	3	$e_3(x) = g_3(x)$ $= 1 + x + x^2 + x^4$
$g_4(x) = 1 + x$	6	$e_2(x) + e_3(x)$ $= (x + x^3 + x^5)g_4(x)$ $= x + x^2 + x^3$ $+ x^4 + x^5 + x^6$
$g_5(x) = 1 + x + x^3$	4	$e_1(x) + e_2(x)$ $= xg_5(x)$ $= x + x^2 + x^4$
$g_6(x) = 1 + x^2 + x^3$	4	$e_1(x) + e_3(x)$ $= x^3 g_6(x)$ $= x^3 + x^5 + x^6$

The seventh idempotent is 1 and its code is the whole space; the eighth idempotent is 0 and its code is just the zero vector. Let us notice several things. One is that every cyclic code of length 7 does have an idempotent generator. Another is that there are certain idempotents, $e_1(x)$, $e_2(x)$, and $e_3(x)$, that are special. If we look carefully, we see that $1 = e_1(x) + e_2(x) + e_3(x)$, $e_i(x)e_j(x) = 0$ if $i \neq j$ and every other idempotent is a sum of these special ones. As we see, these are specific instances of general facts.

Theorem 52. Every cyclic code C has an idempotent generator $e(x)$. Further, the matrix M formed by $e(x)$ and its next $k - 1$ cyclic shifts is a generator matrix for C.

Proof. Let $g(x)$ be the generator polynomial of the cyclic code C. Then $x^n - 1 = g(x)h(x)$ in $F[x]$. By our assumption on n, $x^n - 1$ has distinct factors so that g.c.d.$(g(x), h(x)) = 1$. By the Euclidean algorithm, there are polynomials $a(x)$ and $b(x)$ so that $1 = a(x)g(x) + b(x)h(x)$ in $F[x]$. Let $e(x) = a(x)g(x)$. Clearly $e(x)$ is in C. Multiply the above equation by $a(x)g(x)$ so that $a(x)g(x) = a^2(x)g^2(x) + a(x)b(x)g(x)h(x) = a^2(x)g^2(x)$ in R_n. If $c(x)$ is any codeword in C, then $c(x) = d(x)g(x)$ so that $c(x) = a(x)g(x)c(x) + b(x)d(x)g(x)h(x)$ in $F[x]$ and this equals $a(x)g(x)c(x)$ in R_n. Hence $c(x) = e(x)c(x)$ so that $e(x)$ acts as a unit for C and so generates C.

If M is not a generator matrix for C, then there exists a polynomial $a(x)$ of degree $\leq k - 1$ so that $a(x)e(x) = 0$. But $a(x)e(x)g(x) = a(x)g(x) = 0$ which contradicts Theorem 46.   Q.E.D.

Call an ideal M in a ring R a *minimal ideal* if 0 is the only ideal strictly contained in M. As examples of minimal ideals consider the length 7 codes whose idempotent generators are $e_1(x)$, $e_2(x)$, and $e_3(x)$. Clearly no code other than 0 is contained in $\langle e_1(x) \rangle$ since it has dimension 1. Also, by Theorem 49, we can see that $\langle e_1(x) \rangle$ is not contained in either $\langle e_2(x) \rangle$ or $\langle e_3(x) \rangle$ so that these are minimal ideals by dimension arguments.

If $x^n - 1 = (x - 1)f_1(x) \ldots f_k(x)$, let $\hat{f_i}(x)$ denote the product of all factors except $f_i(x)$.

Theorem 53. If $x^n - 1 = (x - 1)f_1(x) \ldots f_k(x)$ where the $f_i(x)$ are irreducible, then a cyclic code C is a minimal ideal iff it has as generator polynomial $\widehat{f_i}(x)$ or $\widehat{(x - 1)}$.

Proof. This follows from Theorem 49.   Q.E.D.

The code $\langle \widehat{(x + 1)} \rangle$ has generator polynomial $1 + x + x^2 + \cdots + x^{n-1}$ and is the one-dimensional space generated by the all-one vector h.

Let $C_1 + C_2 = \{ c_1(x) + c_2(x)$ where $c_1(x)$ is in C_1 and $c_2(x)$ is in $C_2 \}$. We call this the sum of codes C_1 and C_2.

Theorem 54. Let C_1 and C_2 be cyclic codes with generator polynomials $g_1(x)$ and $g_2(x)$ and idempotent generators $e_1(x)$, and $e_2(x)$. Then $C_1 \cap C_2$ has as generator polynomial l.c.m. $(g_1(x), g_2(x))$ and as idempotent generator $e_1(x)e_2(x)$, and $C_1 + C_2$ has as generator polynomial g.c.d.$(g_1(x), g_2(x))$ and as idempotent generator $e_1(x) + e_2(x) - e_1(x)e_2(x)$.

Proof. We leave the proofs of the statements about generator polynomials to Problem 14. Clearly $e_1(x)e_2(x)$ is in $C_1 \cap C_2$ and $(e_1(x)e_2(x))^2 = e_1(x)^2 e_2(x)^2 = e_1(x)e_2(x)$ so that $e_1(x)e_2(x)$ is an idempotent in $C_1 \cap C_2$. If $c(x)$ is in $C_1 \cap C_2$, then $e_1(x)e_2(x)c(x) = e_1(x)c(x) = c(x)$ so that $e_1(x)e_2(x)$ is a unit for $C_1 \cap C_2$ and so generates $C_1 \cap C_2$. Now $e_1(x) + e_2(x) - e_1(x)e_2(x)$ is in $C_1 + C_2$ and $(e_1(x) + e_2(x) - e_1(x)e_2(x))^2 = e_1(x) + e_2(x) - e_1(x)e_2(x)$ so that $e_1(x) + e_2(x) - e_1(x)e_2(x)$ is an idempotent. If $c(x)$ is in $C_1 + C_2$, then $c(x) = c_1(x) + c_2(x)$ for some $c_1(x)$ in C_1 and some $c_2(x)$ in C_2. Hence

$$
\begin{aligned}
&(c_1(x) + c_2(x))(e_1(x) + e_2(x) - e_1(x)e_2(x)) \\
&= c_1(x)e_1(x) + c_1(x)e_2(x) - c_1(x)e_1(x)e_2(x) \\
&\quad + c_2(x)e_1(x) + c_2(x)e_2(x) - c_2(x)e_1(x)e_2(x) \\
&= c_1(x) + c_1(x)e_2(x) - c_1(x)e_2(x) \\
&\quad + c_2(x)e_1(x) + c_2(x) - c_2(x)e_1(x) \\
&= c_1(x) + c_2(x)
\end{aligned}
$$

so that $e_1(x) + e_2(x) - e_1(x)e_2(x)$ acts as a unit for $C_1 + C_2$ and thus generates it.   Q.E.D.

Theorem 55. If $x^n - 1 = (x - 1)f_1(x)\ldots f_k(x)$ is a factorization of $x^n - 1$ into irreducible factors, then there are $k + 1$ minimal ideals $C_1,\ldots, C_{k+1}$ with generator polynomials $\widehat{f_1}(x),\ldots,\widehat{f_k}(x),\widehat{(x - 1)}$ and idempotent generators $e_1(x),\ldots, e_{k+1}(x)$. These $e_i(x)$ satisfy the following conditions.

(i) $e_i(x)e_j(x) = 0$ if $i \neq j$.

(ii) $1 = \displaystyle\sum_{i=1}^{k+1} e_i(x)$.

Furthermore, any cyclic code C is a sum of minimal ideals C_i and its idempotent e is a sum of the idempotents e_i for the C_i.

Proof. Since the C_i are minimal ideals, $C_i \cap C_j = 0$ for $i \neq j$ so that $e_i e_j = 0$ for $i \neq j$ because $e_i e_j$ is in $C_i \cap C_j$. Now $C_1 + C_2$ has idempotent

$e_1 + e_2 - e_1 e_2 = e_1 + e_2$ and it can be shown that $C_1 + C_2 + \cdots + C_{k+1}$ has idempotent $e_1 + e_2 + \cdots + e_{k+1}$. We know that $C_1 + C_2$ has as generator polynomial g.c.d.$(\widehat{f_1}(x), \widehat{f_2}(x))$ and it follows by finite induction that the generator polynomial of $C_1 + C_2 + \cdots + C_{k+1}$ is the greatest common divisor of $\widehat{f_1}(x), \ldots, \widehat{f_k}(x), \widehat{(x-1)}$. But this greatest common divisor can only be 1 since the factors are distinct. Hence $1 = e_1 + e_2 + \cdots + e_{k+1}$.

If C is any ideal, then C has an idempotent generator $e(x)$. Hence $e(x) = e(x)e_1(x) + \cdots + e(x)e_{k+1}(x)$. The ideal $C \cap C_i$ is contained in C_i and so is either 0 or C_i. If $C \cap C_i = C_i$, then $C_i \subseteq C$ and $ee_i = e_i$; otherwise $ee_i = 0$. Hence $e(x)$ is the sum of the $e_i(x)$ for those i such that $C_i \subset C$ and C itself is the sum of the C_i that are contained in it.   Q.E.D.

If we know the idempotents of the minimal ideals, called *primitive idempotents*, then we can find the idempotent of any ideal by just adding them up. For this reason some effort has been made to find these primitive idempotents [15, Chap. 8].

Now if we have an idempotent generator of a code C, we may want to find the generator polynomial of C, for instance to find the dimension of C. This is given by the following theorem, whose proof we leave to Problem 19.

Theorem 56. If $e(x)$ is the idempotent generator of C, then the generator polynomial $g(x)$ of C equals g.c.d.$(e(x), (x^n - 1))$.

The method described in Section 3.2 can be used to compute this greatest common divisor if necessary. It is often possible to know the dimension of a code with a given idempotent generator without knowing the generator polynomial (see Problem 16). Of course, we can compute all idempotent generators for binary codes immediately from the cyclotomic cosets.

Theorem 57. For a specific n suppose that there are k cyclotomic cosets for n. Then there are 2^k binary cyclic codes. Suppose further that n is a prime p and that m is the smallest integer so that $2^m \equiv 1$ (modulo p). Then $k - 1$ of the cyclotomic cosets have m elements and one has one element. If $x^p - 1 = (x - 1)f_1 \cdots f_{k-1}$ where the f_i are irreducible, then each f_i has degree m and each minimal ideal except $\langle x - 1 \rangle$ has dimension m.

Proof. If there are k cyclotomic cosets, then we can compute 2^k idempotents and each generates a cyclic code. If n is a prime p, then each cyclotomic coset except $\{0\}$ must have m elements since $s2^i \equiv s2^j$ (modulo p) iff $2^i \equiv 2^j$ (modulo p) iff $j - i \equiv m$ (modulo p) iff $j - i$ is a multiple of m. Since we have 2^k cyclic codes, $x^p - 1$ must have k irreducible factors, one of which is $x - 1$. Furthermore, each factor must have degree m that is the dimension of the minimal ideal, $\langle \hat{f}_i(x) \rangle$. Q.E.D.

An analogous theorem holds for codes of prime length over $GF(q)$. Namely, the dimensions and numbers of cyclic codes can be computed from the sizes and numbers of cyclotomic cosets. However, the proof of this is more complicated.

If we have a cyclic code given by its idempotent $e(x)$, we, of course, want to know the idempotent of the dual code. The proof about the idempotent for $\langle h(x) \rangle$ is left to Problem 20.

Theorem 58. Let $x^n - 1 = g(x)h(x)$ and let C be a cyclic code with generator polynomial $g(x)$ and idempotent generator $e(x)$. Then the code with generator polynomial $h(x)$ has idempotent generator $1 - e(x)$ and $C^\perp$ has idempotent generator $1 - e(x^{-1})$.

Proof. It is easy to show that $1 - e(x^{-1})$ is in $C^\perp$ (see Problem 23). The fact that $1 - e(x^{-1})$ is a unit for $C^\perp$ follows from the corresponding fact for $1 - e(x)$.   Q.E.D.

The following theorem about the structure of a minimal ideal is interesting.

Theorem 59. Every minimal ideal M is a field. Let $x^n - 1 = (x - 1)f_1 \ldots f_k$ be the factorization of $x^n - 1$ into irreducible factors. If $M = \langle \hat{f}_i(x) \rangle$, then M can be constructed by using residues modulo the polynomial $f_i(x)$, and if $f_i(x)$ has degree m, then M is isomorphic to the field $GF(2^m)$.

Proof. If $a(x) \neq 0$ is in M, $\langle a(x) \rangle$ is a nonzero ideal in M. Since M is a minimal ideal, $\langle a(x) \rangle = M$. Hence $e(x)$, the idempotent of M, equals $a(x)b(x)$ with $b(x)$ in R_n. If $b(x)$ is in M, it is the inverse of $a(x)$. In any case $b(x)e(x)$ is in M and it is the inverse of $a(x)$.

If $f_i(x)$ has degree m, then M has dimension m and so has 2^m elements. But $f_i(x)$ is an irreducible polynomial of degree m and so can be used to construct $GF(2^m)$ and there is one field of 2^m elements up to isomorphism.   Q.E.D.

The ideal with polynomial generator $\langle f_i(x) \rangle$ is called a *maximal ideal* as it is not contained in any larger ideal except for R_n. Maximal ideals do not play the important role of minimal ideals since the minimal ideals are the building blocks of all ideals in R_n.

Cyclic codes were first studied by Eugene Prange, who determined many of their properties. Many people have worked on these codes since then including W. W. Peterson, who describes many of these contributions in [19].

PROBLEMS

1. Find an element in R_3 that does not have a multiplicative inverse.

2. Let R be a finite commutative ring with a unit. An element $a \neq 0$ in R is called a zero divisor if $ab = 0$ for some $b \neq 0$ in R. Show that R is a field iff it has no zero divisors.

3. Find all binary cyclic codes in R_5.

4. Prove that the integers are a P.I.R.

5. Show that $x^n - 1$ has repeated factors over $GF(2)$ for n even (see Problem 4.12).

6. If C is an (n, k) cyclic code, show that every k successive positions are information positions, if the first k are.

7. If $h(x)$ divides $x^n - 1$ and the reciprocal polynomial of $h(x)$ is $h'(x) = h_0 x^k + h_1 x^{k-1} + \cdots + h_k$, then show that the monic polynomial $1/h_0 h'(x)$ also divides $x^n - 1$.

8. Consider the binary cyclic codes of length 7.

   (a) Give the generator polynomial and a generator matrix for each code.

   (b) Identify dual codes.

   (c) Show all inclusions among these codes, that is, list all cases where $C_i \subset C_j$.

9. Which length 7 binary cyclic codes contain the vector $(0, 1, 0, 0, 1, 1, 1)$?

10. Which binary cyclic codes of length 7 are self-orthogonal?

11. We know that
$$x^{15} - 1 = (x - 1)(1 + x + x^2)(1 + x + x^4)$$
$$\times (1 + x^3 + x^4)(1 + x + x^2 + x^3 + x^4).$$

   (a) How many cyclic codes of length 15 are there?

(b) Give generator polynomials for four of these codes and for their dual codes.

(c) Give the dimensions of the eight codes in part (b).

12. Find a self-orthogonal length 15 binary cyclic code.

13. Prove that an idempotent in an ideal I, which is a unit for I, generates I.

14. Prove the statements in Theorem 54 about generator polynomials for $C_1 \cap C_2$ and $C_1 + C_2$.

15. Verify the statements in Theorem 54 for cyclic codes of length 7.

16. Find all idempotent generators for length 23 binary cyclic codes and for each idempotent generator give the dimension of its code. Find a generator matrix for one of these codes.

17. Find all self-orthogonal binary cyclic codes of length 23.

18. Prove that if S is a union of cyclotomic cosets for n, then so is T where $T = \{ n - i | i \in S \}$.

19. Prove Theorem 56.

20. If $x^n - 1 = g(x)h(x)$ and $\langle g(x) \rangle$ has idempotent generator $e(x)$, show that $\langle h(x) \rangle$ has idempotent generator $1 - e(x)$.

21. Let C_1 and C_2 be cyclic codes with idempotents e_1 and e_2. Show that $C_1 \subseteq C_2$ iff $e_1 e_2 = e_1$.

22. Consider binary cyclic codes of length 15. Some of these codes have the following idempotent generators. $e_1 = x + x^2 + x^4 + x^8$, $e_2 = 1 + x + x^2 + x^4 + x^8$, $e_3 = x^3 + x^6 + x^9 + x^{12}$, $e_4 = x^5 + x^{10}$, $e_5 = 1 + x^5 + x^{10}$, $e_6 = 1 + x^3 + x^6 + x^9 + x^{12}$. Let C_i be the code with idempotent generator e_i.

(a) For which i and j is $C_i \subset C_j$? Why?

(b) Find the idempotent generator of $C_i^\perp$ for $i = 1, 2, 4, 6$.

(c) Which C_i contain only even weight vectors? Why?

23. If $e(x)$ is an idempotent show, by using Theorem 47, that $e(x)$ is orthogonal to $(1 - e(x^{-1}))$.

6

The Group of a Code and Quadratic Residue (Q.R.) Codes

6.1 SOME CYCLIC CODES WE KNOW

In our discussion of cyclic codes, we thoroughly analyzed all cyclic codes of length 7. There are two $(7,4)$ cyclic codes and two $(7,3)$ cyclic codes. We have already seen the perfect $(7,4)$ Hamming code and it did not look cyclic. At least our basis did not consist of cyclic shifts of one vector. Are the cyclic $(7,4)$ codes essentially different from the Hamming $(7,4)$ code or are they equivalent to it (and hence also to each other)? Before guessing at the answer, we look more closely at the $(7,4)$ cyclic codes. The $(7,4)$ cyclic codes C_1 and C_2 have generator polynomials $1 + x + x^3$ and $1 + x^2 + x^3$ and idempotent generators $x + x^2 + x^4$ and $x^3 + x^5 + x^6$, respectively. Now $C_1^\perp$ and $C_2^\perp$ have generator polynomials $(1 + x)(1 + x + x^3)$ and $(1 + x)(1 + x^2 + x^3)$ and, by Theorem 51, we know that these codes are self-orthogonal. The rows of the generator matrices given by the generator polynomials all have weight 4 so that, by Theorem 4, all weights in $C_1^\perp$ and $C_2^\perp$ are divisible by 4, which means that all nonzero weights actually occurring equal 4. Furthermore, we know that $C_1 = C_1^\perp + \langle \mathbf{h} \rangle$, where $\mathbf{h}$ is the all-one vector, and $C_2 = C_2^\perp + \langle \mathbf{h} \rangle$ so that both C_1 and C_2 have seven vectors of weight 3 and one vector of weight 7 in addition to the vectors in $C_1^\perp$ and $C_2^\perp$. Hence C_1 and C_2 have the same weight distribution as the Hamming $(7,4)$ code C. Also, C has the property that $C = C^\perp + \langle \mathbf{h} \rangle$. Although these coincidences do not prove it, it is indeed true that C_1 and C_2 are equivalent to C (see Problem 1).

Recall the double-error-correcting $(15,7)$ B.C.H. code C whose parity check matrix H' is given in Section 3.4. Even though we cannot see from just looking at H' that this code is cyclic, we can check from H'

that C is the code whose generator polynomial is $g(x) = (1 + x + x^4) \times$ $(1 + x + x^2 + x^3 + x^4) = 1 + x^4 + x^6 + x^7 + x^8$. We can see that this is so by checking that the vector $(1, 0, 0, 0, 1, 0, 1, 1, 1, 0, 0, 0, 0, 0, 0)$ and its first six cyclic shifts are orthogonal to each row of H'. The matrix H in Section 3.4 is not the parity check matrix of a cyclic code, but clearly it is equivalent to one since the columns of H' are a rearrangement of the columns of H.

In Section 2.4 generator matrices for the $(24, 12)$ binary Golay code and the $(12, 6)$ ternary Golay code are given. If we puncture these in any coordinate, we obtain the $(23, 12)$ Golay code and the $(11, 6)$ Golay code. They can be defined as cyclic codes that are related to the quadratic residue group, but, in order to do this, we need to know about the group of a code and permutation groups.

6.2 PERMUTATION GROUPS

In Section 4.1 we defined a group. In order to discuss the group of a code, it is necessary to know about special types of groups called permutation groups. Suppose we have n objects arranged in a fixed order. Then a *permutation* of these n objects is a rearrangement of them. So, for example, if $n = 7$, let the objects be seven balls arranged in alphabetical order Ⓐ Ⓑ Ⓒ Ⓓ Ⓔ Ⓕ Ⓖ and placed in positions 1, 2, 3, 4, 5, 6, and 7. Then an example of a permutation π_1 of these balls is the interchange of the first two balls simultaneously with the interchange of the last two balls. Now the balls look like Ⓑ Ⓐ Ⓒ Ⓓ Ⓔ Ⓖ Ⓕ. Another example of a permutation π_2 is the cyclic shift of the original balls. The balls now are arranged as Ⓖ Ⓐ Ⓑ Ⓒ Ⓓ Ⓔ Ⓕ. We obviously need a notation to describe these permutations. Note that we can concisely describe π_1 as $(1, 2)(3)(4)(5)(6, 7)$. This means that the objects in positions 1 and 2 are to be interchanged as are the objects in positions 6 and 7, and positions 3, 4, and 5 are to remain fixed. If we know that we are permuting seven objects, we can write this simply as $(1, 2)(6, 7)$ where it is then understood that the objects in the omitted positions are fixed. Then π_2 has the description $(1, 2, 3, 4, 5, 6, 7)$. This form of a permutation is called cycle form.

If we have two permutations, we can multiply them and obtain another permutation. This amounts to applying the first permutation to the objects and then following this with the second permutation. Thus $(1, 2, 3, 4)(1, 4)$ $= (1, 2, 3)$ and $(1, 2, 4)(2, 3) = (1, 3, 2, 4)$. A group whose elements are permutations is called a *permutation group* if the multiplication may be regarded as first applying one rearrangement and then the second rearrangement. The group of all permutations on n objects is called S_n. It is not hard to show that the order of S_n is $n!$ (Problem 3). Thus S_3 has six elements, which are as follows: the identity, $(1, 2)$, $(1, 3)$, $(2, 3)$, $(1, 2, 3)$, and $(1, 3, 2)$.

If π is a permutation acting on objects $a_1, \ldots, a_n$, then $a_i\pi$ denotes the image of a_i under π. If $a_{i_1}\pi = a_{i_2}, a_{i_2}\pi = a_{i_3}, \ldots, a_{i_k}\pi = a_{i_1}$, then $(a_{i_1} a_{i_2}, \ldots, a_{i_k})$ is called a *cycle* of π. Note that we can start the cycle anywhere so that $(1, 2, 3)(2, 3, 1) = (3, 1, 2)$. Generally we start with the smallest element written first.

Theorem 60. Every permutation π can be written as a product of disjoint cycles. This is the *cycle form* of π.

Proof. If π is a permutation on a set of elements $S = \{a_1, a_2, \ldots, a_n\}$, then consider $a_1, a_1\pi, a_1\pi^2, \ldots$. Since S is finite, we must repeat eventually and the first time this occurs we must have $a_1\pi^i = a_1$. Otherwise we would have $a_1\pi^j = a_1\pi^k$ with $k < j \le i$ and $a_1\pi^{j-k} = a_1$ is an earlier repetition. This gives us the cycle $(a_1, a_1\pi, a_1\pi^2, \ldots, a_1\pi^{i-1})$. If all the elements in S occur in this cycle, we are finished. If not, start with some element a_j not in the cycle of a_1 and determine its cycle. These two cycles cannot contain any common elements by their construction. Continue in this way until all elements in S occur in cycles of π. Since a cycle does nothing to an element not in its list of elements, the product of these cycles in any order must be π.   Q.E.D.

Let P be a set of permutations on n objects. We say that P generates a group G if G is the smallest subgroup of S_n that contains P. S_3 is generated by the permutations $(1, 2)$ and $(1, 2, 3)$. Roughly speaking G is obtained from P by taking all possible products of the elements of P. A group usually has more than one set of generators.

A permutation group G on a set $S = \{a_1, \ldots, a_n\}$ is called *transitive* if, given any two elements a_i and a_j in S, there is a permutation π in G so that $a_i\pi = a_j$. If S is the set of elements between 1 and 7 and $\pi = (1, 2, 3, 4, 5, 6, 7)$, then the group G generated by π is the cyclic group of order 7 consisting of π and its powers. Also G is transitive on S since given i and j in S there is some power of π that sends i into j.

The objects that we permute are the coordinate positions of a code. If $\mathbf{v} = (v_1, \ldots, v_n)$ is a vector and π is a permutation on n objects, then π sends $\mathbf{v}$ into $\mathbf{v}\pi = \mathbf{w} = (w_1, \ldots, w_n)$ with $v_i = w_{i\pi}$. Thus if $\pi = (1, 2, 3, 4, 5, 6, 7)$ and $\mathbf{v} = (0, 1, 1, 0, 1, 0, 0)$, then $\mathbf{v}\pi = (0, 0, 1, 1, 0, 1, 0)$.

A permutation that acts on n objects is said to have *degree n*.

If $\pi_1, \ldots, \pi_k$ are k permutations of degree n, then the *group generated by* $\pi_1, \ldots, \pi_k$ is the smallest subgroup of S_n that contains them. This subgroup must contain all products of powers of the generating permutations.

6.3 THE GROUP OF A CODE

The group of a code is useful in determining the structure of the code, computing weight distributions, classifying codes, and devising decoding algorithms.

Let σ be the cyclic shift $(0, 1, \ldots, n - 1)$. Another way to define a binary (n, k) cyclic code C is to say that C is cyclic iff whenever c is in C so is $c\sigma$. This implies, for a cyclic code C, that cyclically shifting the columns of any generator matrix of C yields another generator matrix of C.

For example, consider the generator matrix G of the binary cyclic $(7, 4)$ code C with generator polynomial $g(x) = 1 + x + x^3$.

$$G = \begin{array}{c} \begin{array}{ccccccc} 0 & 1 & 2 & 3 & 4 & 5 & 6 \end{array} \\ \begin{pmatrix} 1 & 1 & 0 & 1 & 0 & 0 & 0 \\ 0 & 1 & 1 & 0 & 1 & 0 & 0 \\ 0 & 0 & 1 & 1 & 0 & 1 & 0 \\ 0 & 0 & 0 & 1 & 1 & 0 & 1 \end{pmatrix} \end{array}.$$

Applying the permutation $\sigma = (0, 1, 2, 3, 4, 5, 6)$ to the columns of G, we obtain the matrix G'.

$$G' = \begin{array}{c} \begin{array}{ccccccc} 0 & 1 & 2 & 3 & 4 & 5 & 6 \end{array} \\ \begin{pmatrix} 0 & 1 & 1 & 0 & 1 & 0 & 0 \\ 0 & 0 & 1 & 1 & 0 & 1 & 0 \\ 0 & 0 & 0 & 1 & 1 & 0 & 1 \\ 1 & 0 & 0 & 0 & 1 & 1 & 0 \end{pmatrix} \end{array}.$$

Since the first three rows of G' are the last three rows of G and the last row of G' is the sum of the first three rows of G, G' is also a generator matrix for C. Clearly any σ^i applied to the coordinate positions of G will result in another generator matrix of C.

Let C be a binary (n, k) code. Every permutation of the n coordinate positions sends C onto an equivalent (n, k) code or onto itself. It is easy to check that the set of all permutations that send C onto itself is a group, called *the group of C*. It is denoted by $G(C)$. Clearly any element in $G(C)$

applied to the coordinate positions of any generator matrix of C yields another generator matrix of C. The group of C is a subgroup of S_n.

If C is the whole space, $G(C) = S_n$. If $C = \langle \mathbf{h} \rangle$, $G(C)$ is also S_n. Let C be the code with generator matrix G.

$$
\begin{array}{cccccc}
1 & 2 & 3 & 4 & 5 & 6
\end{array}
$$
$$
G = \begin{pmatrix} 1 & 1 & 0 & 0 & 0 & 0 \\ 0 & 0 & 1 & 1 & 0 & 0 \\ 0 & 0 & 0 & 0 & 1 & 1 \end{pmatrix}.
$$

As the rows of G are the only vectors of weight 2 in C, any permutation in $G(C)$ must permute these rows. If we look back again at the columns and call columns 1 and 2 a block, columns 3 and 4 a block, and columns 5 and 6 a block, this means that any permutation in $G(C)$ must either permute these blocks or interchange the columns within a block. Thus $G(C)$ is generated by the permutations $(1, 2)$, $(3, 4)$, $(5, 6)$, $(1, 3)(2, 4)$, and $(1, 5)(2, 6)$ and has order $2^3 \cdot 3! = 48$. The group of a code is often given by generating permutations although it is sometimes quite difficult to find permutations generating the entire group of the code. It is also hard, at times, to determine the order of the group from the generating permutations. Another problem that arises is showing that we do have the entire group of a code. It is often easy to find a subgroup of $G(C)$ as is the case with cyclic codes.

We can now say that a length n code C is cyclic if the group of C contains the cyclic group of order n generated by $\sigma = (0, 1, \ldots, n - 1)$. However, $G(C)$ might be, and usually is, larger than this as we see from Theorem 61. By Problem 7, if g.c.d.$(a, n) = 1$, there is an m so that $a^m \equiv 1 \pmod{n}$. The smallest positive such m is called the *order of a mod n*.

Lemma. Let σ be the cyclic shift permutation of odd degree n, that is, $(i)\sigma = (i + 1) \pmod{n}$. Let τ be the permutation of degree n defined by $(i)\tau = 2i \pmod{n}$. Both σ and τ are considered to act on $0, 1, \ldots, n - 1$. Let m be the order of $2 \bmod n$. Then $\tau \sigma \tau^{-1} = \sigma^{2^{m-1}}$ and $\tau^{-1} \sigma^i \tau = \sigma^{2i}$ for $0 \le i \le n - 1$.

Proof. By Problem 7, an m exists so that $2^m \equiv 1 \pmod{n}$. Notice that the inverse of τ, τ^{-1}, is given by $i\tau^{-1} = 2^{m-1}i \pmod{n}$. This is so as $i\tau\tau^{-1} = i$ and $i\tau^{-1}\tau = i$ for all $i, 0 \le i < n$, which is easy to check since $2^m \equiv 1 \pmod{n}$.

Consider $(i)\tau\sigma\tau^{-1}$. This is $(2i)\sigma\tau^{-1} = (2i + 1)\tau^{-1} = 2^{m-1}(2i + 1) = i + 2^{m-1} \pmod{n} = (i)\sigma^{2^{m-1}}$. Hence $\tau\sigma\tau^{-1} = \sigma^{2^{m-1}}$. It then follows that

$(\tau\sigma\tau^{-1})(\tau\sigma\tau^{-1}) = (\sigma^{2^{m-1}})^2$ so that $\tau\sigma^2\tau^{-1} = \sigma$. Then $\tau^{-1}\sigma\tau = \sigma^2$ and therefore $\tau^{-1}\sigma^i\tau = \sigma^{2i}$.   Q.E.D.

For example, if $n = 7$, $\sigma = (0, 1, 2, 3, 4, 5, 6)$, $\tau = (1, 2, 4)(3, 6, 5)$, and $\tau^{-1} = (1, 4, 2)(3, 5, 6)$. As $2^3 \equiv 1\,(\text{modulo } 7)$, $m = 3$ and $\sigma^{2^{m-1}} = \sigma^{2^2} = \sigma^4 = (0, 4, 1, 5, 2, 6, 3)$. Now

$$\tau\sigma\tau^{-1} = (1, 2, 4)(3, 6, 5)(0, 1, 2, 3, 4, 5, 6)\,(1, 4, 2)(3, 5, 6)$$

$$= (0, 4, 1, 5, 2, 6, 3) = \sigma^4.$$

Using the lemma, we can show that if C is a binary length n cyclic code, then not only is σ in $G(C)$ but τ is also.

Theorem 61. If C is an odd length n binary cyclic code, then the permutation τ defined in the lemma is in $G(C)$. Hence the group G generated by σ and τ is a subgroup of $G(C)$. The order of G is mn.

Proof. Let $e(x)$ be the idempotent generator of C. If $S = \{i$ so that x^i has coefficient 1 in $e(x)\}$, then S is a union of cyclotomic cosets by the lemma to Theorem 52. Hence the vector $e(x)$ has 1's on the same union of cyclotomic cosets. It follows that $e(x)\tau = e(x)$ and $e(x)\tau^{-1} = e(x)$. By the lemma, $\tau^{-1}\sigma^i\tau = \sigma^{2i}$ so that $e(x)\tau^{-1}\sigma^i\tau = e(x)\sigma^{2i}$ and thus $(e(x)\sigma^i)\tau = e(x)\sigma^{2i}$. This means that τ sends $e(x)$ into itself and sends every cyclic shift of $e(x)$ into some cyclic shift of $e(x)$, that is, $e(x)\sigma^i$ goes into, by τ, $e(x)\sigma^{2i}$. Since every vector in C is a linear combination of shifts of $e(x)$ and τ preserves linear combinations, τ is in $G(C)$.

Clearly $G = \langle\sigma, \tau\rangle$ is a subgroup of $G(C)$. Since $\tau^{-1}\sigma^i\tau = \sigma^{2i}$, $\tau^{-2}\sigma^i\tau^2 = \tau^{-1}\sigma^{2i}\tau = \sigma^{2^2 i},\ldots, \tau^{-k}\sigma^i\tau^k = \sigma^{2^k i}$, then $\sigma^i\tau^k = \tau^k\sigma^{2^k i}$. From this it follows that every element in G can be uniquely expressed as a product $\tau^j\sigma^l$. As there are mn of these products, the order of G is mn and the theorem is demonstrated.   Q.E.D.

The lemma holds if we replace 2 by q where $\text{g.c.d.}(q, n) = 1$ and the proof is the same. Theorem 61 also holds for codes of length n over $GF(q)$, $\text{g.c.d.}(q, n) = 1$, with $(i)\tau = qi\,(\text{mod } n)$ but the proof is more complicated.

If a is any integer less than n and $\text{g.c.d.}(a, n) = 1$, then the permutation μ_a defined by $i\mu_a = ai\,(\text{mod } n)$ carries cyclotomic cosets onto cyclotomic cosets (see Problem 8). If $a \equiv 2^i\,(\text{mod } n)$, then this permutation sends any cyclic code onto itself. Suppose a is not a power of $2\,(\text{mod } n)$. We know that the permutation μ_a sends a cyclic code onto an equivalent code and the next theorem says this equivalent code must be cyclic also. It is true for nonbinary codes as well.

Theorem 62. If C is a length n cyclic code, then the permutation μ_a defined by $i\mu_a = ai(\bmod n)$ where g.c.d.$(a, n) = 1$ sends C onto another cyclic code C' or onto C itself.

Proof. The proof is analogous to that of Theorem 61 and uses the fact that $\mu_a \sigma \mu_a^{-1}$ is a power of σ (Problem 12).   Q.E.D.

This shows that the two binary $(7, 4)$ cyclic codes are equivalent.

If C is not binary, then recall that we consider transformations that are more general than permutations. Let C be an (n, k) code over $GF(q)$. In Section 1.2 we defined a monomial transformation acting on n coordinate positions to be a permutation of those positions followed by multiplying some (or none) of them by nonzero elements from $GF(q)$. The group of monomial transformations on a space V over $GF(q)$ has order $(q - 1)^n n!$. Any transformation in this group either sends a length n code C onto an equivalent code or onto itself. The set of all monomial transformations that send C onto itself form a group called the *group of C* and is denoted by $G(C)$. This agrees with the definition of the group of a binary code and extends that definition to codes over $GF(q)$ where $q \neq 2$.

Equivalent codes have groups that are the same up to relabeling.

For example, consider the $(4, 2)$ ternary code C with generator matrix G.

$$\begin{array}{cccc} 1 & 2 & 3 & 4 \end{array}$$
$$G = \begin{pmatrix} 1 & 1 & 1 & 0 \\ 0 & 1 & 2 & 1 \end{pmatrix}.$$

If $\pi = (1, 2, 3)$, then π sends G onto another generator matrix of C. Also the monomial transformation that consists of interchanging the first two columns of G and then multiplying the fourth column by 2 sends G onto another generator matrix of C. These statements can be checked directly by computing these new matrices. If C is a ternary code, then the monomial transformation that multiplies each coordinate position by 2 is always in $G(C)$.

The comments about difficulties in determining the group of a binary code hold for codes over any $GF(q)$.

Theorem 63. $G(C) = G(C^\perp)$.

Proof. This is clear from the definitions of $G(C)$ and $G(C^\perp)$.   Q.E.D.

Corollary. Any permutation π in $G(C)$ sends an information set into an information set.

Proof. Suppose not. Then π sends k independent positions into k dependent positions. As a set of nonzero dependent positions gives a vector in $C^{\perp}$, this means that π would send a vector not in $C^{\perp}$ to one in $C^{\perp}$. This contradicts the theorem.   Q.E.D.

If C is the binary code $\langle \mathbf{h} \rangle$, then $C^{\perp}$ is the code consisting of all even weight vectors. Hence $G(C^{\perp}) = S_n$.

6.4 DEFINITION OF QUADRATIC RESIDUE (Q.R.) CODES

Quadratic residue codes (Q.R. codes) were first defined by Andrew Gleason, who demonstrated many of their important properties in a brief letter. The minimum weights of many modest sized Q.R. codes are known. These are quite high for the codes' lengths, making these codes "good" and this class of codes promising. An interesting question is what happens to the minimum weight d as the length n gets larger and larger. This is a very difficult question to answer for any class of codes. What is wanted in general is a "good" class of codes, that is, a constructive class of $(n, k(n), d(n))$ codes with the values of $d(n)/n$, as n increases, bounded away from 0 while at the same time the rate $k(n)/n$ is bounded away from 0 as n increases. For the Q.R. codes the rate is approximately $\frac{1}{2}$, which is clearly bounded away from 0. Of course, for practical purposes efficient decoding algorithms are needed and, even though the family looks very promising, better decoding algorithms are needed for Q.R. codes.

It is possible to define Q.R. codes over a general finite field but here we consider only binary Q.R. codes. These codes are cyclic codes and are quite easy to construct by their idempotent generators. For this reason we define them in this fashion. Consider the field $GF(p)$ where p is an odd prime and let G be the multiplicative group of nonzero elements in $GF(p)$. Then G has order $p - 1$. Let Q be the subgroup of squares in G. The elements of Q are called *quadratic residues*. Then Q has order $(p - 1)/2$ (Problem 4.16). It is a fact, which is somewhat complicated to demonstrate, that 2 is a quadratic residue iff $p \equiv \pm 1 \pmod{8}$. For such p let H be the subgroup of Q consisting of powers of 2. Just as cyclic codes are codes that are sent onto themselves by the cyclic shift, we want Q.R. codes to be sent onto themselves by the coordinate permutations $i \to ai \pmod{p}$ where a is a quadratic residue. The following theorem is useful in identifying the Q.R. codes.

We are still in the situation where g.c.d.$(a, n) = 1$.

Theorem 64. For any a the permutation μ_a defined by $i\mu_a = ai(\mathrm{mod}\ n)$ preserves the product of polynomials in R_n.

Proof. We already know (Theorem 62) that μ_a sends any cyclic code onto another cyclic code. It is true that μ_a also preserves the product of polynomials in R_n. To see this let

$$b(x) = b_0 + b_1 x + \cdots + b_{n-1} x^{n-1}$$

and

$$c(x) = c_0 + c_1 x + \cdots + c_{n-1} x^{n-1}.$$

Then

$$
\begin{aligned}
b(x)c(x) = & \left(b_0 c_0 + b_1 c_{n-1} + \cdots + b_{n-1} c_1\right) \\
& + \left(b_0 c_1 + b_1 c_0 + \cdots + b_{n-1} c_2\right)x \\
& + \cdots \\
& + \left(b_0 c_{n-1} + b_1 c_{n-2} + \cdots + b_{n-1} c_0\right)x^{n-1}.
\end{aligned}
$$

Let $b'(x), c'(x)$, and $(b(x)c(x))'$ denote the images of $b(x), c(x)$, and $b(x)c(x)$, respectively, under μ_a. Then

$$
\begin{aligned}
b'(x)c'(x) = & \left(b_0 + b_1 x^a + \cdots + b_{n-1} x^{an-a}\right) \\
& \times \left(c_0 + c_1 x^a + \cdots + c_{n-1} x^{an-a}\right) \\
= & \left(b_0 c_0 + b_1 c_{n-1} + \cdots + b_{n-1} c_1\right) \\
& + \left(b_0 c_1 + b_1 c_0 + \cdots + b_{n-1} c_2\right)x^a \\
& + \cdots \\
& + \left(b_0 c_{n-1} + b_1 c_{n-2} + \cdots + b_{n-1} c_0\right)x^{an-a} \\
= & \left(b(x)c(x)\right)'. \qquad \text{Q.E.D.}
\end{aligned}
$$

Corollary. If μ_a sends a cyclic code C with idempotent $e(x)$ onto a code C', then C' is cyclic with idempotent $e(x)\mu_a$.

Proof. This follows from Theorems 62 and 64 since the idempotent is the multiplicative unit of the code.   Q.E.D.

It is quite unusual to be able to tell whether a permutation sends one code onto another just by its effect on one vector, so this is a useful corollary.

For the remainder of this section, we suppose that $p \equiv \pm 1 (\bmod 8)$ so that 2 is a quadratic residue. If a cyclic code C is sent onto itself by all the coordinate permutations determined by quadratic residues, then its idempotent $e(x)$ has to be sent onto itself by all these transformations by the above corollary. Since 2 is a quadratic residue and the product of two residues is a residue, the quadratic residues are a union of cyclotomic cosets. Let m be the order of 2 modulo p. Then each nonzero cyclotomic coset has m elements and there are k of them where $mk = p - 1$. Hence the quadratic residues are a union of $k/2$ cyclotomic cosets and the remaining $k/2$ cyclotomic cosets constitute the *nonresidues*, N. Since the powers appearing in $e(x)$ are a union of cyclotomic cosets, the only $e(x)$ that can be fixed by the quadratic residue permutations (Problem 15) are

$$1 + \sum_{i \in Q} x^i, \qquad \sum_{i \in Q} x^i, \qquad 1 + \sum_{i \in N} x^i, \qquad \sum_{i \in N} x^i,$$

$$1, \qquad 1 + \sum_{i \in Q \cup N} x^i, \qquad \text{and} \qquad \sum_{i \in Q \cup N} x^i.$$

We exclude 1, $1 + \sum_{i \in Q \cup N} x^i$, and $\sum_{i \in Q \cup N} x^i$ as the corresponding codes are R_p, $\langle \mathbf{h} \rangle$, and all even weight vectors, respectively.

Consider the case $p = 31$. Then $C_0 = \{0\}$, $C_1 = \{1, 2, 4, 8, 16\}$, $C_3 = \{3, 6, 12, 24, 17\}$, $C_5 = \{5, 10, 20, 9, 18\}$, $C_7 = \{7, 14, 28, 25, 19\}$, $C_{11} = \{11, 22, 13, 26, 21\}$, and $C_{15} = \{15, 30, 29, 27, 23\}$. Here $H = C_1$, $Q = C_1 \cup C_5 \cup C_7$, and $N = C_3 \cup C_{11} \cup C_{15}$. By observation, we can see that the only idempotents that are sent into themselves by all permutations corresponding to quadratic residues are the ones mentioned above.

Lemma 1. Let 2 be a quadratic residue in $GF(p)$ and let S be a union of cyclotomic cosets for p. For each a in $GF(p)$, let $S(a) = \{ai | i \in S\}$. If $S = S(a)$ for all a in Q, then either $S = \{0\}$ or $S = Q$ or $S = N$ or $S = \{0\} \cup Q$ or $S = \{0\} \cup N$ or $S = Q \cup N$ or $S = \{0\} \cup Q \cup N$. The cyclotomic cosets contained in Q are the cosets of the subgroup H in the group Q.

Proof. Let G be the group of nonzero elements in $GF(p)$. Then G is a cyclic group that has a generator we call g. In this case g^2 generates Q. If the cyclotomic coset containing g^i is in S and i is even, the equation $i + 2k = 2$ has some solution k in $GF(p)$. Hence $g^i g^{2k} = g^2$ and so all of Q is in S. If i is odd, $i + 2k = 1$ has a solution in $GF(p)$ so that g is in S. If n is in N, then any element in N can be expressed as nr for some r in Q. Since g is in S, all of N is in S.   Q.E.D.

Let $e_1(x) = \sum_{i \in Q} x^i$ and $e_2(x) = \sum_{i \in N} x^i$. Clearly $e_1(x)$ and $e_2(x)$ are idempotents. We say that a binary cyclic code of prime length $p \equiv \pm 1 \pmod 8$ is a *Q.R. code* if its idempotent generator is either $e_1(x), e_2(x), 1 + e_1(x)$, or $1 + e_2(x)$. Note that there are four Q.R. codes of length p for p a prime $\equiv \pm 1 \pmod 8$.

With this definition it is easy to give a generator matrix of a length p Q.R. code but we do not know much else. In particular, what is the code's dimension? The following lemma is useful in answering this question.

Lemma 2. A binary cyclic code C that contains an odd weight vector contains the all-one vector $\mathbf{h}$.

Proof. Let $g(x)$ be the generator polynomial of C. By Theorem 50, C contains an odd weight vector iff $x - 1$ does not divide $g(x)$. If C is of length n, let $x^n - 1 = (x - 1)f(x)g(x)$. Now $f(x)g(x) = \mathbf{h}$, which is in C.   Q.E.D.

Theorem 65. -1 is a quadratic residue in $GF(p)$ iff $p \equiv 1 \pmod 4$.

Proof. Let α be a primitive element in $GF(p)$. Then the powers of α give all the nonzero elements of $GF(p)$ and, in particular, $\alpha^{(p-1)/2} = -1$ since this is the element $\neq 1$ whose square is 1. If $p \equiv -1 \pmod 4$, then $p = 4r - 1$ for some r and $(p - 1)/2 = (4r - 2)/2 = 2r - 1$ so that $-1 = \alpha^{2r-1}$ is an odd power of α and thus not a square. If $p \equiv 1 \pmod 4$, then $p = 4r + 1$ for some r and $(p - 1)/2 = 4r/2 = 2r$ and $-1 = (\alpha^r)^2$ is clearly a square.   Q.E.D.

Theorem 66. Let p be a prime $\equiv -1 \pmod 8$. Let $e_1(x) = \sum_{i \in Q} x^i$ and $e_2(x) = \sum_{i \in N} x^i$. Let Q_1 be the Q.R. code with idempotent $e_1(x)$ and Q_2 be the Q.R. code with idempotent $e_2(x)$. We let Q_1' be the Q.R. code with idempotent $1 + e_2(x)$ and Q_2' be the Q.R. code with idempotent $1 + e_1(x)$. Then the four Q.R. codes of length p have the following properties.

(i) Q_1 and Q_2 are equivalent. Q_1' and Q_2' are equivalent.

(ii) $Q_1 \cap Q_2 = \langle \mathbf{h} \rangle$, and $Q_1 + Q_2 = R_p$.

(iii) $\dim Q_1 = \dim Q_2 = (p + 1)/2$.

(iv) $Q_1 = Q_1' + \langle \mathbf{h} \rangle$, $Q_2 = Q_2' + \langle \mathbf{h} \rangle$.

(v) $\dim Q_1' = \dim Q_2' = (p - 1)/2$.

(vi) Q_1' and Q_2' are self-orthogonal and $Q_1'^\perp = Q_1'$, $Q_2'^\perp = Q_2'$.

Proof. By Theorem 62, if $(a, n) = 1$, μ_a sends a cyclic code onto a cyclic code. If we take a to be a fixed nonresidue, then $\mathbf{e}_1(x)\mu_a = \mathbf{e}_2(x)$ and $\mathbf{e}_2(x)\mu_a = \mathbf{e}_1(x)$. By the corollary to Theorem 64 we see that μ_a interchanges Q_1 and Q_2 and similarly Q_1' and Q_2' proving (i).

From the definitions of $\mathbf{e}_1$ and $\mathbf{e}_2$ it is easy to see that

$$(*) \qquad\qquad\qquad \mathbf{h} = 1 + \mathbf{e}_1 + \mathbf{e}_2.$$

Also the weight of either idempotent is $(p - 1)/2$ which is odd when $p \equiv -1 \pmod 8$. Hence by the lemma, $\mathbf{h}$ is in both Q_1 and Q_2. Now $\mathbf{e}_1\mathbf{h} = \mathbf{h}$ by Problem 17, so that multiplying $(*)$ by $\mathbf{e}_1$ we get

$$\mathbf{e}_1\mathbf{h} = \mathbf{h} = \mathbf{e}_1 + \mathbf{e}_1 + \mathbf{e}_1\mathbf{e}_2 = \mathbf{e}_1\mathbf{e}_2,$$

which shows that the idempotent of $Q_1 \cap Q_2$, $\mathbf{e}_1\mathbf{e}_2$, is $\mathbf{h}$. Clearly then $\dim(Q_1 \cap Q_2) = 1$. As Q_1 and Q_2 are equivalent, they have the same dimension, k, say. Now the idempotent of $Q_1 + Q_2$ is $\mathbf{e}_1 + \mathbf{e}_2 - \mathbf{e}_1\mathbf{e}_2 = \mathbf{e}_1 + \mathbf{e}_2 + \mathbf{h}$ (over $GF(2)$ we can disregard the difference between $+$ and $-$) $= 1$ by $(*)$. Hence $Q_1 + Q_2 = R_p$ and has dimension p. This demonstrates (ii).

Now $\dim(Q_1 + Q_2) = \dim(Q_1) + \dim(Q_2) - \dim(Q_1 \cap Q_2)$, which says that $p = 2k - 1$ so that $k = (p + 1)/2$ and (iii) follows.

The idempotent of $Q_1' + \langle \mathbf{h} \rangle$ is $1 + \mathbf{e}_2 + \mathbf{h} + (1 + \mathbf{e}_2)\mathbf{h} = 1 + \mathbf{e}_2 + \mathbf{h}$ by Problem 17 as $1 + \mathbf{e}_2$ has even weight. By $(*)$, $Q_1' + \langle \mathbf{h} \rangle = \langle \mathbf{e}_1 \rangle$ showing (iv).

As $(1 + \mathbf{e}_1)(1 + \mathbf{e}_2) = 1 + \mathbf{e}_1 + \mathbf{e}_2 + \mathbf{h} = 0$ by $(*)$, $Q_1' \cap Q_2' = 0$. The idempotent of $Q_1' + Q_2'$ is $(1 + \mathbf{e}_1) + (1 + \mathbf{e}_2) = \mathbf{e}_1 + \mathbf{e}_2 = 1 + \mathbf{h}$ so that $Q_1' + Q_2'$ is the space of all even-weight vectors which has dimension $p - 1$. Arguing as for (iii) we find that $\dim Q_1' = \dim Q_2' = (p - 1)/2$.

As -1 is a nonresidue since $p \equiv 3 \pmod 4$, we can take $a = -1$ so that $1 - \mathbf{e}_1(x^{-1}) = 1 + \mathbf{e}_2(x)$. Hence $Q_1^{\perp} = Q_1'$ by Theorem 58. Since $Q_1' \subset Q_1$ by (iv) we see that Q_1' and similarly Q_2' are self-orthogonal.   Q.E.D.

Note that this is the situation for $p = 7$ given in Section 5.4.

The case for $p \equiv 1 \pmod 8$ is similar to the above but different in some respects. In this situation the Q.R. codes are equivalent by any permutation given by a nonresidue but it cannot be -1 by Theorem 65.

Theorem 67. Let p be a prime $\equiv 1 \pmod 8$. Let $\mathbf{e}_1(x) = \sum_{i \in Q} x^i$ and $\mathbf{e}_2(x) = \sum_{i \in N} x^i$. Let Q_1 be the Q.R. code with idempotent generator $1 + \mathbf{e}_1(x)$ and Q_2 the Q.R. code with idempotent generator $1 + \mathbf{e}_2(x)$. We let Q_1' be the Q.R. code with idempotent generator $\mathbf{e}_2(x)$ and Q_2' the Q.R.

code with idempotent generator $e_1(x)$. Then the four Q.R. codes of length p have the following properties.

(i) Q_1 and Q_2 are equivalent. Q_1' and Q_2' are equivalent.

(ii) $Q_1 \cap Q_2 = \langle \mathbf{h} \rangle$, and $Q_1 + Q_2 = R_p$.

(iii) Q_1 and Q_2 have dimension $(p + 1)/2$.

(iv) $Q_1 = Q_1' + \langle \mathbf{h} \rangle$, $Q_2 = Q_2' + \langle \mathbf{h} \rangle$.

(v) Q_1' and Q_2' have dimension $(p - 1)/2$.

(vi) $Q_1^{\perp} = Q_2'$ and $Q_2^{\perp} = Q_1'$.

The proof of Theorem 67 is very similar to the proof of Theorem 66. Possibly the most difficult portion is (vi), which is Problem 19.

It should be no surprise that the Hamming $(7, 3)$ and $(7, 4)$ codes are equivalent to Q.R. codes. In fact, the cyclic $(7, 4)$ and $(7, 3)$ codes are Q.R. codes. It is also true (although much less obvious) that the $(23, 12)$ and $(23, 11)$ Q.R. codes are equivalent to the $(23, 12)$ and $(23, 11)$ Golay codes. We first saw (Section 2.4) the extended Golay $(24, 12)$ code and we see this again in the next section.

6.5 EXTENDED Q.R. CODES, SQUARE ROOT BOUND, AND GROUPS OF Q.R. CODES

We extend Q_1 and Q_2 in the usual fashion by adding an overall parity check. We label the new coordinate ∞. The coordinates are now labeled $\infty, 0, 1, \ldots, p - 1$. This is done because these are the points of the projective line (although we do not need to know what this is) and the transformations of the projective line are in the group of each Q.R. code as we see later. Call the extended codes $\overline{Q}_1$ and $\overline{Q}_2$. We can show several facts about these codes.

Theorem 68. $\overline{Q}_1$ and $\overline{Q}_2$ are equivalent $(p + 1, (p + 1)/2)$ codes. If $p \equiv -1 \pmod 8$, $\overline{Q}_1$ and $\overline{Q}_2$ are doubly even codes. If $p \equiv 1 \pmod 8$, $\overline{Q}_1^{\perp} = \overline{Q}_2$, $\overline{Q}_2^{\perp} = \overline{Q}_1^{\perp}$. Clearly $\overline{Q}_1$ and $\overline{Q}_2$ contain only even weight vectors.

Proof. We discuss only $\overline{Q}_1$ as everything said holds for $\overline{Q}_2$ also. As $\dim Q_i = \dim \overline{Q}_i$, $\overline{Q}_1$ and $\overline{Q}_2$ are $(p + 1, (p + 1)/2)$ codes. Recall that $Q_1 = Q_1' + \langle \mathbf{h} \rangle$ where all the vectors in Q_1' have even weight. Hence $\overline{Q}_1$ has the following generator matrix where G_1' is a generator matrix of Q_1'.

∞	0	1	$\cdots$	$p-1$
0				
$\vdots$			G_1'	
0				
1	1		$\cdots$	1

First we consider $p \equiv -1 \pmod 8$. As all the rows of G_1' are cyclic shifts of $1 + \mathbf{e}_2(x)$, they all have weight equal to the weight of $1 + \mathbf{e}_2(x)$. This latter is one more than the number of quadratic residues or $(p+1)/2$. Now $p = -1 + 8r$ for some r so that $(p+1)/2 = 4r$. Since Q_1' is self-orthogonal, the rows of G_1' are orthogonal to each other and clearly to $\mathbf{h}$. Hence, by Theorem 4, $\overline{Q}_1$ is doubly even. When $p \equiv 1 \pmod 8$, $\overline{Q}_1^{\perp} = \overline{Q}_2$ since $Q_1^{\perp} = Q_2'$ and $\overline{Q}_1$ has the following generator matrix where G_1' is a generator matrix of Q_1'.

∞	0	1	$\cdots$	$p-1$
0				
$\vdots$			G_1'	
0				
1	1		$\cdots$	1

Since Q_1 and Q_2 are equivalent, we can extend that permutation to an equivalence between $\overline{Q}_1$ and $\overline{Q}_2$ by leaving ∞ fixed.   Q.E.D.

The projective special linear group is a group of transformations of the projective line that has the $p+1$ points $\infty, 0, 1, \ldots, p-1$ for p a prime. Much is known about this group, things that we simply state here. We define $PSL_2(p)$ to be the group of permutations on $\infty, 0, \ldots, p-1$ for p a prime that is generated by the following permutations of elements i of $GF(p)$.

$$\sigma: \quad i \to i+1 \pmod p, \qquad\qquad \infty \to \infty,$$

$$\mu_a: \quad i \to ai \pmod p \qquad \text{for } a \in Q, \quad \infty \to \infty,$$

$$\rho: \quad i \to -1/i \pmod p, \quad i \neq 0, \qquad 0 \to \infty, \infty \to 0.$$

It is known that $PSL_2(p)$ has order $(p-1)p(p+1)/2$.

Theorem 69 _(Gleason and Prange)._ $PSL_2(p)$ is contained in the group of $\overline{Q}_1$ or of $\overline{Q}_2$.

Proof.   We know that σ and μ_a are in $G(\overline{Q}_i)$, $i = 1, 2$, since these transformations are in $G(Q_i)$ and they leave the ∞ coordinate fixed. To show that ρ leaves the extended Q.R. codes fixed is a bit complicated so we just look at the situation for $p = 7$. The following is a listing of $e_1(x)$ and all its shifts with the added parity check. This includes a generator matrix for $\overline{Q}_1$. We label the rows $r_0, r_1, \ldots, r_6$.

	∞	0	1	2	3	4	5	6
r_0	1	0	1	1	0	1	0	0
r_1	1	0	0	1	1	0	1	0
r_2	1	0	0	0	1	1	0	1
r_3	1	1	0	0	0	1	1	0
r_4	1	0	1	0	0	0	1	1
r_5	1	1	0	1	0	0	0	1
r_6	1	1	1	0	1	0	0	0

Applying ρ to the columns of this matrix, we obtain the following matrix.

∞	0	1	2	3	4	5	6	
0	1	0	0	1	0	1	1	$= r_0 + \mathbf{h}$
0	1	0	1	1	1	0	0	$= r_6 + r_0$
0	1	1	1	0	0	1	0	$= r_3 + r_0$
1	1	0	0	0	1	1	0	$= r_2 + r_0 + \mathbf{h}$
0	1	1	0	0	1	0	1	$= r_5 + r_0$
1	1	1	0	1	0	0	0	$= r_4 + r_0 + \mathbf{h}$
1	1	0	1	0	0	0	1	$= r_1 + r_0 + \mathbf{h}$

Recall that 1, 2, and 4 are residues. There is a pattern emerging that holds in general. When $p \equiv -1 (\bmod 8)$, let M be the matrix with rows r_i, $i = 0, \ldots, p - 1$, where $r_0 = e_1(x)$ and r_i, for $i \neq 0$, equals the ith cyclic shift of $e_1(x)$. Let M', with rows r_i', be the matrix resulting from applying ρ to M. Then it can be shown that $r_0' = r_0 + \mathbf{h}$, $r_i' = r_{-1/i} + r_0$ if i is a residue and $r_i' = r_{-1/i} + r_0 + \mathbf{h}$ if i is not a residue.   Q.E.D.

Theorem 70.   All codes obtained from an extended Q.R. code by puncturing are equivalent.

Proof. We show that $PSL_2(p)$ is transitive on the coordinates of an extended Q.R. code. We can send any finite coordinate onto any other finite coordinate by a power of σ and ρ interchanges 0 and ∞ so that there is a permutation in $PSL_2(p)$ that sends any coordinate position i onto any other coordinate position j. Hence the codes obtained by puncturing the ith coordinate and the jth coordinate are equivalent.   Q.E.D.

Theorem 71. The minimum weight of a Q.R. $(p, (p + 1)/2)$ code is odd. If $p \equiv -1 \pmod 8$, then the number A_i of vectors of weight i in a Q.R. code of length p is 0 unless $i \equiv 0$ or $3 \pmod 4$.

Proof. If $p \equiv -1 \pmod 8$, then the extended Q.R. code is doubly even so that all vectors in it have weight divisible by 4. Hence any vector in a punctured code has weight $\equiv 0$ or $3 \pmod 4$. This proves the second statement of the theorem.

For the first statement suppose that a Q.R. code Q_1 has even minimum weight and that x is a vector in Q_1 of minimum weight d. Consider the extended Q.R. code $\overline{Q}_1$. The vector with 1's where x has 1's and 0 at ∞ is in $\overline{Q}_1$ since d is even. Puncture $\overline{Q}_1$ on a coordinate position where x has a nonzero coordinate. Call the punctured code Q. By the previous theorem, Q is equivalent to Q_1. But Q has a vector in it of weight $d - 1$ (the punctured x). This is a contradiction so that Q_1 must have odd minimum weight.
Q.E.D.

The following theorem is due to Assmus-Mattson and is called the square root bound for Q.R. codes.

Theorem 72. If d is the minimum weight of a Q.R. $(p, (p + 1)/2)$ code of length p, then $d^2 \geq p$. Furthermore, if $p \equiv -1 \pmod 8$, then $d^2 - d + 1 \geq p$.

Proof. Let $a(x)$ be a vector of minimum weight d in Q_1 and let $b(x)$ be a vector of minimum weight d again in Q_2. Then $a(x)b(x)$ is in $Q_1 \cap Q_2 = \langle \mathbf{h} \rangle$. Since d is odd, $a(x)b(x) \neq 0$ (Problem 26) so that $a(x)b(x) = \mathbf{h}$. Hence the weight of $a(x)b(x)$ is p. The number of nonzero coefficients of $a(x)b(x)$ is no more than the number of nonzero products of a coefficient from $a(x)$ and a coefficient from $b(x)$ that is at most d^2 so $d^2 \geq p$.

If $p \equiv -1 \pmod 8$, then μ_{-1} sends Q_1 onto Q_2 so that we can take $b(x) = a(x^{-1})$. Hence if $a(x) = a_0 + a_1 x + \cdots + a_r x^r$, $a(x^{-1}) = a_0 + a_1 x^{-1} + \cdots + a_r x^{-r}$, and $a(x)a(x^{-1})$ has a maximum of $d^2 - (d - 1)$ terms since d of the products $a_i a_j$ add up to 1. Hence $d^2 - (d - 1) \geq p$.
Q.E.D.

We use the square root bound to compute a table of minimum weights for extended Q.R. codes of length ≤ 72. We also use the fact that, for $p \equiv -1 \pmod 8$, the minimum weight of a Q.R. $(p, (p + 1)/2)$ code is $\equiv 3 \pmod 4$. Thus if $p = 23$, $d \geq 7$ as $3^2 - 3 + 1$ is less than 23. Hence since the extended $(24, 12)$ Q.R. code has a vector of weight 8, $d = 8$. If $p = 47$, $d \geq 11$ as $7^2 - 7 + 1$ is less than 47. Thus the extended $(48, 24)$ Q.R. code has $d = 12$.

The square root bound gives a lower bound on d. The minimum weights for the following table are actual minimum weights and these are known because a vector was found in each code (except when $p = 41$) whose weight is that given by the bound.

The minimum weights of some extended binary Q.R. codes are as follows.

$p \equiv -1 \pmod 8$				$p \equiv 1 \pmod 8$			
p	n	k	d	p	n	k	d
7	8	4	4	17	18	9	6
23	24	12	8	41	42	21	10
31	32	16	8				
47	48	24	12				
71	72	36	12				

The square root bound gives the actual minimum weight for these Q.R. codes and gives a great deal of information for Q.R. codes of lengths a couple of hundred. However, as p gets larger, the bound becomes weaker. For larger n it is known that there are Q.R. codes whose minimum weight is greater than the square root bound.

Note that the $(24, 12)$ extended Q.R. code has $d = 8$ just as the Golay code does. We could have defined the Golay code to be the Q.R. code. This code is equivalent to the Golay code given in Section 2.4 although we do not prove it here (see Chapter 10). The extended ternary Golay code is also equivalent to an extended ternary Q.R. code [15].

6.6 PERMUTATION DECODING

Permutation decoding described in [14] and [27] is a decoding procedure that uses the group of a code. It is most useful when the code has a fairly large group of permutations. Let C be an (n, k, d) code whose coordinates are labeled with $0, 1, \ldots, n - 1$. Let $\mathbf{x}$ be the vector sent and $\mathbf{y}$ be the vector received and suppose that $t = [(d - 1)/2]$ or fewer errors have occurred. We may assume that the first k positions form an information set as for a cyclic code. If $\mathbf{y} = (y_0, \ldots, y_{k-1}, \ldots, y_{n-1})$, we use this information set to encode a vector $\mathbf{w}_1 = (y_0, \ldots, y_{k-1}, w_k, \ldots, w_{n-1})$ in C. We then compute the distance between $\mathbf{y}$ and $\mathbf{w}_1$. If this is less than or equal to t, then we decode $\mathbf{y}$ to $\mathbf{w}_1$. If there are no errors in the information set, then the distance between $\mathbf{y}$ and $\mathbf{w}_1$ will be less than or equal to t. By Theorem 15, every set of $n - (d - 1)$ coordinate positions contains an information set so we know that there is an information set that does not contain any of the $\leq t$ positions in error in $\mathbf{y}$. Every permutation in $G(C)$ carries an information set onto an information set and the main idea in this decoding scheme is to use permutations in $G(C)$ to locate an information set in which $\mathbf{y}$ has no errors.

We illustrate this with the $(7, 4, 3)$ Q.R. code with idempotent $\mathbf{e}_1 = (0, 1, 1, 0, 1, 0, 0)$. We know that $1 + \mathbf{e}_2 = (1, 0, 0, 1, 0, 1, 1)$ and its cyclic shifts generate the orthogonal code. From this we can derive the following parity check equations.

$$a_4 = a_0 + a_2 + a_3, \quad a_5 = a_0 + a_1 + a_2, \quad a_6 = a_1 + a_2 + a_3.$$

Suppose that $\mathbf{x} = \mathbf{e}_1$ is the vector sent and that the received vector $\mathbf{y}$ has an error in position 1. We compute $\mathbf{w}_1$ from the parity check equations. When we realize that $d(\mathbf{w}_1, \mathbf{y}) = 2$, we use the permutation σ^2 to get the new information set $\{2, 3, 4, 5\}$ and we use new parity check equations to compute $\mathbf{w}_2$. By applying σ^2 to the old parity checks, the new ones are

$$a_6 = a_2 + a_4 + a_5, \quad a_0 = a_2 + a_3 + a_4, \quad a_1 = a_3 + a_4 + a_5.$$

Realizing that the distance from $\mathbf{y}$ to $\mathbf{w}_2$ is 1 we decode $\mathbf{y}$ to $\mathbf{w}_2$. This is represented in Table 6.1. What we want is the fewest number of permutations so that an error will not appear in either $\{0, 1, 2, 3\}$ or one of its images under these permutations. For this code σ^2 and σ^4 are enough. The three information sets are then $\{0, 1, 2, 3\}$, $\{2, 3, 4, 5\}$, and $\{0, 4, 5, 6\}$.

Let I be an information set for an (n, k, d) code C. We want to choose a smallest set S of permutations in $G(C)$ so that any given set of t coordinate positions is disjoint from at least one image of I under a permutation in S. If C is a binary cyclic code we can search for S through the mn permutations described in Theorem 61. If C is a binary Q.R. code of length p, there are many more permutations available in $PSL_2(p)$ by Theorem 69.

Table 6.1   A Sequence of Steps in Decoding the Q.R. $(7, 4, 3)$ Code Using Permutation Decoding

0	1	2	3	4	5	6	
0	1	1	0	1	0	0	x—the vector sent
0	0	1	0	1	0	0	y—the vector received
0	0	1	0	1	1	1	w_1—the vector computed using $I = \{0, 1, 2, 3\}$
0	1	1	0	1	0	0	w_2—the vector computed using $I\sigma^2 = \{2, 3, 4, 5\}$

The decoding procedure is as follows. Let y be the received vector. Let $S = \{\sigma_1, \ldots, \sigma_r\}$ be a set of permutations in $G(C)$ chosen as described above. Let P be a set of parity check equations. Let I be an information set.

(i) Compute w_1 by encoding the positions in I using P.

(ii) If $d(w_1, y) \leq t$, decode y to w_1. If not, compute $P_2 = P\sigma_1$ giving a new set of parity check equations.

(iii) Compute w_2 by encoding the information positions in $I\sigma_1$ with the parity checks in P_2.

(iv) If $d(w_2, y) \leq t$, decode y to w_2. If not, continue as above until either y is decoded or all the permutations in S have been used. It can happen that y will not be decoded.

The set S is, in general, computed for individual codes. Of course, a set S that is not the minimal one can also be used; it is just not as efficient.

6.7   DECODING THE GOLAY CODE

Our aim here is to decode the $(24, 12)$ binary Golay code C by hand. As there are $2^{12} = 4096$ vectors in this code, finding, by hand, the codeword closest to a received vector is indeed an ambitious aim. This decoding method is described in [33, Chap. 11] and in [43].

We first describe $GF(4)$ which we regard as consisting of 0, 1, ω, and $\bar{\omega}$ which follow the following rules.

$$\bar{\omega} = \omega^2, \qquad \bar{\omega}^2 = \omega, \qquad \omega\bar{\omega} = 1, \qquad \text{and} \qquad 1 + \omega + \bar{\omega} = 0.$$

Before going into the decoding we describe another fascinating code, a $(6, 3, 4)$ code over $GF(4)$ called the Hexacode which we will call Hex for short. We take

$$
\begin{array}{ccc}
\text{I} & \text{II} & \text{III} \\
\overbrace{} & \overbrace{} & \overbrace{}
\end{array}
$$

$$
G = \begin{pmatrix} 1 & 0 & 0 & 1 & \bar{\omega} & \omega \\ 0 & 1 & 0 & 1 & \omega & \bar{\omega} \\ 0 & 0 & 1 & 1 & 1 & 1 \end{pmatrix}
$$

as its generator matrix (the column labels will be explained soon). Clearly Hex is a $(6, 3)$ code and we will show why it has minimum weight 4. But first we verify that certain permutations are in the group of Hex. We call the first two columns block I, the next two block II, and the last two block III. Then any permutation of these blocks is in the group of Hex. We verify this for the permutation (I, II). Applying this permutation to our generator matrix gives the matrix

$$
\begin{pmatrix} 0 & 1 & 1 & 0 & \bar{\omega} & \omega \\ 0 & 1 & 0 & 1 & \omega & \bar{\omega} \\ 1 & 1 & 0 & 0 & 1 & 1 \end{pmatrix}
$$

and we can easily verify that these vectors are in Hex. So in order to show that S_3 considered as permutations of the blocks is in the group of Hex, we would only need to verify that the permutation (I, III) is in the group of Hex for it is known that these permutations generate S_3. Other permutations in Hex's group are interchanges within two blocks. This fact can be verified just as easily (see Problem 29). The permutation $(3, 4)(5, 6)$ applied to the second vector in G gives $(0\ 1\ 1\ 0\ \bar{\omega}\ \omega)$ which we can verify is in Hex. We use this knowledge to recognize all the codewords in Hex, a facility which will be essential to our decoding scheme.

By a counting argument we can show that all nonzero codewords in Hex can be obtained from the following 4 codewords by permuting blocks, interchanges within two blocks, and scalar multiples of such codewords.

If the count in the right-hand column is correct, then the statement is true as there are 63 of these codewords, so that with the zero codeword we get $64 = 4^3$ codewords. We leave the verification of this count to Problem 30. This listing tells us that the minimum weight of Hex is 4 so that Hex is an M.D.S. code. Indeed it is an extension of the M.D.S. code in Problem 4.23. Note that we now know by Corollary 1 to Theorem 15 that every 3 positions in Hex are information positions. We will use this!

Table 6.2 The Hexacodewords

Hexacodeword	Number of this Type
1) 0 1 0 1 ω $\bar{\omega}$	3×12
2) ω $\bar{\omega}$ ω $\bar{\omega}$ ω $\bar{\omega}$	3×4
3) 0 0 1 1 1 1	3×3
4) 1 1 ω ω $\bar{\omega}$ $\bar{\omega}$	3×2

In Section 2.4 we defined a $(24, 12)$ code we called the Golay code and showed it had minimum weight 8. In Section 6.5 we saw an extended Q.R.$(24, 12, 8)$ code which is equivalent to the Golay code as all $(24, 12, 8)$ binary codes are equivalent [21]. In order to decode we give still another description of a code equivalent to the Golay code. We can consider a length 24 binary vector as a 4×6 rectangular array of 0's and 1's (we can spread it out to a length 24 vector any way we like). We say a column (or row) of such an array has even parity if it contains an even number of ones, odd parity otherwise. The dot products of the columns of such an array with the vector

$$\begin{pmatrix} 0 \\ 1 \\ \omega \\ \bar{\omega} \end{pmatrix}$$

gives a vector of length 6 over $GF(4)$ which we call the *projection* of the binary vector. For example the vector

$$\begin{matrix} 0 \\ 1 \\ \omega \\ \bar{\omega} \end{matrix} \begin{pmatrix} 1 & 1 & 0 & 0 & 0 & 0 \\ 0 & 1 & 0 & 1 & 0 & 1 \\ 1 & 1 & 1 & 1 & 0 & 0 \\ 0 & 1 & 1 & 0 & 0 & 1 \end{pmatrix}$$

has projection $\omega\ 0\ 1\ \bar{\omega}\ 0\ \omega$, which we recognize as a Hexacodeword (why?). Note that all columns and the top row have even parity. As we see below, this means that we have a vector in our latest version of the Golay code.

Theorem 73. The set of all binary vectors with the following two properties constitute a $(24, 12, 8)$ code which we call the Golay code C.

(1) All columns and the top row have the same parity.

(2) The projection is in Hex.

Proof. As the set of all vectors with properties (1) and (2) form a code, all we have to prove is that this code has dimension 12 and minimum weight 8. These facts are not difficult to prove and can be done by counting arguments. We begin by counting all vectors in C with even parity. We can specify the first 3 positions in the projection in 4^3 ways and then the other 3 positions are determined. There are precisely 2 columns of even parity which have the same projected value (see our example above). We have only one choice for the last column to preserve the top row parity. Hence there are $4^3 \cdot 2^5 = 2^{11}$ vectors of even parity. Similarly for odd parity giving 2^{12} vectors in C so that C has dimension 12. We leave the proof of minimum weight 8 to Problem 31.　　　　　　　　　　　　　　　Q.E.D.

At last we can start to decode. We know that C can correct any pattern of 3 or fewer errors and detect 4 errors. We have a received vector and we compute its column parities We then compute projected components of those columns we know are correct or which might be correct. We then use Table 6.2 and our pattern recognition abilities (look for zeros) to find the other components of the Hexacodeword. Then change the columns corresponding to these components but maintain the correct parity, and see if we are successful. Let us try an example. Suppose our received vector is the following.

$$
\begin{array}{c}
0 \\ 1 \\ \omega \\ \bar{\omega}
\end{array}
\left(
\begin{array}{cccccc}
1 & 0 & 1 & 0 & 0 & 1 \\
0 & 0 & 1 & 0 & 0 & 0 \\
1 & 0 & 0 & 1 & 0 & 0 \\
0 & 1 & 0 & 0 & 1 & 1
\end{array}
\right).
$$

Notice that we have 3 columns of odd parity and 3 columns of even parity. The only possible explanation for this is that 3 errors have occurred, 1 in each column of a fixed parity. But this means 3 columns of the other parity must be correct. Let us try odd parity. Then the projection looks like—$\bar{\omega} - \omega\bar{\omega}$—and our first task is to fill in the blanks. This one is not hard, it is $\omega\bar{\omega}\bar{\omega}\omega\bar{\omega}\omega$ and if we make a single correction maintaining odd parity in the columns corresponding to blanks we get

$$
\begin{array}{c}
0 \\ 1 \\ \omega \\ \bar{\omega}
\end{array}
\left(
\begin{array}{cccccc}
0 & 0 & 1 & 0 & 0 & 1 \\
0 & 0 & 1 & 0 & 0 & 1 \\
1 & 0 & 1 & 1 & 0 & 0 \\
0 & 1 & 0 & 0 & 1 & 1
\end{array}
\right).
$$
$$
\quad\ \underline{\omega}\quad\ \bar{\omega}\quad\ \underline{\bar{\omega}}\quad\ \omega\quad\ \bar{\omega}\quad\ \underline{\omega}
$$

This is not a vector in C as the top row has even parity. So we now know

Table 6.3

Parity of Columns	Possible Number of Errors	Number of Correct Columns
6 : 0	0, 2, 4	All or 5 out of 6
5 : 1	1, 3	4 out of 5 or 5 of one parity
4 : 2	2, 4	4 of one parity
3 : 3	3	3 of some one parity

that the even parity columns must be correct and the projection looks like $\omega\_1\_ \_\bar{\omega}$. Again we must find the correct Hexacodeword. This one is also not hard, it is $\omega\omega$ 11 $\bar{\omega}\bar{\omega}$ and we get

$$
\begin{array}{c}
\begin{matrix} 0 \\ 1 \\ \omega \\ \bar{\omega} \end{matrix}
\begin{pmatrix}
1 & 0 & 1 & 0 & 1 & 1 \\
0 & 1 & 1 & 0 & 0 & 0 \\
1 & 0 & 0 & 1 & 0 & 0 \\
0 & 1 & 0 & 1 & 1 & 1
\end{pmatrix} \\
\begin{matrix} \omega & \underline{\omega} & 1 & \underline{1} & \bar{\omega} & \bar{\omega} \end{matrix}
\end{array}
$$

giving us the correct codeword. Write down an arbitrary 4×6 array of 0's and 1's and try to decode it. It's fun. The hardest part is finding the Hexacodeword if you know 3 or more correct components. As type 1) is the most numerous, it usually is the place to look at first. The above table might be useful for correcting 1, 2, or 3 errors and detecting 4 errors. The number of correct columns assume 3 or fewer errors. If 4 errors have occurred, there are 6 possible sent vectors and it is possible to find one or all of them. See [43] for details.

PROBLEMS

1. Show that the Hamming $(7, 4)$ code is equivalent to a cyclic code.

2. Find the following products and give the order of the resulting permutation.

   (a) $(1, 2, 4, 6)(3, 4, 5)$.

   (b) $(1, 3)(2, 6)(3, 4)$.

   (c) $(1, 2, 4, 5)(1, 5, 4)$.

3. Prove that the order of S_n is $n!$

4. Is S_n abelian for $n > 2$?

5. (a) Find the order of the group G generated by $(1, 2)(3, 4)$ and $(1, 3)(2, 4)$.

   (b) Is G transitive?

6. (a) What is the order of the group of the binary code with generator matrix G given below?

$$G = \begin{pmatrix} 1 & 1 & 0 \\ 0 & 1 & 1 \\ 1 & 0 & 1 \end{pmatrix}.$$

   (b) Is this group transitive?

7. If g.c.d.$(a, n) = 1$, show that a has an inverse modulo n.

8. If n is an odd integer, consider the partition of the integers $I = \{0, 1, \ldots, n - 1\}$ into cyclotomic cosets given by multiplication by 2. If g.c.d.$(a, n) = 1$, show that the permutation $i \to ai \pmod{n}$ on I sends the set of cyclotomic cosets onto the set of cyclotomic cosets.

9. (a) Show directly that the group of a $(7, 4)$ cyclic code C contains the permutation $(1, 2, 4)(3, 6, 5)$. (This is true for both $(7, 4)$ cyclic codes.)

   (b) What is the order of $(1, 2, 4)(3, 6, 5)$?

   (c) What is the image of C under the permutation $i \to 3i \pmod{7}$?

   (d) What is the image of C under the permutation $i \to 5i \pmod{7}$?

10. (a) What is the order of the group generated by $\sigma = (0, 1, 2, 3, 4, 5, 6)$ and $\tau = (1, 2, 4)(3, 6, 5)$?

   (b) Express $\sigma^2 \tau \sigma^4 \tau^2$ as $\tau^i \sigma^j$.

11. (a) Are the two $(23, 11)$ binary cyclic codes equivalent? Why?

   (b) Are the two $(23, 12)$ binary cyclic codes equivalent? Why?

   (c) What is the order of 2 modulo 23?

12. Suppose that g.c.d.$(a, n) = 1$. Let μ_a be defined by $i\mu_a = ai \pmod{n}$, $i = 0, \ldots, n - 1$ and let σ be the usual cyclic shift.

   (a) Show that there is a smallest positive m so that $a^m \equiv 1 \pmod{n}$.

   (b) Show that $\mu_a \sigma \mu_a^{-1} = \sigma^{a^{m-1}}$.

13. Consider $n = 15$. What happens to the cyclotomic cosets under the permutations $i \to ai \pmod{15}$ for $a = 4, 7$, and 13?

14. **(a)** Find the group of the $(3, 1)$ ternary code that consists of multiples of $(1, 1, 1)$.

    (b) Is this group transitive?

15. Consider the field $GF(p)$ for a prime $p \neq 2$. By Problem 4.16, half the nonzero elements in $GF(p)$ are quadratic residues and half are nonresidues. Show that the product of two residues or two nonresidues is always a residue and that a residue times a nonresidue is a nonresidue.

16. **(a)** Compute the quadratic residues in $GF(23)$.

    (b) Show that any nonresidue in $GF(p)$ can be expressed as nr where n is a fixed nonresidue and r is a variable quadratic residue. The element n can be any nonresidue.

17. Show that if $\mathbf{e}$ is a binary vector of odd length n, then $\mathbf{eh} = \mathbf{h}$ if $\mathbf{e}$ has odd weight and $\mathbf{eh} = 0$ if $\mathbf{e}$ has even weight. $\mathbf{h}$ also has length n.

18. Show that if C_1 and C_2 are binary cyclic codes of length n with idempotents f_1 and f_2 such that $C_1 + C_2 = R_n$, $C_1 \cap C_2 = \langle \mathbf{h} \rangle$, $C_1 = C_1' + \langle \mathbf{h} \rangle$, and $C_2 = C_2' + \langle \mathbf{h} \rangle$ where $\mathbf{h}$ is not in C_1' or C_2', then the idempotent of C_1' is $1 + f_2$ and that of C_2' is $1 + f_1$.

19. Prove Theorem 67, part (vi).

20. If $f(x)$ is the generator polynomial of the binary cyclic code with idempotent generator $e(x)$, show that the reciprocal polynomial of $f(x)$ is the generator polynomial of $\langle e(x^{-1}) \rangle$.

21. If $p \equiv -1 \pmod 8$, then over $GF(2)$, $x^p - 1 = (x - 1)f(x)g(x)$ where $f(x)$ is the generator polynomial of a Q.R. code Q_1. Show that $f(x)$ and $g(x)$ are reciprocal polynomials. What are their degrees? Identify the generator polynomials of the Q.R. codes Q_2, Q_1', and Q_2'.

22. Consider binary cyclic codes of prime length p where $p \equiv -1 \pmod 8$.

    (a) Show that $x^p - 1 = (x - 1)f_1(x) \ldots f_{m/2}(x)g_1(x) \ldots g_{m/2}(x)$ where $f_i(x)$ and $g_i(x)$ are irreducible, reciprocal polynomials.

    (b) What is m when $p = 23$? $p = 31$?

    (c) Describe the generator polynomial of any self-orthogonal binary cyclic code of length p.

23. **(a)** Give idempotent generators for the four binary Q.R. codes of length 23.

    (b) Give the dimension of each of these.

(c) Tell which Q.R. codes of length 23 contain other Q.R. codes of length 23.

(d) Which of these Q.R. codes are self-orthogonal?

24. (a) Answer parts (a), (b), (c), and (d) of Problem 23 for Q.R. codes of length 17.

(b) Give a generator matrix for one Q.R. code of length 17.

25. If $p \equiv 1 (\mod 8)$, why must the idempotent generator of a Q.R. $(p,(p + 1)/2)$ code be either $1 + e_1(x)$ or $1 + e_2(x)$?

26. If $a(x)$ and $b(x)$ are two vectors of odd weight in binary cyclic codes (not necessarily the same code), show that $a(x)b(x) \neq 0$.

27. Give a generator matrix for an extended $(24, 12)$ Q.R. code.

28. Give a lower bound on the minimum weights of $(74, 37)$, $(80, 40)$, $(90, 45)$, and $(98, 49)$ extended Q.R. codes.

29. In Section 6.7 verify that the permutation $(1, 2)(3, 4)$ on the columns of G is in the group of Hex.

30. Verify the numbers in Table 6.2.

31. Show that

(a) Any vector of even parity with a nonzero projection in Hex has weight ≥ 8.

(b) Show that any nonzero vector of even parity whose projection is the zero vector has weight ≥ 8.

(c) Show that any vector of odd parity whose projection is in Hex has weight ≥ 8.

32. Decode the received messages

(a) $$\begin{pmatrix} 1 & 1 & 1 & 0 & 1 & 0 \\ 0 & 0 & 0 & 0 & 1 & 1 \\ 0 & 0 & 0 & 0 & 0 & 1 \\ 0 & 0 & 0 & 0 & 0 & 1 \end{pmatrix}$$

(b) $$\begin{pmatrix} 0 & 1 & 0 & 1 & 1 & 0 \\ 0 & 0 & 0 & 0 & 0 & 0 \\ 0 & 0 & 1 & 1 & 0 & 0 \\ 1 & 0 & 0 & 1 & 1 & 1 \end{pmatrix}$$

for the Golay code.

7

Bose-Chaudhuri-Hocquenghem (B.C.H.) Codes

7.1 CYCLIC CODES GIVEN IN TERMS OF ROOTS

We have seen that cyclic codes can be described in several fashions, that is, in terms of a generator polynomial or as a code left fixed by a cyclic group of permutations. There is yet another way. Consider, for example, the length 7 binary cyclic code C with generator polynomial $f(x) = 1 + x + x^3$. A polynomial is in C iff it is a multiple of $f(x)$. As we saw in Chapter 4, $f(x)$ is the minimal polynomial of an element α in $GF(2^3)$ whose other roots are α^2 and α^4. Hence we can say that a polynomial $h(x)$ is in C iff $h(\alpha) = 0$ or iff $h(\alpha) = h(\alpha^2) = h(\alpha^4) = 0$, because any polynomial whose roots include the roots of $f(x)$ has $f(x)$ as a factor.

Let $\alpha_1, \ldots, \alpha_r$ be a set of elements in a field $F = GF(q^m)$ and let $f_1(x), \ldots, f_r(x)$ be their minimal polynomials. Furthermore, let n be an integer so that each $f_i(x)$ divides $x^n - 1$. Let C be the code of length n consisting of all polynomials $h(x)$ in $F[x]/(x^n - 1)$ so that $h(\alpha_i) = 0$, $i = 1, \ldots, r$. Then C is a cyclic code with generator polynomial $g(x) = $ l.c.m.$(f_1(x), \ldots, f_r(x))$. If the $f_i(x)$ have no common factors, $g(x) = f_1(x) \cdots f_r(x)$. It is clear that any cyclic code C can be specified in this way since we can take the $f_i(x)$ to be the irreducible factors of the generator polynomial of C and α_i to be a root of $f_i(x)$.

We can carry this one step further and use the roots to give a parity check matrix for a cyclic code. Consider again the binary $(7, 4)$ cyclic code C with generator polynomial $f(x) = 1 + x + x^3$ and let α be a root of $f(x)$ in $GF(2^3)$. Then $h(x) = c_0 + c_1 x + c_2 x^2 + \cdots + c_6 x^6$ is in C iff $c_0 + c_1 \alpha + c_2 \alpha^2 + \cdots + c_6 \alpha^6 = 0$. So a vector is in C iff it is orthogonal to $H = (1 \alpha \alpha^2 \cdots \alpha^6)$. But the elements of H are in $GF(2^3)$ and we want them to be in $GF(2)$. We can do this by writing out the α^i, $i = 0, \ldots, 6$ as binary triples. Now

$$H = \begin{pmatrix} 1 & 0 & 0 & 1 & 0 & 1 & 1 \\ 0 & 1 & 0 & 1 & 1 & 1 & 0 \\ 0 & 0 & 1 & 0 & 1 & 1 & 1 \end{pmatrix}$$

and it is indeed a parity check matrix for C. We could do a similar thing and get a different parity check matrix for the other roots α^2 and α^4 of $f(x)$. We compute H_1, the parity check matrix obtained from α^2.

$$H_1 = \begin{pmatrix} 1 & \alpha^2 & \alpha^4 & \alpha^6 & \alpha & \alpha^3 & \alpha^5 \end{pmatrix}$$

$$= \begin{pmatrix} 1 & 0 & 0 & 1 & 0 & 1 & 1 \\ 0 & 0 & 1 & 0 & 1 & 1 & 1 \\ 0 & 1 & 1 & 1 & 0 & 0 & 1 \end{pmatrix}.$$

It is not equal to H, but it is a parity check matrix for C as is easy to check. This is very reminiscent of the parity check matrix for the double-error-correcting B.C.H. code described in Chapter 3. We see why in Section 7.3.

The matrix H_2, whose rows are the combined rows of H and H_1, can also be used as a set of vectors generating $C^\perp$ so that C can be specified as the set of all vectors orthogonal to the rows of H_2. It is not necessary in this case to use all these rows and we just mention it because we define B.C.H. codes in this fashion. On occasion we use more rows than we need because we do not know exactly how many rows are independent.

In our example the field containing the roots is $GF(2^3)$ and the code's length is $n = 2^3 - 1 = 7$. It is not always the case that the code's length is one less than the number of elements in the field. For example, take α to be an element in $GF(2^{11})$ whose minimal polynomial $f(x)$ has degree 11. Since α is in $GF(2^{11})$, $f(x)$ divides $x^{(2^{11}-1)} - 1$. If $f(x)$ divides $x^n - 1$, then the roots of $f(x)$ are roots of $x^n - 1$ so that $f(x)$ can divide $x^n - 1$ when $x^n - 1$ divides $x^{2^{11}-1} - 1$ and this can happen iff n divides $2^{11} - 1 = 89 \cdot 23$ by the second lemma to Theorem 37. Hence we can use α in $GF(2^{11})$ and $f(x)$, its minimal polynomial, to define a cyclic code of length 23.

7.2 VANDERMONDE DETERMINANTS

Vandermonde determinants are needed to provide important information about B.C.H. codes, and they are also used in Chapter 8 to give useful information about weight distributions. The reason for both of these phenomena is that we can determine, by the form of this determinant, whether or not it is nonzero. It is pretty unusual to be able to say this for a determinant given in a general form.

We say that an $n \times n$ determinant D is *Vandermonde* if D has one of the following two forms, D_1 or D_2.

$$
\begin{vmatrix}
1 & 1 & \cdots & 1 \\
\alpha_1 & \alpha_2 & \cdots & \alpha_n \\
\alpha_1^2 & \alpha_2^2 & \cdots & \alpha_n^2 \\
\vdots & \vdots & & \vdots \\
\alpha_1^{n-1} & \alpha_2^{n-1} & \cdots & \alpha_n^{n-1}
\end{vmatrix}
\quad \text{or} \quad
\begin{vmatrix}
1 & \alpha_1 & \alpha_1^2 & \cdots & \alpha_1^{n-1} \\
1 & \alpha_2 & \alpha_2^2 & \cdots & \alpha_2^{n-1} \\
\vdots & \vdots & \vdots & & \vdots \\
1 & \alpha_n & \alpha_n^2 & \cdots & \alpha_n^{n-1}
\end{vmatrix}.
$$

The α_i's are in some field F, which can be finite or infinite.

Theorem 74. The value of a Vandermonde determinant D given above is the product of all $\alpha_i - \alpha_j$ for $i > j$, that is, $D = \prod_{j=1}^{n-1}\prod_{i=j+1}^{n}(\alpha_i - \alpha_j)$.

Proof. It is enough to show this for the second form, D_2 as $D_1 = D_2^T$. Let $n = 2$. Then

$$
\begin{vmatrix}
1 & \alpha_1 \\
1 & \alpha_2
\end{vmatrix}
= \alpha_2 - \alpha_1.
$$

If $n = 3$, we have

$$
\begin{vmatrix}
1 & \alpha_1 & \alpha_1^2 \\
1 & \alpha_2 & \alpha_2^2 \\
1 & \alpha_3 & \alpha_3^2
\end{vmatrix}
=
\begin{vmatrix}
1 & \alpha_1 - \alpha_3 & \alpha_1^2 - \alpha_3\alpha_1 \\
1 & \alpha_2 - \alpha_3 & \alpha_2^2 - \alpha_3\alpha_2 \\
1 & 0 & 0
\end{vmatrix}
=
\begin{vmatrix}
\alpha_1 - \alpha_3 & \alpha_1^2 - \alpha_3\alpha_1 \\
\alpha_2 - \alpha_3 & \alpha_2^2 - \alpha_3\alpha_2
\end{vmatrix}
$$

$$
= (\alpha_3 - \alpha_1)(\alpha_3 - \alpha_2)
\begin{vmatrix}
1 & \alpha_1 \\
1 & \alpha_2
\end{vmatrix}
$$

$$
= (\alpha_3 - \alpha_1)(\alpha_3 - \alpha_2)(\alpha_2 - \alpha_1).
$$

Notice that the second determinant was obtained from the first by subtracting α_3 times the ith column from the $(i + 1)$st column, $i = 2, 1$. In an analogous way an $n \times n$ Vandermonde can be reduced to $(\alpha_n - \alpha_1) \times (\alpha_n - \alpha_2) \cdots (\alpha_n - \alpha_{n-1})$ times an $(n - 1) \times (n - 1)$ Vandermonde and the theorem then follows by induction. Q.E.D.

Corollary. $D = 0$ iff $\alpha_i = \alpha_j$ for distinct i and j.

7.3   DEFINITION AND PROPERTIES OF B.C.H. CODES

B.C.H. codes are a family of multiple-error-correcting codes that were discovered by R. C. Bose and D. K. Ray-Chaudhuri and independently by A. Hocquenghem. They are cyclic codes defined in terms of the roots of their generator polynomials and designed to correct a certain number of errors. Before defining these codes in general, we show that we can construct such a code of length $n = 15$ that is double-error-correcting. Let α be a primitive element in $GF(2^4)$ and consider the code C whose generator polynomial $g(x)$ has α, α^2, α^3, and α^4 as roots. Clearly $g(x)$ could have more roots. Referring to our listing of elements in $GF(16)$ and their minimal polynomials in Chapter 4, we see that $g(x) = (x^4 + x^3 + 1)(x^4 + x^3 + x^2 + x + 1)$ since $x^4 + x^3 + 1$ has α, α^2, α^4, and α^8 as roots and $x^4 + x^3 + x^2 + x + 1$ contributes the roots α^3, hence also α^6, α^{12}, and α^9. C is a $(15, 7)$ code. Why is this code double-error-correcting? We would know this if a parity check matrix H of C has the property that any four columns of H are linearly independent. By its construction we know that all the vectors in C are orthogonal to the rows of the matrix H.

$$
H = \begin{pmatrix}
1 & \alpha & \alpha^2 & \alpha^3 & \cdots & \alpha^{14} \\
1 & \alpha^2 & \alpha^4 & \alpha^6 & \cdots & \alpha^{13} \\
1 & \alpha^3 & \alpha^6 & \alpha^9 & \cdots & \alpha^{12} \\
1 & \alpha^4 & \alpha^8 & \alpha^{12} & \cdots & \alpha^{11}
\end{pmatrix}.
$$

H represents a binary matrix with 15 columns and $4 \times 4 = 16$ rows. Clearly not all rows of H are independent. However, the rows of H contain the rows of a standard parity check matrix for C. As a matrix over $GF(16)$, any four columns of H are independent since the matrix consisting of these four columns is a multiple of a matrix with a Vandermonde determinant. For example, consider the 4×4 matrix M consisting of the second, third, fifth, and eighth columns of H.

$$
|M| = \begin{vmatrix}
\alpha & \alpha^2 & \alpha^4 & \alpha^7 \\
\alpha^2 & \alpha^4 & \alpha^8 & \alpha^{14} \\
\alpha^3 & \alpha^6 & \alpha^{12} & \alpha^6 \\
\alpha^4 & \alpha^8 & \alpha & \alpha^{13}
\end{vmatrix} = \alpha\alpha^2\alpha^4\alpha^7 \begin{vmatrix}
1 & 1 & 1 & 1 \\
\alpha & \alpha^2 & \alpha^4 & \alpha^7 \\
\alpha^2 & \alpha^4 & \alpha^8 & \alpha^{14} \\
\alpha^3 & \alpha^6 & \alpha^{12} & \alpha^6
\end{vmatrix}.
$$

Since $|M|$ is $\alpha\alpha^2\alpha^4\alpha^7|M'|$ where $|M'|$ is Vandermonde, $|M| = \alpha\alpha^2\alpha^4\alpha^7 \times (\alpha^2 - \alpha)(\alpha^4 - \alpha)(\alpha^4 - \alpha^2)(\alpha^7 - \alpha)(\alpha^7 - \alpha^2)(\alpha^7 - \alpha^4)$, which is not zero since α is a primitive element in $GF(16)$. Since any four columns of H are independent over $GF(16)$, they are independent over $GF(2)$, so that the minimum weight of C is ≥ 5 and C is double-error-correcting. We recognize this as the double-error-correcting code constructed in Chapter 3 but we see now how to construct cyclic codes that can correct any specified number of errors.

Let C be a cyclic code of length n over $GF(q)$ where g.c.d.$(n, q) = 1$. Let m be the order of $q \bmod n$ and let α be a primitive element in $GF(q^m)$. C is a *B.C.H. code of designed distance* δ if the generator polynomial $g(x)$ of C is the product of the distinct minimal polynomials of the $\delta - 1$ consecutive elements $\alpha^b, \alpha^{b+1}, \ldots, \alpha^{b+\delta-2}$. If $b = 1$, the $\delta - 1$ consecutive roots are $\alpha, \alpha^2, \ldots, \alpha^{\delta-1}$.

If $n = q^m - 1$, C is called a *primitive B.C.H. code*.

Theorem 75 (B.C.H. Bound). The minimum weight of a B.C.H. code C of designed distance δ is at least δ.

Proof. As in our example, every vector in C is orthogonal to each row of the matrix H.

$$
H = \begin{pmatrix}
1 & \alpha^b & \alpha^{2b} & \alpha^{3b} & \cdots & \alpha^{(n-1)b} \\
1 & \alpha^{b+1} & \alpha^{2(b+1)} & \alpha^{3(b+1)} & \cdots & \alpha^{(n-1)(b+1)} \\
\vdots & \vdots & & & & \vdots \\
1 & \alpha^{b+\delta-2} & & & \cdots & \alpha^{(n-1)(b+\delta-2)}
\end{pmatrix}.
$$

We show that no $d - 1$ or fewer columns of H are linearly dependent over $GF(q^m)$. For this purpose we choose a set of $d - 1$ columns headed by the elements $\alpha^{i_1 b}, \ldots, \alpha^{i_{d-1} b}$ and form the $(d - 1) \times (d - 1)$ determinant consisting of those columns. We factor out the column headings from each column obtaining

$$
\alpha^{b(i_1 + \cdots + i_{d-1})} \begin{vmatrix}
1 & 1 & \cdots & 1 \\
\alpha^{i_1} & \alpha^{i_2} & \cdots & \alpha^{i_{d-1}} \\
\vdots & \vdots & & \vdots \\
\alpha^{(d-2)i_1} & \alpha^{(d-2)i_2} & \cdots & \alpha^{(d-2)i_{d-1}}
\end{vmatrix}.
$$

We see that the matrix consisting of any $\delta - 1$ columns of H is a multiple of a matrix whose determinant is Vandermonde and nonzero since α is a primitive element. Hence any $\delta - 1$ columns of H are independent over $GF(q^m)$ and so over $GF(q)$, which shows that $d \geq \delta$.   Q.E.D.

Note that H is a matrix with $(\delta - 1)m$ rows over $GF(q)$. This is usually more rows than are needed for a parity check matrix of C. This reflects the fact that we do not know the dimension k of C. Since H has $m(\delta - 1)$ rows, $k \geq n - m(\delta - 1)$. This is not too good a bound on k. We can do better in the following theorem, which is part of the reason B.C.H. codes are so important for practical use.

Theorem 76. For any positive integers m and $t \leq 2^{m-1} - 1$, there is a binary B.C.H. code of length $n = 2^m - 1$ that is t-error-correcting and has dimension $\geq n - mt$.

Proof. Take α to be a primitive element in $GF(2^m)$ and let C be the cyclic code with roots, $\alpha, \alpha^2, \ldots, \alpha^{2t-1}$. If $m_i(x)$ is the minimal polynomial of α^i, then the generator polynomial $g(x)$ of C equals l.c.m.$\{m_1(x), m_3(x), \ldots, m_{2t-1}(x)\}$. We need consider only odd i since every even power of α is a root of a minimal polynomial of some odd power of α as C is a binary cyclic code. For example, if $m_1(x)$ is the minimum polynomial of α, then $\alpha^2, \alpha^4, \alpha^8, \ldots$ are all roots of $m_1(x)$. The degree of each $m_i(x)$ is $\leq m$ and there are t of them so that the dimension of C is $\geq n - mt$.   Q.E.D.

This theorem plus good decoding schemes account for much of the usefulness of B.C.H. codes. The decoding schemes are a generalization of the scheme presented in Chapter 3 and one which is described in Section 7.6.

A B.C.H. code of designed distance δ has minimum weight $d \geq \delta$ and it may happen that d is $> \delta$ as the following example shows.

Consider a binary B.C.H. code C whose generator polynomial has roots β, β^2, β^3, and β^4 so that $\delta = 5$ where $\beta = \alpha^{89}$ for α a primitive element in $GF(2^{11})$. Recall that $(2^{11} - 1) = 89 \cdot 23$ so that $\beta^{23} = 1$ and we have a code of length 23. A code with $\delta = 5$ is double-error-correcting, but if we compute the cyclotomic coset C_1 for $n = 23$ containing 1, $C_1 = \{1, 2, 4, 8, 16, 9, 18, 13, 3, \ldots\}$, C_1 contains 11 elements. We know that $x^{23} - 1 = (x - 1)g(x)f(x)$ where $g(x)$ and $f(x)$ each has degree 11. Hence the generator polynomial of C is one of these. Recall that either of these polynomials is known to generate the triple-error-correcting Golay $(23, 12, 7)$ code, so $d = 7$.

7.4 REED-SOLOMON CODES

In defining B.C.H. codes we use two fields, one is the field $GF(q)$ over which the code is defined and the other is the field $GF(q^m)$ in which α can be found. Reed-Solomon codes are an important class of B.C.H. codes where the two fields coincide so that $m = 1$. We only consider the case

$n = q - 1$ and we take α primitive in $GF(q)$. In this situation the minimal polynomial for any α^i is linear. Suppose, for example, that we construct a $(15, 13)$ B.C.H. code C over $GF(16)$ which has roots α and α^2. Then its generator polynomial will be

$$g(x) = (x - \alpha)(x - \alpha^2) = x^2 + \alpha^{13}x + \alpha^3.$$

This is a code of designed distance 3 which is its actual minimum distance as we see a vector of weight 3 in it. As $3 - 1 = 15 - 13$, C is an M.D.S. code.

We define a *Reed-Solomon code* of designed distance d of length $n = q - 1$ over $GF(q)$ to be the code with generator polynomial

$$g(x) = (x - \alpha^b)(x - \alpha^{b+1}) \cdots (x - \alpha^{b+d-1}).$$

Theorem 77. A Reed-Solomon code C of designed distance d has d as its actual minimum weight. Further, C is an M.D.S. code.

Proof. By construction C is an $(n, n - d + 1)$ code. As $n - (n - d + 1) + 1 = d$, C is an M.D.S. code and so must have minimum weight d by the Singleton bound.   Q.E.D.

We see from this that Reed-Solomon codes are quite good and in fact they are often used. In some applications, though, it may be preferable to use a code whose parameters fit that situation better than those of a Reed-Solomon code.

7.5 MORE ON THE MINIMUM DISTANCE

We can actually determine, sometimes, that a B.C.H. code of designed distance δ has distance greater than δ just by looking at the roots. This is based on a recent approach to this question by van Lint and Wilson [41].

Let F be a finite field and let S be a subset of F. We say that a set I_s of subsets of F is *independent with respect to S* if the following holds.

(1) The empty set is in I_s.
(2) If A is in I_s, $A \subset S$, $\beta \in F$, $\beta \notin A$, then $A \cup \{\beta\}$ is in I_s.
(3) If $A \in I_s$, then $\alpha A \in I_s$ for any α in F.

These axioms allow us to build such an I_s element by element.

Theorem 78. Let $f(x)$ be a polynomial with coefficients in $GF(q)$ and let S be the set of its roots in some field $F = GF(q^m)$. Then the weight of $f(x)$

is $\geq$ the size of any set A in a set I_s of subsets of F which are independent with respect to S.

Proof. Suppose that the weight of $f(x)$ is r, then $f(x) = a_1 x^{i_1}$ $+ \cdots + a_r x^{i_r}$ and $f(\gamma) = a_1 \gamma^{i_1} + \cdots + a_r \gamma^{i_r} = 0$ for any γ in S. If A is any subset of F, we let $V(A)$ denote the vector space over F generated by all $(\alpha^{i_1}, \ldots, \alpha^{i_r})$ for α in A. Clearly $\dim V(A) \leq r \leq$ weight of $f(x)$. We want to show that $|A| \leq \dim V(A)$ for any A in a set I_s of subsets of F which are independent with respect to S. We do this by induction on the size of a set A in I_s. If $|A| = 1$, then it is clearly true. Suppose we know that it is true for all sets in I_s of size n and let A be a set in I_s of size $n + 1$. Then $A = A' \cup \{\beta\}$ for some $A' \subset S$, some $\beta \in F$, $\beta \notin S$. By induction we know that $|A'| \leq \dim V(A')$. Since $A' \subset S$, $f(\alpha) = 0$ for any α in A'. By linearity then, $\gamma^{i_1} + \cdots + \gamma^{i_r} = f(\gamma) = 0$ for any $(\gamma^{i_1}, \ldots, \gamma^{i_r})$ in $V(A')$. As $\beta \notin S$, $f(\beta) \neq 0$ so that $\dim V(A) = \dim V(A') + 1$. Hence $|A| \leq \dim V(A)$. \hfill Q.E.D.

We show how this can be used to obtain a better bound on the actual minimum distance of a B.C.H. code under certain circumstances. Consider a $(17, 9)$ B.C.H. code C with generating polynomial $f(x)$. Let $f(x)$ have a root α in some field F where $x^{17} - 1$ splits into linear factors. Then $S = (\alpha, \alpha^2, \alpha^4, \alpha^8, \alpha^9, \alpha^{13}, \alpha^{15}, \alpha^{16})$ is the set of roots of $f(x)$. The B.C.H. bound gives $d \geq 3$. In building our set A we start with the empty set. Taking $\beta = \alpha^3$, we get $\{\alpha^3\}$. Multiplying by α gives us $\{\alpha^4\}$. As $\alpha^4 \in S$, we can get $\{\alpha^4, \alpha^{11}\}$. Multiplying by α^{-2} gives $\{\alpha^2, \alpha^9\}$, another subset of S. We extend this to $\{\alpha^2, \alpha^9, \alpha^{11}\}$ and multiply by α^{-1} getting $\{\alpha, \alpha^8, \alpha^9\}$, again in S. So we add α^6 to get $\{\alpha, \alpha^6, \alpha^8, \alpha^9\}$ and multiply by α^7, giving us still another subset of S, namely $\{\alpha^8, \alpha^{13}, \alpha^{15}, \alpha^{16}\}$. Then $A = \{\alpha^8, \alpha^{13}, \alpha^{14}, \alpha^{15}, \alpha^{16}\}$ is in I_s telling us that the weight of $f(x) \geq 5$. We are still not finished. What about other vectors, $c(x) = a(x)f(x)$, in C? Well, if $c(x)$ has S as its set of roots, the same inequality holds. Certainly the set of roots of $c(x)$ contains S. If it is larger, then it must contain α^3 and all its powers so that $c(x)$ is either **h** of weight 17 or 0. Hence $d \geq 5$. Actually d must be 5 as we know that C is a quadratic residue code (why?). We did not have to go through this in this case but we did for illustrative purposes.

7.6   DECODING B.C.H. CODES

We return to the $(15, 7, 5)$ binary B.C.H. code described in Section 7.3 which we decoded in Section 3.4. There we used the parity check matrix

$$H' = \begin{bmatrix} 1\alpha & \cdots & \alpha^{14} \\ 1\alpha^3 & \cdots & \alpha^{12} \end{bmatrix}.$$

In order to decode a received vector $\mathbf{y}$ we first computed its syndrome, $\text{syn}(\mathbf{y}) = \mathbf{y}H'^T = \begin{bmatrix} y_1 \\ y_3 \end{bmatrix}$, $y_1 = \mathbf{y}(\alpha)$ and $y_3 = \mathbf{y}(\alpha^3)$. We noted that we could determine the locations of the errors by solving an equation whose coefficients we could determine from y_1 and y_3. This is what we now generalize. Our aim is obtaining this equation. Our code is a B.C.H. code C based on a field element α and which has been designed to correct t errors. Suppose we have a received vector $\mathbf{v}$ in which $r \leq t$ errors have occurred. As before we compute $\mathbf{v}(\alpha^i)$ which we now call S_i (in the example we called S_i, y_i) as this is more reminiscent of the word syndrome. Notice that $\mathbf{v} = \mathbf{c} + \mathbf{e}$ where $\mathbf{c}$ is in C and $\mathbf{e}$ is an error vector. Now $\mathbf{v}(\alpha) = \mathbf{c}(\alpha) + \mathbf{e}(\alpha)$.

$$\mathbf{e}(\alpha) = e_{i_1}\alpha^{i_1} + e_{i_2}\alpha^{i_2} + \cdots + e_{i_r}\alpha^{i_r}$$

where there are errors of magnitude $e_{i_1}, \ldots, e_{i_r}$ (which are one for binary codes) in unknown error locations $i_1, \ldots, i_r$. For nonbinary codes the magnitudes are also unknown. In order to handle this problem we introduce the notation $Y_l = e_{i_l}$ and $X_l = \alpha^{i_l}$—the *error-location numbers*. We do know, by their meaning, that the X_i's are distinct. The S_i are known and we get the following set of equations:

$$S_1 = Y_1 X_1 + Y_2 X_2 + \cdots + Y_r X_r$$
$$S_2 = Y_1 X_1^2 + Y_2 X_2^2 + \cdots + Y_r X_r^2$$
$$\vdots$$
$$S_{2t} = Y_1 X_1^{2t} + Y_2 X_2^{2t} + \cdots + Y_r X_r^{2t}.$$

This is a set of $2t$ nonlinear equations in r unknown error locations $X_1, \ldots, X_r$ and r unknown error magnitudes $Y_1, \ldots, Y_r$. This looks pretty hard. But this system must have at least one solution. Actually it has a unique solution. Our aim is to find these $2r$ unknowns given the known $S_1, \ldots, S_{2t}$. For this purpose we define the *error-locator polynomial*

(i)
$$s(x) = (1 - xX_1)(1 - xX_2) \cdots (1 - xX_r)$$
$$= 1 + s_1 x + \cdots + s_r x^r.$$

Notice that $s(x)$ has zeros at the inverses of the error locations. We will first try to compute $s_1, \ldots, s_r$ from the unknown syndromes $S_1, \ldots, S_{2t}$. Then we try to find roots of $s(x)$ in our field. Multiply both sides of (i) by $Y_i X_i^{j+r}$ and let $x = X_i^{-1}$. As $s(X_i^{-1}) = 0$, we get

$$0 = Y_i X_i^{j+r}\left(1 + s_1 X_i^{-1} + s_2 X_i^{-2} + \cdots + s_{r-1} X_i^{-(r-1)} + s_r X_i^{-r}\right)$$
$$= Y_i\left(X_i^{j+r} + s_1 X_i^{j+r-1} + \cdots + s_r X_i^j\right).$$

This is so for each i and j. We sum these equations from $i = 1$ to r obtaining the following system.

$$\sum_{i=1}^{r} Y_i X_i^{j+r} + s_1 \sum_{i=1}^{r} Y_i X_i^{j+r-1} + \cdots + s_r \sum_{i=1}^{r} Y_i X_i^{j} = 0.$$

We recognize this as the equation

$$S_{j+r} + s_1 S_{j+r-1} + s_2 S_{j+r-2} + \cdots + s_r S_j = 0$$

and we know S_j if $j \leq 2t$. So we get the following equations:

(ii) $s_1 S_{j+r-1} + s_2 S_{j+r-2} + \cdots + s_r S_j = -S_{j+r}$ for $j = 1, \ldots, r$.

We can write this set of equations as the following matrix equation.

(iii)
$$\begin{pmatrix} S_1 & S_2 & \cdots & S_r \\ S_2 & S_3 & \cdots & S_{r+1} \\ \vdots & \vdots & & \\ S_r & S_{r+1} & \cdots & S_{2r+1} \end{pmatrix} \begin{pmatrix} s_r \\ s_{r-1} \\ \vdots \\ s_1 \end{pmatrix} = \begin{pmatrix} -S_{r+1} \\ -S_{r+2} \\ \vdots \\ -S_{2r} \end{pmatrix}.$$

Now a magical thing happens. We can actually tell how many errors have occurred if this is less than t.

Theorem 79. The matrix of syndromes

$$M = \begin{pmatrix} S_1 & S_2 & \cdots & S_m \\ S_2 & S_3 & \cdots & S_{m+1} \\ \vdots & & & \vdots \\ S_n & & \cdots & S_{2m+1} \end{pmatrix}$$

is nonsingular if $m \leq r$, the number of errors which have actually occurred. If $m > r$, M is singular.

Proof. Let

$$V = \begin{pmatrix} 1 & \cdots & 1 \\ X_1 & \cdots & X_m \\ \vdots & & \vdots \\ X_1^{m-1} & \cdots & X_m^{m-1} \end{pmatrix}$$

and

$$
D = \begin{pmatrix}
Y_1 X_1 & 0 & \cdots & 0 \\
0 & Y_2 X_2 & \cdots & 0 \\
\vdots & & & \vdots \\
0 & & \cdots & Y_m X_m
\end{pmatrix}.
$$

Then $M = VDV^T$. This fact can be verified by computing the ijth element of VDV^T and noting that it is the ijth element of M. Hence $|M| = |V| |D| |V|$. If $m > r$, then $|D| = 0$ so that $|M| = 0$. If $m = r$, $|D| \neq 0$ and $|V| \neq 0$ as the X_i are different and nonzero which only happens when $m \leq r$. Hence $|M| \neq 0$. Q.E.D.

This theorem is the basis of a Peterson-Gorenstein-Zierler decoding scheme [31] for B.C.H. codes. So to decode a received vector we first determine the number of errors which have occurred. We start with the largest possible value, t. We compute $|M|$ with $m = t$. If $|M| = 0$, we let $m = t - 1$ and so on until a nonzero determinant is obtained. Now the actual number, r, of errors is known. At this point we can compute $s(x)$ by using the system of equations (ii). If it is easier, we can invert M and by (iii) we get $(s_r, s_{r-1}, \ldots, s_1)^T = M^{-1}(-S_{r+1}, -S_{r+2}, \ldots, -S_{2r})^T$. Then we find the roots of $s(x)$. This can be done by just searching throughout the field. If the code is binary, we are finished. If not, we must still find the Y_i's.

We state our decoding algorithm only for binary B.C.H. codes with roots $\alpha, \alpha^2, \ldots, \alpha^{2t-1}$. Let $\mathbf{v}$ be a received vector.

(1) Compute $\mathbf{v}(\alpha^i) = S_i$, $i = 1, \ldots, 2t$.
(2) Determine the maximum number r so that

$$
M = \begin{pmatrix}
S_1 & S_2 & \cdots & S_r \\
S_2 & S_3 & \cdots & S_{r+1} \\
\vdots & \vdots & & \vdots \\
S_r & S_{r+1} & \cdots & S_{2r-1}
\end{pmatrix}
$$

   is nonsingular. Start with $r = t$. Then r is the number of errors which have occurred.
(3) Find the coefficients of the error-locator polynomial by either using (ii) or computing M^{-1} and using (iii).
(4) Solve $s(x) = 0$ by searching throughout the field or by any other way you can think of.
(5) Find the error locations and correct the errors.

Steps (2) and (3) are the hardest and there are several other schemes for decoding B.C.H. codes which do not compute determinants [see 31]. In fact, there has been much work done on decoding B.C.H. codes since these codes are used in many practical applications. There are various generalizations of B.C.H. codes, to Goppa codes and alternant codes, and the decoding schemes have also been generalized.

We return to the $(15, 7, 5)$ B.C.H. code of Section 3.4 where we had a received vector y with $y(\alpha) = \alpha^5$ and $y(\alpha^3) = \alpha^7$. Then $S_1 = \alpha^5$, $S_2 = \alpha^{10}$, $S_3 = \alpha^7$, and $S_4 = \alpha^5$. Since $t = 2$, the first determinant we look at is

$$|M| = \begin{vmatrix} \alpha^5 & \alpha^{10} \\ \alpha^{10} & \alpha^7 \end{vmatrix} = \alpha^{12} + \alpha^5 = \alpha^3 \neq 0.$$

This tells us that two errors have occurred. In this situation

$$M^{-1} = \begin{pmatrix} \alpha^4 & \alpha^7 \\ \alpha^7 & \alpha^2 \end{pmatrix}$$

is easy to compute and

$$M^{-1}\begin{pmatrix} \alpha^7 \\ \alpha^5 \end{pmatrix} = \begin{pmatrix} \alpha^8 \\ \alpha^5 \end{pmatrix}.$$

Hence $s(x) = 1 + \alpha^5 x + \alpha^8 x^2$ and a search through $GF(16)$ yields the roots α^9 and α^{13}. Hence the errors are at positions numbered 8 and 12 where the numbering starts at 0. This is exactly what we found before.

Suppose that we consider a length 15 triple-error-correcting code and that our received vector is $v(x) = x^3 + x^9$. Then $S_1 = v(\alpha) = \alpha^{11}$, $S_2 = S_1^2 = \alpha^7$, $S_3 = v(\alpha^3) = \alpha^{13}$, $S_4 = S_2^2 = \alpha^{14}$, and $S_5 = v(\alpha^5) = 0$. The first M we look at is

$$M = \begin{pmatrix} \alpha^{11} & \alpha^7 & \alpha^{13} \\ \alpha^7 & \alpha^{13} & \alpha^{14} \\ \alpha^{13} & \alpha^{14} & 0 \end{pmatrix}.$$

As $|M| = 0$, 3 errors did not occur. The next M is

$$M = \begin{pmatrix} \alpha^{11} & \alpha^7 \\ \alpha^7 & \alpha^{13} \end{pmatrix}$$

and $|M| \neq 0$. So 2 errors did occur and we can correct them as above. But we really should be able to correct them without doing any of this (why?).

PROBLEMS

1. Let α be an element in $GF(2^8)$ whose minimal polynomial $f(x)$ has degree 8. What can be the length n of a cyclic code consisting of all polynomials $h(x)$ of degree $< n$ so that $h(\alpha) = 0$?

2. A Q.R. code C of length 47 is a cyclic code. Hence we can define C as consisting of all binary polynomials $h(x)$ of degree less than 47 so that $h(\alpha_i) = 0$, $i = 1, \ldots, r$. Describe these α_i.

3. Give a generator matrix for the double-error-correcting B.C.H. code described in Section 7.3. What is its actual minimum weight? Why?

4. (a) Give a generator polynomial of a triple-error-correcting binary B.C.H. code of length 15.

   (b) What is the dimension of this code?

   (c) Give a generator matrix for this code.

5. (a) What is the dimension of a quadruple-error-correcting B.C.H. code C of length 15?

   (b) What is the actual d of C?

6. (a) What is the dimension of a binary double-error-correcting B.C.H. code of length 31?

   (b) What is the dimension of a triple-error-correcting B.C.H. code of length 31?

   (c) What is the dimension of a quadruple-error-correcting B.C.H. code C of length 31?

7. (a) Give a generating polynomial of a single-error-correcting ternary B.C.H. code of length 8.

   (b) Give a generator matrix of this code.

8. Describe a Reed-Solomon $(7, 3)$ code over $GF(8)$ by giving its generator polynomial. How many errors will it correct?

9. Find a generator polynomial for a double-error-correcting Reed-Solomon code over $GF(16)$. Give its length and dimension.

10. Do Problems 15 and 16 from Chapter 3 using the decoding algorithm of Section 7.6.

11. Let α be a primitive element of $GF(16)$ and let $g(x) = 1 + x^2 + x^5 + x^6 + x^8 + x^9 + x^{10}$ be a generator polynomial of a $(15, 5)$ B.C.H. code. Suppose the word $\mathbf{v} = (1, 0, 1, 1, 0, 1, 0, 1, 1, 0, 0, 1, 0, 0, 1)$ is received. Determine the correct word which was sent.

8

Weight Distributions

8.1 PRELIMINARY CONCEPTS AND A THEOREM ON WEIGHTS IN HOMOGENEOUS CODES

When using a code it is important to know the probability of correct decoding. To be able to compute this in a practical situation, it is necessary to know the weight distribution of the code. Thus there has been a great deal of effort to determine the weight distributions of specific codes, a very difficult task for any but modest sized codes. To give an idea of the difficulties involved, it is possible to compute, in a reasonable amount of time, the weight distribution of a specified (40, 20) binary code on a large computer, but larger codes usually require extra knowledge to obtain their weight distributions. Theoretical knowledge does help to compute the weight distributions of certain codes. We explore much of this knowledge in this chapter.

The MacWilliams-Pless equations relate the weight distribution of a code C to the weight distribution of its dual code $C^\perp$. When $C = C^\perp$ these equations give strong constraints on the weight distribution of C, which, with other knowledge, often lead to the explicit weight distribution. These are most easily determined over $GF(2)$ or $GF(3)$ by the Gleason polynomials, which generate the weight enumerators of self-dual codes.

We first give some needed preliminaries. Recall that in Chapter 2 we defined the binomial coefficient $\binom{n}{r}$ to be the number of subsets of size r of a set of size n and that this equals $n!/(r!(n-r)!)$. By its definition this assumes that n and r are integers with $n \geq r \geq 0$. We extend this definition to $\binom{n}{r}$ for $r > n$ and say that in this situation $\binom{n}{r} = 0$. Note that $\binom{n}{0} = 1$ since $0! = 1$. Binomial coefficients arise in many different contexts where enumerations occur and they satisfy many identities. One obvious identity is $\binom{n}{r} = \binom{n}{n-r}$. Another well known identity is $\binom{n}{r} = \binom{n-1}{r}$ $+ \binom{n-1}{r-1}$. By using this identity, binomial coefficients can be generated in terms of previously generated binomial coefficients (see Problem 2). Binomial coefficients occur prominently in the MacWilliams equations. Stirling numbers of the second kind occur in the Pless power moments.

A *Stirling number of the second kind* is denoted by $S(r, \nu)$. If $r \geq \nu \geq 0$, then $\nu! S(r, \nu)$ is the number of ways of placing r distinct objects into ν distinct cells with no cell left empty. By definition,

$$S(r, \nu) = \frac{1}{\nu!} \sum_{i=0}^{\nu} (-1)^{\nu-i} \binom{\nu}{i} i^r.$$

As with the binomial coefficients, it is possible to generate Stirling numbers from previously generated ones. We give the identity that makes this possible and a few rows of the table that we can compute from this identity. First we have the initial conditions $S(0,0) = 1$, $S(r,0) = 0$ for $r \neq 0$, and $S(1, 1) = 1$. The recursion satisfied by the Stirling numbers is $S(r + 1, \nu) = \nu S(r, \nu) + S(r, \nu - 1)$ for $r \geq \nu \geq 1$. Since $S(1, 1) = 1$ and $S(r, 1) = S(r - 1, 1)$ for $r > 1$, it follows by induction that $S(r, 1) = 1$ for all r. The first few Stirling numbers can be generated from the initial conditions and the recursion relation and are given in Table 8.1.

We turn now to the theorem on homogeneous codes. Let C be a code of length $n + 1$ (we see why later) and let M_i be the matrix whose rows are the vectors in C of weight i, if any exist. Then C is called *homogeneous* if for each weight i, each column of M_i has the same weight. The following theorem is due to Eugene Prange.

Theorem 80. Let C be a homogeneous code of length $n + 1$ and let A_i denote the number of vectors of weight i in C. Let C' be a punctured code of C and let a_i denote the number of vectors of weight i in C'. Then if

Table 8.1 Some Stirling Numbers of the Second Kind

$\nu \rightarrow$						
r	1	2	3	4	5	6
1	1					
2	1	1				
3	1	3	1			
4	1	7	6	1		
5	1	15	25	10	1	
6	1	31	90	65	15	1

$A_1 = 0,$

(i) $$a_i = \frac{(n + 1 - i)}{(n + 1)} A_i + \frac{(i + 1)}{(n + 1)} A_{i+1}.$$

If B is a subcode of C obtained by requiring that some coordinate equal zero and if we let b_i denote the number of vectors of weight i in B, then we have

(ii) $$b_i = \frac{(n + 1 - i)}{(n + 1)} A_i.$$

If we add the further assumption that C is a binary code with only even weight vectors, then we have

(iii) $$A_{2j} = a_{2j} + a_{2j-1}$$

(iv) $$a_{2j-1} = \frac{2j}{(n + 1)} A_{2j}$$

(v) $$a_{2j} = \frac{(n + 1 - 2j)}{(n + 1)} A_{2j}$$

(vi) $$2j a_{2j} = (n + 1 - 2j) a_{2j-1}.$$

Proof. The number of nonzero elements in the matrix M_i equals iA_i since M_i has A_i rows of weight i. By the homogeneity assumption, each column of M_i has the same weight, say r. Hence $(n + 1)r = iA_i$ so that $r = (i/(n + 1))A_i$. From this we see that each column of M_i has $((n + 1 - i)/(n + 1))A_i$ zeroes. A vector of weight i in C' arises either from a vector of weight i in C with 0 on the punctured coordinate or a vector of weight $i + 1$ in C with a nonzero element on the punctured coordinate. This demonstrates (i). Since a vector of weight i in B is a vector of weight i in C with 0 on a fixed coordinate, (ii) holds. We consider the special case where C is a binary code with only even weight vectors and C' is a punctured code. Then the punctured code can have vectors of weight $2j$ and $2j - 1$ and these must come about by deleting one coordinate from an even weight vector of weight $2j$. This proves (iii). If we let $i = 2j - 1$ in (i), then $A_{2j-1} = 0$ by assumption so that (iv) holds. If we let $i = 2j$ in (i), then A_{2j+1} is 0 and we get (v). By direct computation (vi) follows from (iv) and (v).   Q.E.D.

A code whose group is transitive is homogeneous and indeed this is the way in which we usually know that a code is homogeneous. Since the group of an extended binary Q.R. code contains $PSL_2(p)$ and this group is transitive (Problem 5), our theorem can be applied to extended Q.R. codes. The following corollary is part of Theorem 71, but this proof is simpler.

Corollary. Any binary Q.R.$(p, (p + 1)/2)$ code has odd minimum weight d. Further, the code contains vectors of even weight $d + 1$.

Proof. This statement about binary Q.R. codes of odd length follows from (iv) in the theorem and Theorem 69.

It is also true that any primitive, binary B.C.H. code of length $2^m - 1$ has odd minimum weight d since the extended code has a transitive group [15, p. 236]. They also have vectors of even weight $d + 1$ [see Problem 6].   Q.E.D.

It can also be shown that extended binary B.C.H. codes have transitive groups so that the binary B.C.H. codes have odd minimum weight. We illustrate Theorem 80 on the $(7, 4)$ binary Q.R. code C'. Since $PSL_2(7)$ is transitive on the coordinate indices of the $(8, 4)$ extended Q.R. code C, we can apply the theorem to weights in C and C'. Cases (iii), (iv), (v), and (vi) in the theorem hold and we verify these results for this situation. It is known that $A_0 = A_8 = 1$, $A_4 = 14$, and $a_0 = a_7 = 1$, $a_3 = a_4 = 7$. Condition (iii) of Theorem 80, states that $A_4 = 14 = a_3 + a_4$. Condition (iv) is the equation $a_3 = \frac{4}{8}A_4 = 7$. Condition (v) is the statement $a_4 = ((8 - 4)/8)A_4 = 7$, and condition (vi) is $4a_4 = (8 - 4)a_3 = 4a_3$. For larger codes we could obtain new information about weights from partial information.

8.2 THE MACWILLIAMS EQUATIONS

The MacWilliams identities [13] give a surprising and important relationship between the weight distribution of a code C and the weight distribution of the dual code $C^\perp$. They hold for codes over any finite field. We state them first for $GF(2)$ in order to get a feeling for why they hold. Let A_i be the number of vectors of weight i in C and B_i the number of vectors of weight i in $C^\perp$. For C an (n, k) binary code, there are two sets of MacWilliams identities, given below, each consisting of $n + 1$ equations.

$$\sum_{j=0}^{n} \binom{j}{\nu} A_j = 2^{k-\nu} \sum_{j=0}^{n} (-1)^j \binom{n-j}{n-\nu} B_j \tag{1}$$

$$\sum_{j=0}^{n} \binom{n-j}{n-\nu} B_j = 2^{\nu-k} \sum_{j=0}^{n} \binom{n-j}{\nu} A_j \tag{2}$$

$$\nu = 0, \ldots, n.$$

Since we are only interested in solutions that are weight distributions of codes, we can let $A_0 = B_0 = 1$. We do this whenever we wish.

We consider the first few equations in (1). In the case that $\nu = 0$ we get $\sum_{j=0}^{n} A_j = 2^k B_0 = 2^k$. In fact we know this. It just says that there are 2^k vectors in an (n, k) binary code. Let us go on.

$$\nu = 1: \qquad \sum_{j=0}^{n} jA_j = 2^{k-1}(n - B_1).$$

This is not too bad either. If $B_1 = 0$, that is, if there are no zero columns in C, then this is Problem 1.20. Let M be the matrix of all codewords in C. The left side of the equation counts the number of ones in M as each A_i is the number of rows of M of weight i. Each column of M consists of either half 1's and half 0's (Problem 1.19) or is entirely 0. As there are n columns and B_1 is the number of zero columns of M, the right side holds even when $B_1 \neq 0$. This looks fascinating. Let us continue.

$$\nu = 2: \qquad \sum_{j=0}^{n} \binom{j}{2} A_j = 2^{k-2}\left(\binom{n}{2} - (n - 1)B_1 + B_2\right).$$

Things are getting more complicated here. Recall that B_2 is the number of pairs of equal columns in C, possibly equal zero columns and possibly equal nonzero columns. If both B_1 and B_2 are 0, the equation is still not too bad. The left side of our identity is the sum of the number of pairs of 1's in any row of M, for example a row of weight i would have $\binom{i}{2}$ pairs of 1's. For the right side, consider two unequal columns of M. As no column is zero, this is a matrix with two columns and 2^k rows, and as for the case of one column, it can be shown that $\frac{1}{4}$ of the rows are 00, $\frac{1}{4}$ are 01, $\frac{1}{4}$ are 10, and $\frac{1}{4}$ are 11. Hence M has $(2^k/2^2)\binom{n}{2}$ pairs of 1's. If $B_1 = r \neq 0$ and the only repeated columns are zero columns so that $B_2 = \binom{r}{2}$, by the above argument, the right side should be $2^{k-2}\binom{n-r}{2}$, which it is since $\binom{n}{2} - (n - 1)r + \binom{r}{2} = \binom{n-r}{2}$. Of course, there can be repeated columns that are not zero columns and the pairs can still be counted but the counting gets more complicated.

There are many proofs of (1) and (2) utilizing sophisticated mathematical techniques. We give an elementary proof due to Brualdi, Pless, and Beissinger [32]. But we need some notation and a few lemmas first. If C is a length n code over $GF(q)$ and I is a subset of $\{1, \ldots, n\}$ with $|I| = \nu$, then we let $C(I)$ be the code of length ν consisting of the vectors $C(I) = (c_{i_1}, c_{i_2}, \ldots, c_{i_\nu})$ where $\mathbf{c} = (c_1, \ldots, c_n)$ is in C and $i_1, \ldots, i_\nu$ are in I. We have seen something like this before when we punctured a code. In that case I consists of all but one coordinate and $C(I)$ is the punctured code.

Lemma 1. Let D be the subcode of $C^\perp$ which is 0 on all positions not in I, then $C(I)^\perp = D(I)$.

Proof. Clearly $D(I) \subseteq C(I)^\perp$. Take any vector $\mathbf{d}'$ in $C(I)^\perp$. It is of length ν and if we extend it to a length n vector $\mathbf{d}$ by adjoining $n - \nu$ zeros, then $\mathbf{d}$ certainly is in D.

Lemma 2. If $0 \le j \le \nu \le n$, then $\sum_{|I|=\nu} B_j(I) = \dbinom{n-j}{\nu-j} B_j$.

Proof. Take a vector $\mathbf{d}$ of weight j in $C^\perp$. Then $\mathbf{d}$ has $n - j$ zero positions so that there are $\dbinom{n-j}{\nu-j}$ sets I of size ν which include the nonzero positions of $\mathbf{d}$. Thus $\mathbf{d}$ gives rise to $\dbinom{n-j}{\nu-j}$ vectors of weight j in codes $C(I)^\perp$ where $|I| = \nu$. If $\mathbf{d}'$ is a vector in such a $C(I)^\perp$, then by Lemma 1, $\mathbf{d}'$ came from a vector in $C^\perp$ by adjoining $n - j$ zeros.   Q.E.D.

We suppose that C is an (n, k) code over $GF(q)$ and that M is the matrix of all codewords in C. Then M is a $q^k \times n$ matrix. Let $M(I)$ be the submatrix of M whose columns consist of those columns of M whose labels are in I. If $|I| = \nu$, $M(I)$ is a $q^k \times \nu$ matrix. All codewords in $C(I)$ occur as rows of $M(I)$ but the same codeword occurs several times. If we call the dimension of $C(I)$ k_I, then the following lemma tells us how many times.

Lemma 3. Each codeword of $C(I)$ occurs exactly q^{k-k_I} times as a row of $M(I)$.

Proof. We can suppose that the first ν positions are the positions in I since C is certainly equivalent to such a code. Then C has a generator matrix of the following form:

$$G = \begin{pmatrix} A & B \\ 0 & D \end{pmatrix},$$

where A, a $k_I \times \nu$ matrix, is a generator matrix of $C(I)$. Now every row of M is a linear combination of rows of G and $M(I)$ consists of the first ν

columns of M. Let c be a linear combination of the first k_I rows of G. Then c plus any of the q^{k-k_I} linear combinations of the last $k - k_I$ rows of G gives a vector in M with the same values in their first ν positions.

$$\text{Q.E.D.}$$

We let ν be an integer with $0 \le \nu \le n$. We see that a row of M of weight j has $\binom{n-j}{\nu}$ ν-tuples of zeros. Hence the number of ν-tuples of zeros in the rows of M equals

$$\sum_{j=0}^{n} \binom{n-j}{\nu} A_j .$$

We can also count the number of ν-tuples of zeros in the rows of M by counting the number of zero rows of $M(I)$ for each subset I of $\{1, \ldots, n\}$ of cardinality ν.

Theorem 81. The number of ν-tuples of zeros in the rows of the codeword matrix M of C equals

$$q^{k-\nu} \sum_{j=0}^{n} \binom{n-j}{\nu-j} B_j \qquad 0 \le \nu \le n .$$

Proof. We know that

$$q^{k-\nu} \sum_{j=0}^{n} \binom{n-j}{\nu-j} B_j = q^{k-\nu} \sum_{j=0}^{n} \sum_{|I|=\nu} B_j(I) \quad \text{(by Lemma 2)}$$

$$= q^{k-\nu} \sum_{|I|=\nu} \sum_{j=0}^{n} B_j(I)$$

$$= q^{k-\nu} \sum_{|I|=\nu} q^{\nu-k_I} \quad \text{since } \dim C(I)^{\perp} = \nu - k_I$$

$$= \sum_{|I|=\nu} q^{k-k_I} .$$

But by Lemma 3, q^{k-k_I} is the number of zero rows of $M(I)$ and hence $\sum_{|I|=\nu} q^{k-k_I}$ is the number of ν-tuples of zeros in the rows of M. Q.E.D.

As over $GF(2)$, there are two sets of MacWilliams identities over $GF(q)$. We give only one of them; the other set of identities can be derived from this set.

Corollary. (MacWilliams). Let C be an (n, k) code over $GF(q)$ with A_i the number of vectors of weight i in C and B_i the number of vectors of weight i in $C^\perp$. The following equations relate the $\{A_i\}$ and $\{B_i\}$.

$$\sum_{j=0}^{n} \binom{n-j}{\nu} A_j = q^{k-\nu} \sum_{j=0}^{n} \binom{n-j}{\nu-j} B_j$$

where $\nu = 0, \ldots, n$.

Another useful way to regard weight distributions is as polynomials called weight enumerators. Let C be a length n code with A_i again the number of vectors in C of weight i. A polynomial in x and y is *homogeneous* of degree n if the powers of x and y in each term add up to n. Define the *weight enumerator* of C to be the following homogeneous polynomial. $W_C(x, y) = A_0 x^n + A_1 x^{n-1} y + A_2 x^{n-2} y^2 + \cdots + A_n y^n$.

For C an (n, k) binary code, let $|C| = 2^k$. In these terms the MacWilliams identities can be expressed in either of the following two elegant forms.

$$W_{C^\perp}(x, y) = \frac{1}{|C|} W_C(x + y, x - y) \tag{4}$$

or

$$\sum_{i=0}^{n} B_i x^{n-i} y^i = \frac{1}{|C|} \sum_{j=0}^{n} A_j (x + y)^{n-j} (x - y)^j. \tag{5}$$

These formulas are also symmetric in A and B. By expressing both sides of (4) as weight enumerator polynomials, it can be seen that (4) and (5) say exactly the same thing. The MacWilliams identities are equivalent to either (4) or (5) as can be seen by equating corresponding coefficients. We see why this is so for a few coefficients. First for $\nu = 0$. Then $B_0 = 2^{-k}\sum_{j=0}^{n} A_j$. We see that B_0 is the coefficient of x^n on the left side of (5) and the coefficient of x^n on the right side of (5) is $1/|C|\sum_{j=0}^{n} A_j$ so (5) is correct for the coefficient of x^n. When $\nu = 1$ we have $nB_0 + B_1 = 2^{1-k}\sum_{j=0}^{n}(n - j)A_j$ so that $B_1 = 2^{1-k}\sum_{j=0}^{n}(n - j)A_j - nB_0 = 2^{1-k}\sum_{j=0}^{n}(n - j)A_j - n/2^k\sum_{j=0}^{n} A_j = 2^{-k}\sum_{j=0}^{n}(n - 2j)/A_j$ which is the coefficient of $x^{n-1} y$ on the left side of (5). The coefficient of $x^{n-1} y$ on the right side of (5) equals

$$\frac{1}{|C|} \sum_{j=0}^{n} \left((n - j) x^{n-j-1} y \cdot x^j A_j + x^{n-j}(-j) x^{j-1} y A_j \right)$$

$$= \frac{1}{|C|} \sum_{j=0}^{n} (n - 2j) A_j x^{n-1} y.$$

This check can be performed for any coefficient (see Problem 13). In Section 8.4 this form of the MacWilliams formulas is used to prove some nice facts.

8.3 PLESS POWER MOMENTS

The Pless power moments are an infinite family of equations relating the weight distribution of C to the weight distribution of $C^{\perp}$. This family of equations is equivalent to the MacWilliams equations. This form has certain advantages in that a unique solution to the identities is often evident.

We have already seen the beginning of the first form of the power moments, (P_1). The first equation in (P_1) for the binary case is $\sum_{j=0}^{n} A_j = 2^k$ and the second equation is $\sum_{j=0}^{n} j A_j = 2^{k-1}(n - B_1)$.

Theorem 82 (Pless Power Moments) [20]. Let C be an (n, k) code over $GF(q)$ with A_i the number of vectors of weight i in C and B_i the number of vectors of weight i in $C^{\perp}$. Let $\gamma = q - 1$. The following equations relate the $\{A_i\}$ and the $\{B_i\}$.

$$(P_1) \quad \sum_{j=0}^{n} j^r A_j = \sum_{j=0}^{n} (-1)^j B_j \left(\sum_{\nu=0}^{r} \nu! S(r, \nu) q^{k-\nu} \gamma^{\nu-j} \binom{n - j}{n - \nu} \right)$$

and

$$(P_2) \quad \sum_{j=0}^{n} (n - j)^r A_j = \sum_{j=0}^{n} B_j \left(\sum_{\nu=0}^{r} \nu! S(r, \nu) q^{k-\nu} \binom{n - j}{n - \nu} \right).$$

As there is one equation in either (P_1) or (P_2) for any r, this is an infinite family of equations. If $r < n$, then $\sum_{j=0}^{n}$ on the right sides of (P_1) and (P_2) can be replaced by $\sum_{j=0}^{r}$. When $q = 2$, clearly $\gamma = 1$.

Proof. We prove that the MacWilliams equations imply (P_2). Conversely (P_2) implies the MacWilliams equations. There is a known identity that says

$$(n - j)^r = \sum_{\nu=0}^{r} \nu! \binom{n - j}{\nu} S(r, \nu).$$

Hence

$$(n - j)^r A_j = \sum_{\nu=0}^{r} \nu! \binom{n - j}{\nu} S(r, \nu) A_j$$

so that

$$\sum_{j=0}^{n} (n-j)^r A_j = \sum_{j=0}^{n} \sum_{\nu=0}^{r} \nu! \binom{n-j}{\nu} S(r,\nu) A_j.$$

By interchanging the order of summation in the right side, we have

$$\sum_{j=0}^{n} (n-j)^r A_j = \sum_{\nu=0}^{r} \nu! S(r,\nu) \left(\sum_{j=0}^{n} \binom{n-j}{\nu} A_j \right)$$

$$= \sum_{\nu=0}^{r} \nu! S(r,\nu) \left(q^{k-\nu} \sum_{j=0}^{n} \binom{n-j}{n-\nu} B_j \right)$$

by the MacWilliams identities. By again interchanging the order of summation, this is equal to

$$\sum_{j=0}^{n} B_j \left(\sum_{\nu=1}^{r} \nu! S(r,\nu) q^{k-\nu} \binom{n-j}{n-\nu} \right). \qquad\text{Q.E.D.}$$

In order to work out a few examples, we give the first three equations in (P_1) for binary codes. We repeat the first two equations.

$$r = 0: \quad \sum_{j=0}^{n} A_j = 2^k$$

$$r = 1: \quad \sum_{j=0}^{n} j A_j = 2^{k-1}(n - B_1)$$

$$r = 2: \quad \sum_{j=0}^{n} j^2 A_j = B_0 \left(0! S(2,0) 2^k \binom{n}{n} \right.$$

$$+ 1! S(2,1) 2^{k-1} n + 2! S(2,2) 2^{k-2} \binom{n}{n-2} \Big)$$

$$- B_1 \left(1! S(2,1) 2^{k-1} \binom{n-1}{n-1} + 2! S(2,2) S^{k-2} \binom{n-1}{n-2} \right)$$

$$+ B_2 \left(2! S(2,2) 2^{k-2} \binom{n-2}{n-2} \right)$$

$$= 2^{k-2} n(n+1) - 2^{k-1} n B_1 + 2^{k-1} B_2.$$

Why is this form useful? Let us try it when $n = 8$, $C = C^{\perp}$, and $d = 4$. We can suppose that $A_0 = B_0 = 1$. Since $d = 4$, $A_1 = B_1 = 0$, and $A_2 = B_0 = 0$ so that the first three equations in (P_1) are as follows.

$$A_4 + A_6 + A_8 = 15$$
$$4A_4 + 6A_6 + 8A_8 = 64$$
$$4^2 A_4 + 6^2 A_6 + 8^2 A_8 = 288.$$

The determinant of this system is

$$D = \begin{vmatrix} 1 & 1 & 1 \\ 4 & 6 & 8 \\ 4^2 & 6^2 & 8^2 \end{vmatrix}.$$

This is a Vandermonde determinant that is not zero so that the system has a unique solution. We could solve it, but since we know the weight distribution of the $(8, 4)$ Hamming code and this code satisfies the conditions above, its weight distribution, $A_0 = A_8 = 1$ and $A_4 = 14$, must be the solution. Note that even though a weight distribution is unique, it does not follow that a code with this weight distribution is unique. There are cases known where inequivalent codes have the same weight distribution. It can be proven, however, that the Hamming $(8, 4)$ code C is the unique code with its weight distribution; that is, any $(8, 4)$ code with this weight distribution must be equivalent to C.

Let us try this again. Let $n = 24$, $k = 12$, $d = 8$, and suppose that C is doubly even. In this situation $B_1 = B_2 = 0$ as $C = C^{\perp}$. We again have three equations in three unknowns, A_8, A_{12}, and A_{16}. The determinant of this system is Vandermonde so that its value is easily seen to be nonzero. We again have a unique solution and this must be the weight distribution of the Golay code. It can be proven that a code with this weight distribution is equivalent to the Golay code [21].

The following is a useful theorem.

Theorem 83 [20].   A unique solution to the power moments exists under the conditions that s or fewer A_i's are unknown and that $B_1, B_2, \ldots, B_{s-1}$ are known.

Proof.   In (P_1) the first s equations in s unknowns have a coefficient matrix whose determinant is Vandermonde. This determinant is not 0 so that there is a unique solution for the A_i's. Each further B_j occurs one at a time in the succeeding equations and hence can be solved for.   Q.E.D.

In our examples above the $(s - 1)$ B_i's that we knew were all 0. This happens quite often when the B_i's are known through a knowledge of the minimum weight of $C^\perp$.

If we let C_1 be the $(24, 12, 8)$ Golay code then a punctured code C_2 of C_1 is a $(23, 12, 7)$ Golay code. By Theorem 71 the only nonzero weights in C_2 are 7, 8, 11 12, 15, and 16. Since $C_1 = C_1^\perp$, the vectors in $C_2^\perp$ are the vectors of even weight in C_2 so that $B_1 = B_2 = \cdots = B_6 = 0$ and the weight distribution of C_2 is also unique. From the table in Section 6.5 we see that the $(32, 16)$ binary Q.R. code C has minimum weight 8. Since C is doubly even, the only possible nonzero weights are 8, 12, 16, 20, 24, and 32. Since $B_1 = B_2 = B_3 = B_4 = 0$, the weight distribution of C is also unique. Not all weight distributions are unique. The $(72, 36)$ binary Q.R. code has minimum weight 12 and there are many possible weight distributions for a $(72, 36, 12)$ doubly-even code. However, the weight distribution of a doubly even $(72, 36, 16)$ code is unique (see Problem 16). Furthermore, this weight distribution consists of nonnegative integers. However, even though many people have looked for it, no code has been found with this weight distribution and no one has shown that such a code cannot exist.

The weight distribution of any code C must satisfy both the MacWilliams equations and the Pless power moments. However, a solution to these equations need not be the weight distribution of any code. Clearly a solution with negative numbers could not be the weight distribution of a code. But even solutions with positive integral values need not be. We discuss this further in the next section.

8.4 GLEASON POLYNOMIALS

The Gleason polynomials are weight enumerators that generate the weight distributions of self-dual codes over $GF(2)$ and $GF(3)$. Self-dual codes are important codes because many of the best algebraic codes are self-dual, for example the extended Hamming code, the extended Golay codes, and the extended binary Q.R. codes when $p \equiv -1 \pmod 8$. Interesting ternary self-dual codes are the symmetry codes [22] and the ternary Q.R. codes. Self-dual codes are important because it is known that this class of codes satisfy a Varshamov-Gilbert bound [16, 24]. Therefore it is worth looking here for good codes. Furthermore, more is known about these codes; for example, information about their weight distribution is given by the Gleason polynomials. The Gleason polynomials are important theoretically and they also simplify the computation of the weight distributions of self-dual codes considerably.

We need a few definitions first. Let G_1 be a generator matrix of an (n_1, k_1) code C_1 and let G_2 be a generator matrix of an (n_2, k_2) code C_2. Then the *direct sum* of C_1 and C_2, written $C_1 \oplus C_2$, is the $(n_1 + n_2, k_1 + k_2)$ code with generator matrix

$$\begin{pmatrix} G_1 & 0 \\ 0 & G_2 \end{pmatrix}.$$

We let C^r denote the direct sum of C with itself r times. If the minimum weight of C_1 is d_1 and the minimum weight of C_2 is d_2, then it is easy to see that the minimum weight of $C_1 \oplus C_2$ is the minimum of d_1 and d_2. If $W_{C_i}(x, y)$ is the weight enumerator polynomial of C_i, $i = 1, 2$ then the weight enumerator polynomial of $C_1 \oplus C_2$ is $W_{C_1}(x, y)W_{C_2}(x, y)$ (Problem 17).

From now on we refer to weight enumerator polynomials both as $W_C(x, y)$ and $g(x, y)$. If $g(x, y)$ is the weight enumerator polynomial of a length n code C, the coefficient of $x^{n-i}y^i$ is understood to be A_i, the number of vectors of weight i in C. Let $g_1(x, y)$ and $g_2(x, y)$ be homogeneous polynomials of degrees r_1 and r_2 where r_1 and r_2 both divide n. Let S be the set of all pairs (i, j) with $r_1 i + r_2 j = n$ and $i, j \geq 0$. If we denote complex numbers by α_i and let $R \subseteq S$, then a polynomial

$$h(x, y) = \sum_{(i, j) \in R} \alpha_i g_1(x, y)^i g_2(x, y)^j$$

is called a *combination of* $g_1(x, y)$ and $g_2(x, y)$. Clearly $h(x, y)$ has degree n and is homogeneous. Various combinations can be seen in the examples that follow.

The Gleason polynomials are certain weight enumerator polynomials such that any weight enumerator polynomial is a combination of them. Before stating this theorem in general, we look at a few examples for the first situation, self-dual codes over $GF(2)$. Gleason's theorem states that the weight enumerator of a binary self-dual code is a combination of the polynomials $g_1(x, y) = x^2 + y^2$ and $g_2(x, y) = x^8 + 14x^4y^4 + y^8$. We examine what this means for small values of n.

$n = 2$ $x^2 + y^2$ is the weight enumerator of the $(2, 1)$ self-dual code C_1 consisting of 0 and **h**.

$n = 4$ $(x^2 + y^2)^2$ is the weight enumerator of the $(4, 2)$ self-dual code C_1^2.

$n = 6$ $(x^2 + y^2)^3$ is the weight enumerator of the self-dual $(6, 3)$ code C_1^3.

$n = 8$ Here any combination of $g_1(x, y)$ and $g_2(x, y)$ has the form

$$\alpha\left(x^8 + 14x^4y^4 + y^8\right) + \beta\left(x^2 + y^2\right)^4 = (\alpha + \beta)x^8 + 4\beta x^6y^2$$
$$+ (14\alpha + 6\beta)x^4y^4 + 4\beta x^2y^6 + (\alpha + \beta)y^8 \quad (7)$$

for α and β fixed complex numbers. We determine all solutions to (7) that could be weight distributions of codes.

First A_0 must be 1. Hence $\alpha + \beta = 1$. The computation could be tabulated as follows.

	A_0	A_2	A_4	A_6	A_8
α	1	0	14	0	1
β	1	4	6	4	1

Hence $A_2 = 4\beta$ so that $\beta \geq 0$ and 4β is an integer. Now $A_4 = 14\alpha + 6\beta = 14 - 8\beta$, which tells us that $\beta < 2$. The only possibilities for β are then 0, $\frac{1}{4}, \frac{1}{2}, \frac{3}{4}, 1, \frac{5}{4}, \frac{3}{2}$, and $\frac{7}{4}$, which give the following eight solutions to (7). The columns of the matrix below are the solutions to (7) that could be the weight distributions of $(8, 4)$ self-dual codes.

	1	2	3	4	5	6	7	8
A_0	1	1	1	1	1	1	1	1
A_2	0	1	2	3	4	5	6	7
A_4	14	12	10	8	6	4	2	0
A_6	0	1	2	3	4	5	6	7
A_8	1	1	1	1	1	1	1	1

As a matter of fact, only solutions 1 and 5 represent the weight distributions of self-dual $(8, 4)$ codes. Solution 1 is the weight distribution of the Hamming $(8, 4)$ code C_2 and solution 5 is the weight distribution of C_1^4.

Clearly $A_2 \leq 4$ for a self-dual $(8, 4)$ code, which eliminates solutions 6, 7, and 8. Other arguments eliminate solutions 2, 3, and 4 (Problem 19).

Note how much easier it is to use the Gleason polynomials to find the possible weight distributions of $(8, 4)$ self-dual codes than it would have been to solve either the MacWilliams equations or the power moment identities. It is an interesting open problem whether further restrictions can be placed on the Gleason polynomials so that there are fewer solutions but the set of solutions would still contain all the weight distributions of self-dual codes. Before giving an elementary proof of the first case in Gleason's theorem, we require the following lemma.

Lemma. Any combination of $g_1(x, y)$ and $g_2(x, y)$ with coefficients that add to 1 is a solution of the power moments.

Proof. Clearly $g_1(x, y)$ is a solution to the power moments for $n = 2$ as it is the weight enumerator of C_1. Since $g_1(x, y)^j$ is the weight enumerator of the self-dual $(2j, j)$ code C_1^j, it is also a solution to the power moments for $n = 2j$. As $g_2(x, y)$ is the weight enumerator of a self-dual code, the Hamming $(8, 4)$ code C_2, a similar argument shows that $g_2(x, y)^j$ is a solution of the power moments for $n = 8j$. The power moments are a system of linear equations so that any combination of solutions whose coefficients add to 1 is likewise a solution. For example, if (a_1, b_1, c_1) and (a_2, b_2, c_2) are solutions to the first two equations in (6), then so is $(\alpha a_1 + \beta a_2, \alpha b_1 + \beta b_2, \alpha c_1 + \beta c_2)$ where $\alpha + \beta = 1$. We consider just the first two equations in (6) as all three equations have a unique solution. In other words, the solutions of the power moments for a fixed n constitute an affine subspace of complex n-dimensional space (see the Appendix). Q.E.D.

Gleason's theorem has three parts for three situations. As we are interested in combinations of the Gleason polynomials that are weight enumerators of self-dual codes, A_0 must equal 1 so the only combinations that can occur are those with coefficients adding to one. We suppose this condition holds for all combinations in the following.

Theorem 84 (Gleason) [7]. We consider the following three cases.

(i) The weight enumerator of any self-dual code over $GF(2)$ is a combination of

$$g_1(x, y) = x^2 + y^2 \quad \text{and}$$
$$g_2(x, y) = x^8 + 14x^4y^4 + y^8.$$

(ii) The weight enumerator of any doubly even code over $GF(2)$ is a combination of

$$g_2(x, y) \text{ and } g_3(x, y) = x^{24} + 759x^{16}y^8 + 2576x^{12}y^{12} + 759x^8y^{16} + y^{24}.$$

(iii) The weight enumerator of any self-dual code over $GF(3)$ is a combination of

$$g_4(x, y) = x^4 + 8xy^3 \quad \text{and}$$
$$g_5(x, y) = x^{12} + 264x^6y^6 + 440x^3y^9 + 24y^{12}.$$

Proof. We prove (i) from an elementary point of view. First some comments. Note that this theorem implies that self-dual codes in situation (i) exist only when n is even, in situation (ii) only when n is divisible by 8, and in situation (iii) only when n is divisible by 4. We can replace the $g_i(x, y)$ by other polynomials for ease of computation. In situation (i) a polynomial that is often used in place of $g_2(x, y)$ is $x^2y^2(x^2 - y^2)^2$. In situation (ii) $g_3(x, y)$ can be replaced by $x^4y^4(x^4 - y^4)^4$. And in situation (iii) $g_5(x, y)$ can be replaced by $y^3(x^3 - y^3)^3$.

We prove the first case now. By the lemma we know that all combinations of the Gleason polynomials are solutions to the power moments. To complete the proof of case (i) we show that the set of combinations of the Gleason polynomials equals the set of solutions to the power moments with certain assumptions about the A_i. Let C be a self-dual binary code with weights A_i. Since we are only interested in solutions that can be weight distributions of such codes, we make certain assumptions that must be satisfied by the weight distribution of any self-dual binary code. We assume that $A_i = 0$ for i odd and that $A_i = A_{n-i}$ (since the all-one vector is in C) for all $i \leq n$. Note that these conditions are automatically satisfied by combinations of the Gleason polynomials. Clearly we are only interested in solutions to the power moments for which $B_i = A_i$.

Since all weights in C are even, there are at most $n/2 + 1$ nonzero A_i. If $A_0, A_2, \ldots, A_{2(j-1)}$ are known, so are $A_{n-2(j-1)}, \ldots, A_n$ by the assumption that $A_i = A_{n-i}$. Thus if these A_i's were known there would be $n/2 + 1 - 2j$ unknowns. By the uniqueness Theorem 83, there is a unique solution whenever $2j \geq n/2 + 1 - 2j$ or $j \geq (n + 2)/8$. Hence there are as many solutions to the power moments as there are specifications of $A_0, A_2, \ldots, A_{2(j-1)}$. Since we are interested in weight distributions, we can think of these as $A_0 = 1$ and $A_2, \ldots, A_{2(j-1)}$ as being non-negative integers. Let us now look at combinations of the Gleason polynomials. For $n = 8$, these are of the form $\alpha(x^2 + y^2)^4 + \beta(x^8 + 14x^4y^4 + y^8)$ so that a unique solution exists whenever α and β are specified. If $\alpha + \beta = 1$ so that $A_0 = 1$, there is one choice for α (or β). Note: $1 = [8/8]$. When $n = 10$ all combinations look like $\alpha(x^2 + y^2)^5 + \beta(x^2 + y^2)(x^8 + 14x^4y^4 + y^8)$ so that there is again one free choice, $[10/8]$.

This number changes when $n = 16$ as the combinations now are $\alpha g_1(x, y)^8 + \beta g_1(x, y)^4 g_2(x, y) + \gamma g_2(x, y)^2$ so if we let $\alpha + \beta + \gamma = 1$ (so that $A_0 = 1$), then we have two choices ($2 = [16/8]$) of α, β, and γ. In both cases, if we let $A_0 = 1$, there are $[n/8]$ choices that determine all combinations of either the Gleason polynomials or solutions to the power moments. As all combinations of the Gleason polynomials are solutions to the power moments, the two sets are equal and case (i) holds.   Q.E.D.

Note that $g_3(x, y)$ is the weight enumerator of the binary $(24, 12, 8)$ Golay code, $g_5(x, y)$ is the weight enumerator of the ternary $(12, 6, 6)$ Golay code, and $x^4 + 8xy^3$ is the weight enumerator of the $(4, 2, 3)$ ternary self-dual code called C_2 in Section 1.2. This proof is instructive as it also figures in the proof of the following corollary.

Corollary. The largest minimum weight d a self-dual $(n, n/2)$ code can have is as follows.

   (i) A self-dual $(n, n/2)$ code over $GF(2)$: $d = 2[n/8] + 2$.
   (ii) A doubly even $(n, n/2)$ code over $GF(2)$: $d = 4[n/24] + 4$.
   (iii) A self-dual $(n, n/2)$ code over $GF(3)$: $d = 3[n/12] + 3$.

Proof. The largest possible minimum weight d occurs at that point when the assumption that $A_i = 0$, $i \neq 0$, and $i < d$ leads to a uniquely determined weight distribution. Consider the situation for a $(24, 12)$ doubly even code. If we suppose $A_0 = 1$, $A_2 = A_4 = A_6 = 0$, and $A_i = A_{24-i}$, then a unique solution to the power moments exists. This solution has a nonzero A_8. Thus if we added to our assumptions the assumption that $A_8 = 0$, there would be no solution to the power moments. By the proof of the theorem in case (i), there is a unique solution to the power moments when $j \geq (n + 2)/8$, that is when $A_0 = 1$, and $A_2 = A_4 = \cdots = A_{2(j-1)} = 0$. Hence the largest that d can be is the smallest $2j$ with $2j \geq (n + 2)/4$. The smallest even integer with this property, for even n, is $2[n/8] + 2$ (Problem 23). The other cases are shown similarly.

Of course it is still possible that when we calculate the unique weight distribution of one of these codes with the highest possible minimum weight, that the minimum weight would be larger still. For example, in the doubly-even case it could be that the calculation gives $A_{4[n/24]+4} = 0$ so that the minimum weight would be $4[n/24] + 8$ or higher.

That this is not so was shown by Mallows and Sloane who actually computed this unique weight distribution [42]. The other two situations are also considered.   Q.E.D.

We call a self-dual code that has the largest possible minimum weight an *extremal code*. The value of the minimum weight d for an extremal code is given by the corollary. We see that the doubly even Golay $(24, 12, 8)$ code and the ternary Golay $(12, 6, 6)$ code are extremal codes. The Hamming $(8, 4, 4)$ code is extremal as is the doubly even Q.R. $(48, 24, 12)$ code. It is indeed nice to know that a given code is extremal. The Q.R. $(72, 36, 12)$ code is not extremal. Indeed, 72 is the smallest number that is divisible by 24 where it is not known whether an extremal, doubly even $(72, 36, 16)$ code exists. It is also not known whether an extremal doubly even $(96, 48, 20)$ code exists.

The combination of the Gleason polynomials that has the largest minimum weight (given by the above corollary) is called an *extremal weight enumerator*. In the ternary case, John Pierce computed the extremal weight enumerator for $n = 72$ and discovered that one of the coefficients was negative. This naturally shows that an extremal ternary $(72, 36, 21)$ code cannot exist. Subsequently, Mallows, Odlyzko, and Sloane [17] have shown that there cannot exist extremal codes for n very large as extremal weight enumerators with negative coefficients appear.

We have given an elementary proof of Gleason's theorem, but there is an elegant proof of it using invariant theory and we just give the flavor of it here. If C is a binary self-dual code (case (i)),

$$W_C(x, y) = \frac{1}{|C^{\perp}|} W_{C^{\perp}}(x + y, x - y) \quad \text{since } C = C^{\perp}$$

$$= \frac{1}{2^{n/2}} W_{C^{\perp}}(x + y, x - y) = W_C\left(\frac{(x + y)}{\sqrt{2}}, \frac{(x - y)}{\sqrt{2}}\right).$$

This shows that such a weight enumerator is sent onto itself by a transformation $1/\sqrt{2}\begin{pmatrix} 1 & 1 \\ 1 & -1 \end{pmatrix}$ acting on the pair $\begin{pmatrix} x \\ y \end{pmatrix}$. This enumerator is also invariant under the transformation $\begin{pmatrix} 1 & 0 \\ 0 & -1 \end{pmatrix}$, which sends y onto $-y$ since only even weights occur. These two matrices generate a group of order 16. The proof then proceeds to show that the subring of homogeneous polynomials, which is invariant under this group, is finitely generated by $g_1(x, y)$ and $g_2(x, y)$. This account is not a proof; it is given to show the use of the form (4) of the MacWilliams identities. For these proofs see Berlekamp, MacWilliams, and Sloane [3] and Gleason [7]. Also in the former are proofs for all parts of Theorem 84. Our proof for situation (i) is similar to one of these.

PROBLEMS

1. Prove that $\binom{n}{r} = \binom{n}{n-r}$.

2. Prove the identity $\binom{n}{r} = \binom{n-1}{r} + \binom{n-1}{r-1}$.

3. Using the identity in Problem 1, compute $\binom{n}{r}$ for $0 \le r \le n \le 6$. Arrange your answer in a triangle (called Pascal's triangle) as follows.

$$\binom{0}{0}$$

$$\binom{1}{0} \qquad \binom{1}{1}$$

$$\binom{2}{0} \qquad \binom{2}{1} \qquad \binom{2}{2}$$

$$\vdots$$

$$\binom{6}{0} \qquad\qquad\qquad\qquad\qquad \binom{6}{6}$$

4. Compute the next line in the table of Stirling numbers of the second kind.

5. Why is $PSL_2(p)$ transitive on the $p + 1$ points (or coordinate indices) $\infty, 0, \ldots, p - 1$?

6. If C is a binary code whose extended code has a transitive group, show that C has odd minimum weight d and vectors of even weight $d + 1$.

7. The group of the $(24, 12)$ binary Golay code C is M_{24}, which is known to be transitive (it is actually one of a few fivefold transitive groups). The weight distribution of C is $A_0 = A_{24} = 1$, $A_8 = A_{16} = 759$, $A_{12} = 2576$. What is the weight distribution of the $(23, 12)$ Golay code?

8. If C is the binary code with generator matrix

$$G = \begin{pmatrix} 1 & 1 & 0 & 0 \\ 0 & 0 & 1 & 1 \end{pmatrix},$$

verify the identities in (1) for $v = 0, 1, 2, 3$, and 4.

9. Show that $\binom{n}{2} - (n - 1)r + \binom{r}{2} = \binom{n - r}{2}$.

10. Let C be the $(15, 11)$ binary Hamming code.

   (a) Show that all nonzero vectors in $C^{\perp}$ have weight 8.

   (b) Determine A_0, A_1, and A_2 for C.

   (c) Choose an appropriate form of the MacWilliams identities so you can solve for the A_i one at a time and then determine the weight distribution of C.

11. Prove the identity in (1) for binary codes for $v = 3$ under the assumption that any set of three or fewer dependent columns in a generator matrix of C are zero columns.

12. Derive the first three identities in (1) from the identities in (2).

13. Verify that the coefficient of $x^{n-2}y^2$ on both sides of (5) are equal.

14. By solving the power moments, verify the weight distribution of the Golay $(24, 12)$ code given in Problem 7.

15. Why is the weight distribution of the binary Q.R. $(48, 24)$ code unique?

16. Why does a doubly even $(72, 36, 16)$ code, if one exists, have a unique weight distribution?

17. If $W_{C_1}(x, y)$ is the weight enumerator of C_1 and $W_{C_2}(x, y)$ is the weight enumerator of C_2, show that the weight enumerator of $C_1 \oplus C_2$ is $W_{C_1}(x, y)W_{C_2}(x, y)$.

18. Using the formula for $W_C(x, y)$ show that $W_{(C^{\perp})^{\perp}}(x, y) = W_C(x, y)$.

19. Show that the solutions 2, 3, and 4 in the table of possible weight distributions of $(8, 4)$ self-dual codes cannot be weight distributions of self-dual $(8, 4)$ codes.

20. Using the Gleason polynomials, find all possible weight distributions of self-dual binary $(10, 5)$ codes.

21. Using the Gleason polynomials, find the weight distribution of a $(24, 12, 4)$ doubly even code with $A_4 = 6$.

22. Show that $x^2y^2(x^2 - y^2)^2$ can be used in place of $g_2(x, y)$ in situation (i) of Theorem 84.

23. If n is a positive even integer $\neq 2$, show that the smallest even integer equal to or exceeding $(n + 2)/4$ is $2[n/8] + 2$.

9

Designs

9.1 DESIGNS

Designs, or more precisely t-designs, are interesting combinatorial structures that originated in the design of agricultural experiments. The commonly used parameter v designates varieties, as of wheat. One of the main problems in t-designs is the question of their existence. Projective planes are 2-designs. Many 3-designs are known. It is interesting to find 4-designs. Until the mid-sixties only a few 5-designs were known, which arose from the few known 5-transitive groups, the Mathieu groups.

We can view t-designs as generalizations of projective planes. A *projective plane* consists of two types of objects, points and collections of points called lines, satisfying the following conditions.

   (i) Every two points lie on exactly one line.
   (ii) Every two lines intersect in exactly one point.
   (iii) Every line contains at least three points.
   (iv) There are at least three points not on one line.

If we try to construct the smallest projective plane satisfying these axioms, we obtain the diagram in Figure 9.1. This has seven points and seven lines (the six lines drawn and the central circle).

A t-(v, k, λ) *design* consists of a set of v points, a set of blocks (instead of lines) where each block has k points so that every t points are contained in exactly λ blocks. A 2-$(v, k, 1)$, $v > k \geq 3$, design is a projective plane. Other designs are of special interest. When $\lambda = 1$, the t-design is called a *Steiner system* and is denoted by $S(t, k, v)$. It can be shown that every projective plane is an $S(2, n + 1, n^2 + n + 1)$. This is called a projective plane of order n. Our example is an $S(2, 3, 7)$, a projective plane of order 2.

In order for a t-(v, k, λ) design to exist, various numerical conditions have to hold; for instance, the λ_i's defined in the next theorem must be integers.

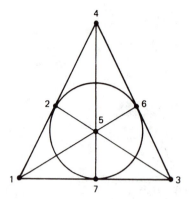

Figure 9.1 The smallest projective plane.

Theorem 85. A t-(v, k, λ) design $\mathscr{D}$ is also an i-(v, k, λ_i) design for $1 \le i < t$. Furthermore,

$$\lambda_i = \frac{\lambda \binom{v - i}{t - i}}{\binom{k - i}{t - i}} = \frac{\lambda(v - i) \cdots (v - t + 1)}{(k - i) \cdots (k - t + 1)}.$$

Proof. We need only show that the theorem is true for $i = t - 1$. The theorem for $i = t - 2$ would then follow from the fact that $\mathscr{D}$ is a $(t - 1)$-design and so on for the other values of i. Given any $t - 1$ points, there are $v - (t - 1)$ points from which we can choose to get t points. Each such set of t points is contained in λ blocks. For any block we could have chosen the additional point in the block in $k - (t - 1)$ ways. Thus

$$\lambda_{t-1} = \frac{\lambda(v - t + 1)}{(k - t + 1)}. \qquad \text{Q.E.D.}$$

Even though the λ_i of Theorem 85 must all be integers for a t-(v, k, λ) design to exist; if they are integers, this is no guarantee that the design exists.

Let b be the number of blocks in a t-(v, k, λ) design.

Corollary. $b = \lambda \binom{v}{t} \Big/ \binom{k}{t}$.

Proof. The number of t-subsets of v points is $\binom{v}{t}$. Each of these is in λ blocks and there are $\binom{k}{t}$ t-subsets in a given block. Q.E.D.

Let r be the number of blocks containing a particular point.

Corollary. $bk = vr$.

Proof. This follows from the last corollary since $r = \lambda_1$.

Suppose we have a t-(v, k, λ) design $\mathcal{D}$; then $r = \lambda_1$ is the number of blocks containing a fixed point P_1. Hence the number of blocks not containing P_1 is $b - r$. Let us now pick two points P_1 and P_2. The number of blocks that contain both of these points is λ_2. The number of blocks that contain P_2 but not P_1 (or P_1 but not P_2) is then $\lambda_1 - \lambda_2$ and the number of blocks that do not contain either P_1 or P_2 is $(b - r) - (\lambda_1 - \lambda_2) = b - 2r + \lambda_2$. We can continue like this. In order to clarify things, we make the next definition.

Let $P_1, \ldots, P_i$ be fixed points. For $t \geq i \geq j \geq 0$ we define *block intersection numbers* λ_{ij} to be the numbers of blocks that contain $P_1, \ldots, P_j$ but not $P_{j+1}, \ldots, P_i$. Theorem 86 shows that these numbers are well defined.

The λ_{ij} are called block intersection numbers since, if $P_1, \ldots, P_i$ are in a fixed block, they give information about the intersections of blocks; see Theorem 87. If $j = 0$, λ_{i0} is the number of blocks that do not contain $P_1, \ldots, P_i$. We let $\lambda_{00} = b$. In these terms $\lambda_i = \lambda_{ii}$. By our previous discussion, $\lambda_{10} = b - r = \lambda_{00} - \lambda_{11}$, $\lambda_{21} = \lambda_{11} - \lambda_{22}$, and $\lambda_{20} = \lambda_{10} - \lambda_{21}$. We write this information as a triangle in bold lines for the seven point projective plane in Figure 9.2. For this case $\lambda_{00} = b = \binom{7}{2} \big/ \binom{3}{2} = 7$, the number of lines, $\lambda_{11} = r = bk/v = 7 \cdot 3/7 = 3$, the number of lines containing one fixed point, and $\lambda_{10} = \lambda_{00} - \lambda_{11} = 4$ is the number of lines that do not contain one fixed point. Continuing, $\lambda_{22} = 1$ is the number of lines

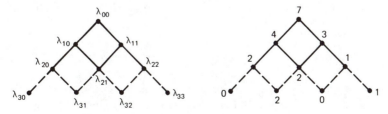

Figure 9.2 The Pascal triangle for the seven point projective plane.

containing two fixed points, $\lambda_{21} = 3 - 1 = 2$ is the number of lines containing P_2 but not P_1, and $\lambda_{20} = 4 - 2$ is the number of lines containing neither P_1 nor P_2. These numbers can be checked with Figure 9.1. We make these observations into the following useful theorem.

Theorem 86. Let $\mathscr{D}$ be a t-(v, k, λ) design and let $t \geq i \geq j \geq 0$. Then the block intersection numbers are independent of the i points chosen. Furthermore, $\lambda_{i(j-1)} = \lambda_{(i-1)(j-1)} - \lambda_{ij}$.

Proof. By definition, $\lambda_{ii} = \lambda_i$ and these are independent of the points chosen since $i \leq t$ and $\mathscr{D}$ is an i-design by Theorem 85. If $i = 0$, $\lambda_{00} = b$. We say that $\lambda_{i'j'}$ precedes λ_{ij} if $i > i'$ or if $i = i'$ and $j < j'$. Suppose the theorem holds for all $\lambda_{i'j'}$ that precede $\lambda_{i(j-1)}$. Then we show that it holds for $\lambda_{i(j-1)}$. Note that $\lambda_{(i-1)(j-1)}$ precedes λ_{ij}, which precedes $\lambda_{i(j-1)}$. Choose i points $P_1, \ldots, P_i$. Then $\lambda_{i(j-1)}$ is the number of blocks that contain $P_1, \ldots, P_{j-1}$ and do not contain $P_j, \ldots, P_i$. Both $\lambda_{(i-1)(j-1)}$ and λ_{ij} are independent of the points chosen by assumption. So $\lambda_{(i-1)(j-1)}$ is the number of blocks that contain $P_1, \ldots, P_{j-1}$ but do not contain $P_j, \ldots, P_{i-1}$ and λ_{ij} is the number of blocks that contain $P_1, \ldots, P_{j-1}, P_i$ but not $P_j, \ldots, P_{i-1}$. Clearly $\lambda_{(i-1)(j-1)} = \lambda_{i(j-1)} + \lambda_{ij}$ as a block that contains $P_1, \ldots, P_{j-1}$ but not $P_j, \ldots, P_{i-1}$ can either contain P_i or not.   Q.E.D.

The λ_{ij} can be arranged in a triangle called Pascal's triangle and the numbers in it can be computed in the following order. The top, λ_{00}, is b. Then $\lambda_{11} = \lambda_1$ is computed. From this and λ_{00}, λ_{10} can be computed. Next λ_{22} is known and working to the left each λ_{2j} can be computed. After the ith row is computed, $\lambda_{(i+1)(i+1)}$ is calculated and the entire $\lambda_{(i+1)j}$ can be determined by working to the left of $\lambda_{(i+1)(i+1)}$.

Theorem 87. Let $\mathscr{D}$ be a Steiner $S(t, k, v)$ system. For $k \geq i \geq j \geq 0$, let $P_1, \ldots, P_i$ be a set of i fixed points contained in a block of $\mathscr{D}$. Let λ_{ij}, defined in terms of i points contained in a block of $\mathscr{D}$, have the same meaning as the block intersection numbers, λ_{ij}. Then $\lambda_{ii} = \lambda_i$ for $i \leq t$ and $\lambda_{ii} = 1$ for $k \geq i > t$ and $\lambda_{i(j-1)} = \lambda_{(i-1)(j-1)} - \lambda_{ij}$.

Proof. Theorem 87 follows from Theorem 86 when $t \geq i \geq j \geq 0$. Theorem 87 states that the Pascal triangle can be extended to k levels when $\mathscr{D}$ is a Steiner system. That $\lambda_{ii} = 1$ for $k \geq i \geq t$ follows from the fact that t points determine a unique block. The rest follows since the ith row is calculated from λ_{ii} and the previous row.

For the seven point projective plane this means that we can carry the triangle down one more level since here $k = 3$ and $t = 2$. This is indicated with dotted lines in Figure 9.2.

Theorem 88. If $\mathscr{D}$ is a t-(v, k, λ) design, let the blocks in $\mathscr{D}_1$ be all blocks in $\mathscr{D}$ that contain one fixed point and omit that point. Then $\mathscr{D}_1$ is a $(t - 1)$-$(v - 1, k - 1, \lambda)$ design called a *derived design*.

Proof. This follows from the Pascal triangle for $\mathscr{D}$. In fact the Pascal triangle for $\mathscr{D}_1$ has its apex at λ_{11}, its first row is λ_{21}, λ_{22}, the rest of its triangle being that part of the Pascal triangle for $\mathscr{D}$ that remains after omitting $\mathscr{D}$'s left side.

We can continue in this fashion. If we let the blocks of $\mathscr{D}_2$ consist of all the blocks of $\mathscr{D}$ that contain two fixed points, then $\mathscr{D}_2$ is a derived design of $\mathscr{D}_1$ and its Pascal triangle has its apex at λ_{22}.

The block intersection numbers give useful information for codes as we see after we see the connection between codes and designs, the topic of the next section.

9.2 DESIGNS AND CODES

It is quite interesting that there is a connection between designs and codes. This leads to the construction of new designs using knowledge about codes and the existence of designs in codes can be used for decoding purposes. It also gives other information about codes. Well, what is the connection? Even though there is more than one way to relate codes to designs, the following way has yielded the most results. We start with a binary code since this is most easily visualized, although a similar connection holds between nonbinary codes and designs.

A binary vector x of weight w is said to determine the block of w points corresponding to the positions where x has nonzero coordinates. We say that vectors of a fixed weight w in a binary code of length n *hold a t-design* if the blocks determined by these vectors are the blocks of a t-design on n points. This means that there must exist a t and a λ so that every set of t coordinate positions occur as nonzero positions for exactly λ vectors of weight w. Clearly it is not necessarily so that vectors of weight w in a code hold a design. It is interesting when they do, and it is important to be able to recognize that a design is there when it is.

If we try to construct a small example, we might look at the seven vectors of weight 3 in our favorite example for everything, the Hamming

(7, 4) code. Of course, this works. Notice that the smallest projective plane, a 2-(7, 3, 1) design, has seven points, seven lines, three points on a line, and three lines through a point. Consider the seven vectors of weight 3 in the representation of the (7, 4, 3) code as a cyclic code.

	1	2	3	4	5	6	7
1	1				1	1	
2		1				1	1
3	1		1				1
4	1	1		1			
5		1	1		1		
6			1	1		1	
7				1	1		1

We know that spheres of radius 1 about the codewords are disjoint and cover the space. Hence every vector of weight 2 is in a sphere about a unique codeword. But the only codeword at distance 1 from a weight 2 vector is a weight 3 codeword. Hence the vectors of weight 3 hold a 2-(7, 3, 1) design. The values of λ_{ij} in Figure 9.2 can be verified directly. Clearly these vectors are a representation of the projective plane of order 2. In Figure 9.1 we have numbered the points of the plane to make this fact obvious.

This is part of a general theorem that tells us that certain codes must contain designs. It should be no surprise that these codes are the perfect codes.

Theorem 89. If C is a perfect binary (n, k, d) code, then the vectors of weight d hold a Steiner system of type $S(t + 1, d, n)$ for $t = (d - 1)/2$.

Proof. Since the spheres of radius t about codewords are disjoint and cover the space, every vector of weight $t + 1$ is in a unique sphere about a codeword. This codeword must have weight d. Since d is odd, $t = (d - 1)/2$ (prove this).

Corollary. The vectors of weight 3 in a Hamming $(2^r - 1, 2^r - 1 - r, 3)$ code, H_r, hold a Steiner system of type $S(2, 3, 2^r - 1)$.

Corollary. The vectors of weight 7 in the Golay $(23, 12, 7)$ code hold a Steiner system of type $S(4, 7, 23)$.

Corollary. If C is a perfect binary (n, k, d) code, then

$$A_d = \binom{n}{t + 1} \bigg/ \binom{d}{t + 1}.$$

Proof. This is so since $A_d = b$, which is given by the corollary to Theorem 85.

From this we can compute the number of vectors of weight 7 in the Golay $(23, 12, 7)$ code and this is $\binom{23}{4} / \binom{7}{4} = 253$. Determining the number of vectors of weight 3 in H_r is left to Problem 4.

Recall that Theorem 9 gave conditions on n, k, and t in order for a perfect t-error-correcting binary code to exist. Combining the results of Theorems 85 and 89 gives the following additional conditions that n and t must satisfy.

Theorem 90. In order for a perfect t-error-correcting binary code of length n to exist the numbers

$$\frac{\binom{n - i}{t + 1 - i}}{\binom{2t + 1 - i}{t + 1 - i}}$$

for $1 \leq i \leq t$ must all be integers.

Proof. This is a straightforward application of the two theorems.

Recall that the possibility of a length 90 perfect double-error-correcting code was raised in Section 2.2 as $n = 90$ and $t = 2$ satisfy Theorem 9. If we take $n = 90$, $t = 2$, and $i = 2$ in Theorem 90,

$$\frac{\binom{n - i}{t + 1 - i}}{\binom{2t + 1 - i}{t + 1 - i}} = \frac{88}{3},$$

which is not an integer. Hence this possibility is ruled out.

We already see one way to find designs in codes, namely the minimum weight vectors in perfect codes hold designs, but there are not many multiple-error-correcting perfect codes. It was unexpected that a simple computation, based on weight distributions, would reveal designs in codes. This is given in the next section. For many interesting connections between designs and codes see [6, 37].

9.3   THE ASSMUS-MATTSON THEOREM AND A DESIGN-DECODING SCHEME

Even though the vectors of a fixed weight in a code hold a design, it may be quite difficult to know that this is so if the code is not perfect. If we suspect, somehow, that vectors of a certain weight w in a code hold a t-design, we could store these vectors in a computer and count how many times each t-set is contained in each vector. This is a lot of work and may not even be possible to perform for some large codes that do contain designs. It is nice, therefore, to be able to determine by a simple calculation that there are designs in codes. This computation is based on knowledge, which we have for a number of self-dual codes, of the weight distribution of the code. If the conditions of the Assmus-Mattson theorem [1] are fulfilled, then we know that vectors of specified weights in the code hold designs. If they are not fulfilled, vectors might still hold designs. Of course, the numerical conditions of Theorem 85 would have to be satisfied, but we would not then know that the designs existed. It is interesting that many 5-designs have been found in codes and Theorem 93 shows that they must exist in certain extremal self-dual codes.

Theorem 91.   If $\mathscr{D}$ is a t-(v, k, λ) design, let the blocks of $\mathscr{D}'$ be the complements of the blocks in $\mathscr{D}$. Then $\mathscr{D}'$ is a t-$(v, v - k, \lambda')$ design where

$$\lambda' = \frac{\lambda \binom{v - k}{t}}{\binom{k}{t}}.$$

Proof.   We can see from the block intersection numbers that $\mathscr{D}'$ is a t-design as $\lambda' = \lambda_{t0}$, which is independent of the t-set chosen. Since b is the same for both designs, by the corollary to Theorem 85, $b = \lambda\binom{v}{t}\Big/\binom{k}{t} = \lambda'\binom{v}{t}\Big/\binom{v - k}{t}$ and, we get the equation for λ' directly.

If $\mathscr{D}$ is the set of seven lines in the order 2 projective plane, then the blocks of $\mathscr{D}'$ are those sets of four points whose complements are lines; for example $\{3, 5, 6, 7\}$ is a block of $\mathscr{D}'$.

The following is a modified version of the Assmus-Mattson theorem in the binary case.

Theorem 92.   Let C be an (n, k, d) binary code and let $0 < t < d$. Let B_i be the number of vectors of weight i in $C^\perp$ and let

$$s = |\{ i | B_i \neq 0 \text{ and } 0 < i \leq n - t \}|.$$

If $s \leq d - t$, then the vectors of weight d in C hold a t-design and the vectors of any weight i in $C^\perp$ such that $i \leq n - t$ and $B_i \neq 0$ hold a t-design.

Proof.   Let T be a set of t coordinate positions and I the remaining $n - t$ coordinate positions. Then $C(I)$ is the code obtained from C by removing these t coordinate positions. Since any $n - d + 1$ columns of C contain k independent columns (Theorem 15) and $t < d$, $C(I)$ is an $(n - t, k)$ code. Clearly the minimum weight of $C(I)$ is greater than or equal to $d - t$. Consider now the subcode D of $C^\perp$, which is 0 on all the positions in T. By Lemma 1 to Theorem 81, $C(I)$ and $D(I)$ are dual codes.

Let B_i' be the number of vectors of weight i in $D(I)$. Then $B_i' \leq B_i$, and if s' is the number of i so that $B_i' \neq 0$, then $s' \leq s$. Since we have assumed that $s \leq d - t$, we have $s' \leq d - t$; hence s' is less than or equal to the minimum weight of $C(I)$. This is a perfect situation to apply the uniqueness Theorem 83 to the codes $C(I)$ and $D(I)$. Doing so, we obtain a unique solution to the power moments for their weight distributions. This solution just depends on the dimensions, k and $n - k - t$, of the two codes. Thus it is the same for any set of t-coordinates chosen.

Consider the vectors of weight d in C, all of which have 1's on a fixed T of size t. Each of these gives rise to a vector of weight $d - t$ in $C(I)$. Conversely every vector of weight $d - t$ in $C(I)$ must have come from a vector of weight d in C that is 1 on these t coordinates since d is the minimum weight. Since the number of vectors of weight $d - t$ in $C(I)$ is independent of the set T chosen, the vectors of weight d in C hold a t-design.

Let $c_1, \ldots, c_s$ be the complements of vectors of weight w in $C^\perp$. We show that these vectors hold a t-design. By Theorem 91, it then follows that the vectors of weight w in $C^\perp$ hold a t-design. Consider all c_i's that are 1 throughout T. Each such c_i is the complement of a vector of weight w in D. Hence the number of these is a constant independent of the particular T chosen since the weight distribution of D is the same as the weight distribution of $D(I)$, and this distribution is independent of T.   Q.E.D.

We give some examples illustrating how easy it is to use this theorem. Let C be the $(24, 12, 8)$ Golay code and let $t = 5$. Here $C = C^\perp$ and $B_i \neq 0$ for $i \leq 25 - 5 = 19$ when $i = 8$, 12, and 16. Hence $s = 3$. Since

Table 9.1 Block Intersection Numbers for the Octads in the (24, 12) Golay Code

								759									Apex
							506		253								1
						330		176		77							2
					210		120		56		21						3
				130		80		40		16		5					4
			78		52		28		12		4		1				5
		46		32		20		8		4		0		1			6
	30		16		16		4		4		0		0		1		7
30		0		16		0		4		0		0		0		1	8

$3 \leq 8 - 5 = 3$, the vectors of any nonzero weight in $C(= C^{\perp})$ hold 5-designs.

We know that the vectors of weight 7 in the $(23, 12)$ Golay code C' hold a 4-design since the code is perfect, but what about the vectors of other weights in C'? If we let B_i be the number of vectors of weight i in $(C')^{\perp}$, then $B_i = 0$ unless $i = 8$, 12, or 16. If we take $t = 4$, $n - t = 23 - 4 = 19$ and $s = 3$. Since 3 equals $d - t = 7 - 4$, vectors of all weights in $(C')^{\perp}$ hold 4-designs. As $(C')^{\perp} \subset C'$, the vectors of weights 8, 12, and 16 in C' hold 4-designs. The design held by vectors of weight 16 is complementary to the design held by vectors of weight 7. The vectors of weights 11 and 15 also hold 4-designs (see Problem 10).

We give the Pascal triangle, Table 9.1, for the 5-design $\mathscr{D}$ held by the vectors of weight 8, called *octads*, in the $(24, 12)$ Golay code C. Note that the last line of Table 9.1 shows that two octads intersect in either four, two, or no places. There is also a Pascal triangle for the design held by the vectors of weight 12 in C. The design held by the vectors of weight 16 is complementary to $\mathscr{D}$ so that its Pascal triangle can be obtained from Table 9.1 by reflecting the triangle in a verticle line through its apex. Notice that the 4-design held by the vectors of weight 7 in the $(23, 12)$ Golay code C' is a derived design of $\mathscr{D}$ and its Pascal triangle is that subtriangle with apex at 253. The triangle with apex at 506 is also a design (see Problem 12).

We can use Table 9.1 to construct a decoding scheme [8] for C. If y is a received vector, using this scheme, we test each coordinate until we can decode y. Since C is self-dual, we use the vectors in C as parity checks, in particular the 253 octads, which contain the point we are testing. Table 9.2 gives the results of these parity checks under the circumstances described. Suppose we are testing the first position. If there are no errors, then the 253 dot products are zero. If there is one error in the first position, then all the

Table 9.2   The Boxes Give the Number of Ones Obtained by Taking the Dot Products of the 253 Octads Containing Position i Under the Given Circumstances

	Number of Errors				
Position i Tested Is	0	1	2	3	4
Correct	0	77	112	125	128
Incorrect	x	253	176	141	128

253 octads would have dot product one with y. If the single error is in position i, $i \neq 1$, then exactly 77 of these octads contain position i and so have dot product one with y. If there are two errors, one in position i and one in position j, i, $j \neq 1$, then by Table 9.1, 56 of the octads contain i and not j and 56 contain j and not i so that $2 \cdot 56 = 112$ of the parity checks will be one. The other entries can be explained similarly (see Problem 16). Using this scheme, we can decode three or fewer errors and detect four or more. When we finish testing the first position, we know how many errors have occurred, and we then test the positions in sequence until the errors are corrected. Since C is cyclic, the octads for each new position are the cyclic shift of the previous set of octads.

Many of the designs found in binary codes were found in doubly even codes since there are fewer $B_i \neq 0$ as $B_i = 0$ if $i \not\equiv 0 \pmod{4}$ so that the Assmus-Mattson theorem can be used to detect the presence of these designs. It is interesting that the next theorem says that 5-designs always exist in certain extremal doubly even codes. Notice that the proof shows that higher designs could not be detected by the Assmus-Mattson theorem even if they were present in these codes.

Theorem 93.   If C is an extremal doubly even code whose length is divisible by 24, then the vectors of any weight in C hold t-designs for $t \leq 5$.

Proof.   Let C be a $(24r = n, 12r)$ extremal, doubly even code. Then C has minimum weight $d = 4r + 4$ (Theorem 84, corollary). Let B_i be the number of vectors of weight i in $C^\perp = C$. Then the number of $B_i \neq 0$ for $i \neq 0$, $i < n - 5$, is $n/4 - d/2 + 1 = 6r - (2r + 2) + 1 = 4r - 1 = s$. Now $s \leq d - 5 = 4r - 1$.   Q.E.D.

A similar theorem can be demonstrated for extremal ternary self-dual codes whose lengths are divisible by 12. In this situation also it is not possible to detect t-designs in these codes for $t > 5$ by using the Assmus-Mattson theorem even if such designs were held by vectors in these codes.

9.4 SYMMETRY CODES

The symmetry codes [22] are an infinite family of ternary codes, and 5-designs have been found in the first five symmetry codes by the Assmus-Mattson theorem. We first define the symmetry codes and then state the Assmus-Mattson theorem for the general case.

The construction of these codes is based on quadratic residues in $GF(p)$ and the $p \times p$ *Jacobsthal matrix* $Q = (q_{ij})$. We label the rows and columns of Q with the integers $0, 1, \ldots, p - 1$ and describe its entries in terms of the *Legendre symbol* χ, which is defined on the elements of $GF(p)$ as follows; $\chi(0) = 0$, $\chi(i) = 1$ if i is a quadratic residue and $\chi(i) = -1$ if i is not a quadratic residue. Then we let q_{ij} equal $\chi(j - i)$. As an example, we give Q for $p = 5$.

$$
\begin{array}{c|ccccc}
 & 0 & 1 & 2 & 3 & 4 \\
\hline
0 & 0 & 1 & -1 & -1 & 1 \\
1 & 1 & 0 & 1 & -1 & -1 \\
2 & -1 & 1 & 0 & 1 & -1 \\
3 & -1 & -1 & 1 & 0 & 1 \\
4 & 1 & -1 & -1 & 1 & 0
\end{array}.
$$

Note that each row except the first is a cyclic shift of the previous row. We have all the cyclic shifts of the first row. This is true for all the Q matrices.

In order to prove things we need a lemma.

Lemma. In $GF(p)$, if $c \neq 0$, $\sum_{b=0}^{p-1} \chi(b)\chi(b + c) = -1$.

Proof. Since a product of two residues or two nonresidues is a quadratic residue and the product of a quadratic residue by a nonresidue is a nonresidue (Problem 6.15), $\chi(xy) = \chi(x)\chi(y)$ for all x and y in $GF(p)$.

$$
\sum_{b=0}^{p-1} \chi(b)\chi(b + c) = \sum_{b=1}^{p-1} \chi(b)\chi(b + c) \tag{1}
$$

since $\chi(0) = 0$. For $b \neq 0$, let $z = (b + c)/b$ in $GF(p)$. If c is fixed this has a unique solution for z given b. As b varies from 1 through $p - 1$, z

assumes all values in $GF(p)$ except the number 1. Hence

$$\sum_{b=1}^{p-1} \chi(b)\chi(b+c) = \sum_{b=1}^{p-1} \chi(b)\chi(bz) = \sum_{b=1}^{p-1} \chi(b)^2\chi(z) = \sum_{z=0,\, z\neq 1}^{p-1} \chi(z)$$

$$= \sum_{z=0}^{p-1} \chi(z) - \chi(1) = -\chi(1) = -1. \qquad \text{Q.E.D.}$$

Let J be the $p \times p$ matrix all of whose entries are 1.

Theorem 94. $QQ' = pI - J$ and $QJ = JQ = 0$.

Proof. Let $P = QQ' = (p_{ij})$. By definition,

$$p_{ij} = \sum_{k=0}^{p-1} q_{ik}q_{jk} = \sum_{k=0}^{p-1} \chi(k-i)\chi(k-j) = -1, \quad \text{if } i \neq j$$

by the lemma with $b = k - i$ and $c = i - j$. Each p_{ii} is the weight of row i of Q, which is $p - 1$ so that $P = pI - J$. Since each row and column of Q has $(p-1)/2$ 1's and $(p-1)/2$ -1's, $QJ = JQ = 0$.

Let S_p be the $(p+1) \times (p+1)$ matrix

$$\begin{pmatrix} 0 & 1 & \cdots & 1 \\ \chi(-1) & & & \\ \vdots & & Q & \\ \chi(-1) & & & \end{pmatrix}.$$

The *symmetry code* $C(p)$ is defined to be the $(2p+2, p+1)$ ternary code with generator matrix (I, S_p) for p a prime congruent to 2 (mod 3). This defines an infinite family of codes. They can be defined more generally for $p^n \equiv 2$ (mod 3) but we consider only $n = 1$. The first few such p's are 5, 11, 17, 23, and 29. The corresponding codes are $(12,6)$, $(24,12)$, $(36,18)$, $(48,24)$, and $(60,30)$ codes. The $(12,6)$ code is the ternary Golay code whose basis (I, A) is given in Section 2.4. Notice that A is actually S_5.

Theorem 95. Each symmetry code $C(p)$ is self-dual; hence the weight of each vector in $C(p)$ is divisible by 3.

Proof. Since $QQ^t = (pI - J)$, $S_p S_p^t = pI = -I$ (mod 3) (Problem 18) where the last equation involves $(p + 1) \times (p + 1)$ matrices. This equation implies that every two rows of (I, S_p) are orthogonal to each other. Every row r of (I, S_p) is orthogonal to itself as $r \cdot r$ is the weight of r (mod 3). But $wt(r) = p + 1 \equiv 0$ (mod 3) by the assumption on p. The result then follows from Theorem 3.

Theorem 96. If $p \equiv 1$ (mod 4), $C(p)$ has $(-S_p, I)$ as a generator matrix and, if $p \equiv 3$ (mod 4), $C(p)$ has (S_p, I) as a generator matrix.

Proof. Since (I, S_p) is a generator matrix for $C(p)$, $(-S_p^t, I)$ is a generator matrix for $C(p)^\perp = C(p)$ by the last theorem. If $p \equiv 1$ (mod 4), $S_p = S_p^t$ (Problem 19) and, if $p \equiv 3$ (mod 4), $S_p = -S_p^t$ (problem 19).
$$\text{Q.E.D.}$$

This theorem can be used to prove easily that the minimum weight of $C(5)$ is 6 (Problem 2.27). The analysis used is similar to the proof, given in Section 2.4, that the (24, 12) Golay code has minimum weight 8. Theorem 95 was also used [22] to reduce the number of combinations of basis vectors needed to determine the minimum weight, on a computer, for $C(11)$, $C(17)$, $C(23)$, and $C(29)$. The minimum weights obtained were 9, 12, 15, and 18, respectively, so that the first five symmetry codes are extremal self-dual codes, which makes the family look quite promising. The minimum weights of the next symmetry codes are not known nor is there any information on the ratio $d(p)/(2p + 2)$ as p gets large where $d(p)$ is the minimum weight of $C(p)$.

This information about minimum weight allows us to find 5-designs in the symmetry codes as we shall soon see. First we describe how vectors in a nonbinary code hold a t-design. The set of w coordinates where a codeword is nonzero is called the *support* of the codeword. If C is a code over $GF(q)$, then the vectors of weight w in C are said to *hold a t-design* if the supports of these vectors are the blocks of a t-design. We state a modified version of the Assmus-Mattson theorem for codes over a general finite field $GF(q)$. The condition on w_0 is needed if $q \neq 2$ to insure that two vectors with the same support are scalar multiples of each other.

Theorem 97. Let C and $C^\perp$ be codes of length n over $GF(q)$ with minimum weights d and e, respectively. Let w_0 be the largest integer so that

$$w_0 - \left[\frac{(w_0 + (q - 2))}{q - 1} \right] < e.$$

Table 9.3   Block Intersection Numbers for the $S(5, 6, 12)$ Held by the Vectors of Weight 6 in the Ternary Golay $(12, 6, 6)$ Code

				132					Apex
			66		66				1
		30		36		30			2
	12		18		18		12		3
	4	8		10		8	4		4
1		3	5		5		3	1	5
1	0		3	2		3		0	1	6

Let s be the number of weights $B_i \neq 0$ in $C^\perp$ where $0 < i \le n - t$. Suppose $s \le d - t$. Then the vectors of weight d in C hold a t-design and the vectors of each weight w in $C^\perp$ where $B_w \neq 0$ and $e \le w \le \min\{n - t, w_0\}$ hold a t-design.

The proof is similar to that of Theorem 92.

Consider the Golay $(12, 6, 6)$ code, which is the first symmetry code $C(5)$. This is a self-dual code whose nonzero vectors have weights 6, 9, 12. If $t = 5$, then $n - t = 12 - 5 = 7$, and $s = 1$. This equals $d - t = 6 - 5$. Hence the vectors of weight 6 hold a 5-design. See Table 9.3 for the Pascal triangle of this design. The second symmetry code $C(11)$ is a $(24, 12, 9)$ self-dual code whose nonzero vectors have weights 9, 12, 15, 18, 21, and 24. If $t = 5$, $n - t = 24 - 5 = 19$ so that $s = 4$ and $d - t = 9 - 5 = 4 = s$. Hence vectors of weights 9, 12, and 15 in $C(11)$ hold 5-designs. Similarly 5-designs can be found in the next three symmetry codes (Problem 20).

PROBLEMS

1. Give the geometric meaning of the last line of the Pascal triangle of the order 2 projective plane (Figure 9.2).

2. Compute the Pascal triangle down to four rows (the apex is not counted as a row) for the projective plane of order 3.

3. Give a geometrical interpretation of the results of Problem 2.

4. How many vectors of weight 3 does H_r have?

5. If the vectors of weight r in a binary code C hold a t-(n, r, λ) design and there are A_r vectors of weight r in C, show that $\lambda = A_r \binom{r}{t} \Big/ \binom{n}{t}$.

6. Show that the vectors of weight 4 in the Hamming $(8, 4, 4)$ code hold an $S(3, 4, 8)$ system.

7. Draw the Pascal triangle for the $S(3, 4, 8)$ system.

8. Which other designs besides the Steiner system $S(4, 7, 23)$ are held by vectors of weight 7 in the $(23, 12)$ Golay code? Give all their relevant parameters.

9. If $\mathscr{D}'$ is the complementary design to the design $\mathscr{D}$ of lines in the order 2 projective plane, what is λ'? How many blocks are in $\mathscr{D}'$?

10. Show that the vectors of weights 11 and 15 in the Golay $(23, 12)$ code hold 4-designs.

11. Let C be the $(32, 16, 8)$ binary Q.R. code.

   (a) By the Assmus-Mattson theorem, do the vectors of any weights hold designs? Which ones?

   (b) Find λ for these designs. ($A_8 = 620$, $A_{12} = 13888$, $A_{16} = 36518$).

   (c) Identify complementary designs.

12. Consider the subtriangle of Table 9.1 that has its apex at 506. This is the Pascal triangle of a design in the $(23, 12)$ Golay code. Identify this design.

13. Describe a design derived from the 4-$(23, 7, 1)$ design.

14. Find the coset weight distribution of the $(24, 12, 8)$ Golay code.

15. Using the weight distribution of the Golay $(24, 12, 8)$ code C and Table 9.1, find the weight distribution of a coset of weight 1 of C.

16. Explain the entries in Table 9.2.

17. Let C be an extremal ternary self-dual code with minimum weight d and let A_i denote the number of vectors of weight i in C. Compute the number s of $A_i \neq 0$ where $d \leq i \leq n - 5$. Compare this with $d - 5$.

18. Show that $S_p S_p^t = pI$.

19. Show that if $p \equiv 1 \pmod 4$, then $S_p = S_p^t$ and if $p \equiv 3 \pmod 4$, then $S_p = -S_p^t$ (hint: use Theorem 65).

20. Using the Assmus-Mattson theorem, find designs in the $(36, 18, 12)$, $(48, 24, 15)$, and $(60, 30, 18)$ symmetry codes.

21. If the vectors of weight r in a ternary code C of length n hold a t-design and A_r is the number of vectors of weight r in C, show that

$$\lambda = \frac{A_r}{2} \frac{\binom{r}{t}}{\binom{n}{t}}$$

if any two vectors of weight r in C with the same support are multiples of each other.

22. Using the generator matrix (I, S_p) and Theorem 96, find elements in the group of $C(p)$.

23. Justify the entries in Table 9.3.

10

Some Codes Are Unique

10.1 THE HAMMING CODE AND THE TERNARY GOLAY CODE ARE UNIQUE

As we noted in Chapter 8, there are occasions when the weight distribution is unique, but this does not mean that a code with this weight distribution is unique. In fact there are examples of codes that have the same weight distribution but are not equivalent. We say that an (n, k, d) *code* over $GF(q)$ with certain properties is *unique* if any two (n, k, d) codes over $GF(q)$ with these properties are equivalent. Note that if a code is unique, then it is completely determined by n, k, d, and these properties. On many occasions the set of properties is not specified so that n, k, and d are enough to completely determine a unique code. If we want to use codes practically, it is often of interest to know whether an (n, k, d) code is unique or, if not, how many inequivalent (n, k, d) codes there are. These are interesting questions from a purely theoretical point of view also. The analogous question is also interesting for designs.

Two t-(v, k, λ) *designs* are said to be *equivalent* if there is a permutation of the v points that sends any block of one design onto a block of the other design. We say that a t-(v, k, λ) *design* $\mathscr{D}$ is *unique* if any other t-(v, k, λ) design is equivalent to $\mathscr{D}$. An example of a unique design is the $(2, 3, 7)$ Steiner system. Consider Table 10.1. Label the seven points by the integers from 1 through 7. Then without loss of generality we can suppose that the first block is $\{1, 2, 3\}$. Figure 9.2 gives the block intersection numbers for this design. From this we see that any two blocks have one point in common and that exactly three blocks contain any point. This shows that, up to a permutation of the points, the second and third blocks are in the design. Similar arguments (Problem 1) show that the last four blocks in the figure can be assumed to be in the design. Hence the 2-$(7, 3, 1)$ design is unique.

Table 10.1   The $(2, 3, 7)$ Steiner System

	Points						
Blocks	1	2	3	4	5	6	7
1	1	1	1				
2	1			1	1		
3	1					1	1
4		1		1		1	
5		1			1		1
6			1	1			1
7			1		1	1	

It is equally easy to show that the $(7, 4, 3)$ Hamming code C is unique. Consider Table 10.2. Any Hamming code has four independent columns and, by permuting coordinates, we may assume these are the first four columns. Hence some basis of C has the first four columns given in Table 10.2. Since three is the minimum weight in the Hamming code, we can choose the first vector in Table 10.2 to be in the basis. Then any other vector in this basis of C must have either three 1's in positions 5, 6, and 7 or two 1's that cannot both be in positions 6 and 7. Hence up to a permutation of the coordinates, Table 10.2 is a basis of the Hamming $(7, 4, 3)$ code so that this code is unique. Clearly the blocks of an $S(2, 3, 7)$ design generate a $(7, 4, 3)$ code. In our examples the blocks of Table 10.1 generate the code of Table 10.2.

Consider now an $S(3, 4, 8)$ design. By the corollary to Theorem 85 there are 14 blocks, so it would be tedious to write them all down to see if this design is unique. We try another approach. The last line of the Pascal triangle for this design (Problem 9.7) is 10201. Hence any two blocks either intersect in two points or in no points. If now we consider the blocks as vectors of weight 4 in a length 8 binary code, then the blocks generate a self-orthogonal code C in which all weights are divisible by 4 by Theorem 4. Clearly the dimension of C is ≤ 4. But A_4 is $\geq$ the number of blocks,

Table 10.2   A Basis for the Hamming $(7, 4, 3)$ Code

1	2	3	4	5	6	7
1	0	0	0	0	1	1
0	1	0	0	1	0	1
0	0	1	0	1	1	0
0	0	0	1	1	1	1

Table 10.3   A Basis for the Hamming (8, 4, 4) Code

1	2	3	4	5	6	7	8
1	0	0	0	0	1	1	1
0	1	0	0	1	0	1	1
0	0	1	0	1	1	0	1
0	0	0	1	1	1	1	0

which is 14. Since the number of vectors in C is a power of 2, the dimension of C is 4 so that C has a total of 16 vectors. Hence C is an $(8, 4, 4)$ code. We can show that it is unique, as for the $(7, 4, 3)$ code, by showing that a basis is determined up to a permutation of the columns. This basis is given in Table 10.3. Since all the vectors of weight 4 in C are the blocks of the $S(3, 4, 8)$ design, we have also shown that this design is unique.

Formulas are known [25] for the number N of doubly even $(n, n/2)$ codes, also for the number of self-dual $(n, n/2)$ codes over both $GF(2)$ and $GF(3)$ [21]; however we now compute directly the number of doubly even $(8, 4)$ codes. We do this by considering how many different bases we can choose for such a code C. Since C must contain $\mathbf{h}$, we only count those bases of C that contain $\mathbf{h}$. There are $\binom{8}{4} = 70$ choices for the second basis vector $\mathbf{x}_1$ (see Table 10.4). Then there are $\binom{4}{2}\binom{4}{2}$ ways of choosing $\mathbf{x}_2$ since $\mathbf{x}_2$ must have two 1's where $\mathbf{x}_1$ has 1's and two 1's where $\mathbf{x}_2$ has 0's. Up to equivalence $\mathbf{x}_1$ and $\mathbf{x}_2$ are as in Table 10.4. Now to be independent of $\mathbf{h}$, $\mathbf{x}_1$, and $\mathbf{x}_2$ and still be orthogonal to them, there are $2 \cdot 2 \cdot 2 \cdot 2 = 16$ choices for $\mathbf{x}_3$. Hence we have $70 \cdot 36 \cdot 16$ possible bases (containing $\mathbf{h}$) for C. To determine the number of these codes, we must divide by the number of such bases a particular C has. Since C has $2^4 = 16$ vectors and $\mathbf{h}$ is the first basis vector, there are 14 nonzero vectors to choose for the second basis vector. These now span a space of dimension 2 containing 4 vectors, so there are 12 choices for the third basis vector and 8 for the fourth. Hence there are $(70 \cdot 36 \cdot 16)/(14 \cdot 12 \cdot 8) = 2 \cdot 3 \cdot 5$ doubly even $(8, 4)$ codes.

Table 10.4   A General Basis for a Doubly Even (8, 4) Code

1	2	3	4	5	6	7	8	
1	1	1	1	1	1	1	1	$\mathbf{h}$
1	1	1	1					$\mathbf{x}_1$
1	1			1	1			$\mathbf{x}_2$
1		1		1		1		$\mathbf{x}_3$

Consider the entire group of coordinate permutations, S_8, which has order 8!. Each permutation in S_8 applied to the Hamming code carries it either onto itself or onto an equivalent code. In general, if C' is a length n binary code whose group G' has order $o(G')$, then the number of codes equivalent to C' is

$$\frac{n!}{o(G')}. \tag{1}$$

Since the (8, 4) Hamming code is unique, every (8, 4, 4) code is equivalent to it and its group G has order $8!/(2 \cdot 3 \cdot 5) = 8 \cdot 7 \cdot 6 \cdot 4$. In Section 6.5 we saw that G contains $PSL_2(7)$, which has order $7 \cdot 6 \cdot 4$. This shows that G is larger than $PSL_2(7)$ and has order 8 times as much. In this case we could determine the order of the group of a code from knowing that the code is unique. In many other cases the reverse is done in order to classify all $(n, n/2)$ doubly even codes for a given n. Knowledge of the entire group of a code yields the number of codes equivalent to it by (1). If this is not N, then other doubly even $(n, n/2)$ codes exist. When another code is found, its entire group is computed giving the number of codes equivalent to it. This process continues until N is reached, at which point it is known that all doubly even $(n, n/2)$ codes have been found [23].

It is also true that any ternary (12, 6, 6) code is unique [21]. However, we prove the following weaker theorem, which is easier to demonstrate.

Theorem 98. A ternary self-dual (12, 6, 6) code is unique.

Proof. Since C is a self-dual, all weights are divisible by 3. Hence C only contains vectors of weights 0, 6, 9, and 12. By Theorem 97, the vectors in C of weight 6 hold a 5-design. C is an extremal code so that its weight distribution is uniquely determined and it turns out that $A_6 = 264$. This means that the design has 132 blocks since a vector and its negative are the support of the same block. By Problem 9.21, $\lambda = A_6 \binom{6}{5} / \left(2\binom{12}{5} \right) = 1$ so that this design is an $S(5, 6, 12)$.

Since C has dimension 6, it can be assumed, by permuting coordinates, that C has a basis of the form (I, A) where both I and A are 6×6 matrices. Clearly the rows of A must have weight 5, and we can suppose that the first row of A is 0 1 1 1 1 1. By the last line of Table 9.3, we know that any two blocks of an $S(5, 6, 12)$ design intersect in either zero, two, three, or four points. This means that any two rows of A must have four nonzero entries in common. Since any two rows of the basis must be orthogonal, up to equivalence, the second row of A can be chosen to be 1 0 1 2 2 1. In fact, using the two facts that every two rows must be orthogonal and have four nonzero entries in common, it can be shown (Problem 5) that C is equivalent to a code whose basis is (I, A) where

$$
A = \begin{pmatrix}
0 & 1 & 1 & 1 & 1 & 1 \\
1 & 0 & 1 & 2 & 2 & 1 \\
1 & 1 & 0 & 1 & 2 & 2 \\
1 & 2 & 1 & 0 & 1 & 2 \\
1 & 2 & 2 & 1 & 0 & 1 \\
1 & 1 & 2 & 2 & 1 & 0
\end{pmatrix}.
$$

The $S(5, 6, 12)$ design is also unique but this is harder to show. Even though the vectors of weight 6 in C hold an $S(5, 6, 12)$, we cannot conclude from this that any other $S(5, 6, 12)$ design is held by vectors of weight 6 in a code equivalent to the ternary Golay code. So the code's uniqueness does not imply that the design is unique. In Section 10.2 we see a situation where this does hold.

10.2 THE STEINER SYSTEM $S(5, 8, 24)$ IS UNIQUE AND SO IS A BINARY $(24, 12, 8)$ CODE

The Steiner system $S(5, 8, 24)$ is a very interesting combinatorial configuration for many reasons. One of these is that its group is the Mathieu group, M_{24}, one of the few five-transitive groups (other than a symmetric or alternating group). It is also associated with the interesting Golay codes. This design is unique, but historically this has been quite difficult to demonstrate. As we saw in Section 10.1, it can be easier to show that a code is unique than to show that a design is unique. Here we give a new, elementary proof that this Steiner system is unique. This proof depends on showing that the code generated by the blocks of such a system is a unique $(24, 12, 8)$ code.

We start with a particular Steiner $S(5, 8, 24)$ system and we consider the blocks as binary vectors of length 24 and weight 8. The possible ways these vectors can intersect is given by the last line of the block intersection numbers for this design (see Table 9.1). We note that these blocks can intersect in no or two or four places. Let C denote the length 24 code generated by these blocks. By Theorem 4, C is self-orthogonal and all weights in C are divisible by 4. We can actually prove much more about C, which we do in several lemmas. Let any vector of weight 4, length 24, be called a *tetrad*. We call a set of six tetrads a *sextet* if the sum of any two tetrads is a block of the $S(5, 8, 24)$ system. Clearly the tetrads in a sextet are disjoint. The all-one vector $\mathbf{h}$ is the sum of all tetrads in a sextet.

Lemma 1.   Any tetrad $\mathbf{t}$ determines five other tetrads, $\mathbf{t}_1, \mathbf{t}_2, \mathbf{t}_2, \mathbf{t}_4, \mathbf{t}_5$ so that $\mathbf{t} + \mathbf{t}_i$, $i = 1, \ldots, 5$ is a block and the six tetrads are mutually disjoint.

Proof.   Let $\mathbf{t}$ be any tetrad and consider the four points where $\mathbf{t}$ has 1's. A fifth point determines a unique block in our $S(5, 8, 24)$. We now have two tetrads $\mathbf{t}$ and $\mathbf{t}_1$ whose sum is the block $\mathbf{b}_1$, say. Consider the four points of $\mathbf{t}$ and a fifth point outside $\mathbf{b}_1$. This determines a unique block $\mathbf{b}_2$ where $\mathbf{b}_2 = \mathbf{t} + \mathbf{t}_2$, $\mathbf{t}_2$ a tetrad. Since any two nondisjoint blocks intersect in either two or four points, $\mathbf{b}_1$ and $\mathbf{b}_2$ must intersect in the four points of $\mathbf{t}$. We can continue in this fashion and construct three other tetrads $\mathbf{t}_i$, $i = 3, 4, 5$ so that $\mathbf{t} + \mathbf{t}_i$ is a block. Clearly all our tetrads are disjoint.   Q.E.D.

Lemma 2. C has minimum weight 8.

Proof.   Since all weights in C are divisible by 4, if C does not have minimum weight 8, it has minimum weight 4. If $\mathbf{v}$ is a vector of weight 4 in C, let $\mathbf{t}$ be a tetrad that has three 1's in common with $\mathbf{v}$. By Lemma 1, there are five other tetrads $\mathbf{t}_i$, $i = 1, \ldots, 5$ so that $\mathbf{t} + \mathbf{t}_i$ is a block, hence a codeword. It is not hard to see that only one of these can have four points in common with $\mathbf{v}$. All the other $\mathbf{t} + \mathbf{t}_i$ meet $\mathbf{v}$ in three points. This contradicts the fact that C is self-orthogonal.   Q.E.D.

Call a vector of weight 8 in C an *octad*.

Lemma 3.   The octads of C consist precisely of the blocks of the Steiner system used to generate C. Any tetrad is contained in one sextet. Also the all-one vector $\mathbf{h}$ is in C.

Proof.   Clearly the blocks are octads. We show that the process of generating C does not produce any new octads. Suppose not. Let $\mathbf{v}$ be an octad that is not a block. Choose five points in $\mathbf{v}$. This determines a unique block $\mathbf{b}$ and, since C is self-orthogonal, $\mathbf{v}$ and $\mathbf{b}$ must have an even number of points in common. As $\mathbf{v} \neq \mathbf{b}$, this must be six points. But then $\mathbf{v} + \mathbf{b}$ has weight 4, which contradicts Lemma 2.

We see now that each $\mathbf{t}_i + \mathbf{t}_j$, $i \neq j$, is an octad, hence a block.   Q.E.D.

Lemma 4.   The dimension of C is 12.

Proof. Since C is self-orthogonal, its dimension is ≤ 12. To show that it is 12, we demonstrate that C has exactly 2^{12} cosets. Recall that the sum of two elements in one coset of a binary code is itself in the code. This implies, since C has minimum weight 8, that all vectors of weights 1, 2, and 3 are in distinct cosets and no vector of weight 4 can be in a coset of lower weight. Hence there are $\binom{24}{1} = 24$ cosets of weight 1, $\binom{24}{2} = 276$ cosets of weight 2, and $\binom{24}{3} = 2024$ cosets of weight 3. In order to determine the number of weight 4 cosets we have to compute the number of weight 4 vectors in one weight 4 coset. In this case this number is the same for any weight 4 coset. By Lemma 3, any tetrad is contained in exactly one sextet so that there are six weight 4 vectors in any coset that contains a weight 4 vector. Hence there are $\binom{24}{4}\big/6 = 1771$ cosets of weight 4. No vector of weight 5 can be a coset leader since it is contained in an octad and thus would be in a weight 3 coset. For similar reasons no vector of weight greater than 5 can be a coset leader (Problem 7). We now have a total of 4095 cosets and with C itself this gives $2^{12} = 4096$ cosets.   Q.E.D.

Theorem 99. The Steiner system $S(5, 8, 24)$ is unique.

Proof. Koch [36] proved this by showing that up to equivalence we can choose twelve blocks of an $S(5, 8, 24)$ which are linearly independent. We also give such a listing in Table 10.5. We regard the blocks as octads in the binary code C generated by the blocks of an $S(5, 8, 24)$.

Table 10.5 Twelve Independent Octads in an $S(5, 8, 24)$

	1	2	3	4	5	6	7	8	9	10	11	12	13	14	15	16	17	18	19	20	21	22	23	24
1	1	1	1	1	1	1	1	1																
2	1	1	1	1					1	1	1	1												
3	1	1	1		1				1				1	1	1									
4	1	1		1	1				1							1	1	1						
5	1		1	1	1				1										1	1	1			
6		1	1	1	1				1													1	1	1
7	1	1	1			1			1							1			1		1			
8	1	1		1		1			1				1						1		1			
9	1		1	1		1			1						1			1						1
10	1	1			1	1			1	1										1				1
11	1			1		1	1		1		1						1					1		
12	1	1	1					1	1									1			1		1	

Clearly we can choose the first octad to occupy the first eight positions. There is a unique octad which contains the five points $1, 2, 3, 4, 9$. As any two octads have either two or four points in common, the second octad cannot have any more points in common with the first octad and we label the other three points $10, 11, 12$. The third octad is chosen to contain the five points $1, 2, 3, 5, 9$ and up to equivalence the last three points can be labeled $13, 14, 15$. A similar argument gives the octads 4, 5, and 6. We choose octad 7 to contain the points $1, 2, 3, 6, 9$ and we see that it must meet each of the octads 4, 5, and 6 exactly once and, up to equivalence, we can choose the other points to be $16, 19, 22$. We leave the construction of octads $8, 9, 10$ for Problem 8. Octad 11 is not too difficult. The last octad is more complicated; there are two choices but they generate equivalent codes. We give one of the choices. We still have to show that these octads are linearly independent. This can be done by putting the matrix consisting of these 12 octads into row-echelon form. This is pretty tedious but elementary.

By the lemmas, C has dimension 12 and by the listing C is unique. As any octad in C is a block, an $S(5, 8, 24)$ is unique.   Q.E.D.

Theorem 100.   A binary $(24, 12, 8)$ code C is unique.

Proof. We show that every five points are contained in a unique octad in C. For this reason we puncture C in some coordinate, which we call ∞, so that the resulting punctured code C' has dimension 12. Then C' has minimum weight 7 or 8 and spheres of radius 3 about codewords are disjoint. Since there are 2^{12} codewords and

$$2^{12}\left[\binom{23}{0} + \binom{23}{1} + \binom{23}{2} + \binom{23}{3}\right] = 2^{23},$$

C' is a perfect code. Hence these spheres cover the space so that the minimum weight of C' must be 7 since vectors of weight 4 cannot be in spheres of radius 3 about vectors of weight 8 or higher. By Theorem 89, we know that the vectors of weight 7 hold a Steiner system of type $S(4, 7, 23)$.

We are now ready to return to C. Consider a set S of five points that contains ∞. This set without ∞ is contained in a unique vector $\mathbf{v}$ of weight 7 in C' since the weight 7 vectors are an $S(4, 7, 23)$ system. Since C has minimum weight 8, $\mathbf{v}$ must have a one at ∞ so that S is contained in a unique octad of C. Now let S be a set of five points none of which is ∞. Then S must be contained in a unique sphere of radius 3 about either a codeword $\mathbf{v}$ of weight 7 or a codeword $\mathbf{w}$ of weight 8 in C'. Clearly $\mathbf{v}$ must have a 1 at ∞, in which case S is contained in a unique octad in C. If $\mathbf{w}$ has a 0 at ∞, S is again contained in a unique octad in C. We show that this must be the case. If $\mathbf{w}$ has a 1 at ∞, pick four other points in $\mathbf{w}$. These five points are contained in a unique octad $\mathbf{x}$ in C by the 4-design in C'. Now $wt(\mathbf{x} + \mathbf{w}) \leq 7$, which contradicts the fact that C has minimum weight 8. Hence $\mathbf{w}$ must have a 0 at ∞ and the octads of C hold a 5-design. By the proof of Theorem 99, C is unique. Q.E.D.

The Steiner system $S(4, 7, 23)$ is also unique but it takes a bit of work to show this. However, it is easy to show that a binary $(23, 12, 7)$ code is unique.

Theorem 101. A binary $(23, 12, 7)$ code C' is unique.

Proof. Extend C' to a $(24, 12)$ code C by adding an overall parity check to each vector. Clearly the minimum weight of C is 8. By Theorem 100, C is unique. C' is a punctured code of C. Since C is unique, it is equivalent to a $(24, 12)$ Q.R. code that has minimum weight 8 (see Section 6.5). By Theorem 69, the group of C contains $PSL_2(23)$ and by Theorem 70 any two codes punctured from C are equivalent. Hence any punctured code of C is unique. Q.E.D.

Actually the group of C is M_{24}, which is 5-transitive, but we have not needed this fact. Even though we obtain a Steiner $S(4, 7, 23)$ system by considering all blocks that contain a fixed point, that is, as a derived design, it does not follow from this, although it is true, that any $S(4, 7, 23)$ system can be obtained in this fashion. We do not pursue this further as we are mainly interested in codes. We proved that an $S(5, 8, 24)$ system was unique in order to prove that the binary Golay code is unique, and also because it is nice to be able to use the new coding techniques to demonstrate this result in an elementary fashion.

10.3 "GLUE"

We discuss briefly the theory of "gluing" because it is interesting and we will see that the Golay $(24, 12, 8)$ code can be regarded as two codes glued together.

If X is a generator matrix, we let $\{X\}$ denote the code it generates. If C_1 is a code of length n_1 with generator matrix A and C_2 is a code of length n_2 with generator matrix B, then we say that a code C of length $n_1 + n_2$ is obtained from *gluing* C_1 to C_2 (or C_2 to C_1) if C has a generator matrix

$$G = \begin{pmatrix} A & 0 \\ 0 & B \\ D & E \end{pmatrix}$$

where $\{D\} \subset C_1^{\perp}$ and $\{E\} \subset C_2^{\perp}$. Vectors in $\{DE\}$ are called *glue vectors* and $\{DE\}$ is called the *glue space*. As G is a generator matrix of C, the rows of G are linearly independent so that no vector in $\{DE\}$ is in $\{A0\}$ or in $\{0B\}$. In the classifications mentioned in Section 10.1, gluing is used extensively to obtain new self-dual codes of length n from known self-orthogonal codes of smaller lengths. That this is possible can be seen from the next theorem.

Theorem 102. Let C be obtained from gluing two self-orthogonal codes C_1 and C_2 together. If $\{DE\}$ generates a self-orthogonal code, then C is self-orthogonal.

This theorem is clear from the definitions. For example, if we let both A and B be the all-one vector of weight 4, then we could glue these together as follows.

1	2	3	4	5	6	7	8
1	1	1	1	0	0	0	0
0	0	0	0	1	1	1	1
1	1	0	0	1	1	0	0
1	0	1	0	1	0	1	0

Clearly any weight 2 vector is orthogonal to the all-one vector of weight 4 and is a glue vector. Since the dimension of the glue space is 2, the glued code C is self-dual. We do not necessarily obtain a self-dual code by gluing self-orthogonal codes together unless the dimension of the glue space is enough when added to the dimensions of C_1 and C_2 to be $n/2$. The following is a useful gluing theorem [26].

Theorem 103. Let C be an $(n, n/2)$ self-dual code and let $n = n_1 + n_2$. Let $A0$ be a basis of the largest subcode of C, which is 0 on the last n_2 coordinate indices, and let $0B$ be a basis of the largest subcode of C, which is 0 on the first n_1 coordinate indices. Then C has a generator matrix of the following form.

$$G = \begin{array}{cc} n_1 & n_2 \\ \begin{pmatrix} A & 0 \\ 0 & B \\ D & E \end{pmatrix}. \end{array}$$

Let k_x be the dimension of a code generated by a basis labeled X. Then the following statements hold.

   (i) $k_d = k_e$.
   (ii) $k_a + k_b + k_d = n/2$.
   (iii) $\{A \cup D\} = \{A\}^\perp$ and $\{B \cup E\} = \{B\}^\perp$.

Proof. The existence of G is immediate since we can extend the independent vectors given by

$$\begin{pmatrix} A & 0 \\ 0 & B \end{pmatrix}$$

to a basis of C.

We show (i) by proving that both k_d and k_e equal the dimension of $\{DE\}$. If not, then some linear combination of the vectors in DE is 0 on either the first n_1 coordinates or on the second n_2 coordinates. Suppose the first holds. Then some vector $\mathbf{0v}$ is in $\{DE\}$. But $\mathbf{0v}$ is in $\{0B\}$ since $0B$ is the basis of the largest subspace of C that is 0 on the first n_1 coordinates. This is impossible since $\{DE\}$ and $\{0B\}$ intersect in only the zero vector. Hence $k_d = k_e$. Statement (ii) holds since $k_a + k_b +$ the dimension of $\{DE\}$ equals the dimension of C, $n/2$.

To show (iii) note that $\{A\}$ is self-orthogonal since $\{A0\}$ is contained in the self-orthogonal code C. Similarly $\{B\}$ is self-orthogonal. Since $\{D\}$ is orthogonal to $\{A\}$, $\{A \cup D\} \subset \{A\}^\perp$ and analogously $\{B \cup E\} \subset \{B\}^\perp$. Since A and D are disjoint, the dimension of $\{A \cup D\}$ is $k_a + k_d$ and we have $2k_a + k_d \le n_1$. For similar reasons $2k_b + k_e = 2k_b + k_d \le n_2$. Adding these equations gives $2k_a + 2k_b + 2k_d \le n_1 + n_2 = n$. Since $k_a + k_b + k_d = n/2$, we have equality in all three equations and statement (iii) holds.

In our example, $k_a = k_b = 1$, $k_d = k_e = 2$, and $n = 8$.

We return to C the binary Golay $(24, 12, 8)$ code. By permuting the coordinates of C, if necessary, we can suppose that there is an octad in C that has 1's on the first eight coordinate positions. We call this octad $A0$. Let $0B$ be a basis of the largest subcode of C whose vectors are 0 on these first eight positions.

Clearly $\{B\}$ is a self-orthogonal code of length 16. It has the all-one vector of length 16 in it since this is the sum of the all-one vector in C and our fixed octad. Since the minimum weight of C is 8 and $\{0B\}$ is contained in C, $\{B\}$ can only contain vectors of weights 0, 8, and 16. We can see in Table 9.1 that 30 octads are disjoint from a fixed octad so 30 is the number of weight 8 vectors in $\{B\}$. As the only other vectors in $\{B\}$ are the zero vector and the weight 16 vector, $\{B\}$ is a $(16, 5, 8)$ code. We show that, up to a permutation of its coordinates, B can be taken to be the following five vectors.

	1	2	3	4	5	6	7	8	9	10	11	12	13	14	15	16
$\mathbf{h}$	1	1	1	1	1	1	1	1	1	1	1	1	1	1	1	1
$\mathbf{v}_1$	1	1	1	1	1	1	1	1								
$\mathbf{v}_2$	1	1	1	1					1	1	1	1				
$\mathbf{v}_3$	1	1			1	1			1	1			1	1		
$\mathbf{v}_4$	1		1		1		1		1		1		1		1	

The first vector is obvious. We can permute the coordinates so that some octad occurs in the first eight positions giving $\mathbf{v}_1$. All the octads in $\{B\}$ are blocks of the Steiner system so that any other octad in $\{B\}$ must intersect $\mathbf{v}_1$ in either two or four points. An intersection of two points is impossible since then the sum of the two octads would have weight 12, an impossibility in $\{B\}$. Hence, by permuting coordinates, we can choose $\mathbf{v}_2$ as the third basis vector. The fourth basis vector must have four nonzero positions in common with $\mathbf{v}_1$ and $\mathbf{v}_2$ and can be chosen as $\mathbf{v}_3$ (Problem 10). Analogous arguments give $\mathbf{v}_4$ (Problem 11).

We see that C has a generator matrix G of the following form.

$$G = \begin{pmatrix} A & 0 \\ 0 & B \\ D & E \end{pmatrix}$$

where $k_a = 1$, $k_b = 5$, and $k_d = k_e = 6$. By a similar type of reasoning we can choose

$$D = \quad \begin{array}{cccccccc} 1 & 2 & 3 & 4 & 5 & 6 & 7 & 8 \end{array}$$
$$\begin{pmatrix} 1 & 1 & 0 & 0 & 0 & 0 & 0 & 0 \\ 1 & 0 & 1 & 0 & 0 & 0 & 0 & 0 \\ 1 & 0 & 0 & 1 & 0 & 0 & 0 & 0 \\ 1 & 0 & 0 & 0 & 1 & 0 & 0 & 0 \\ 1 & 0 & 0 & 0 & 0 & 1 & 0 & 0 \\ 1 & 0 & 0 & 0 & 0 & 0 & 1 & 0 \end{pmatrix}.$$

Theorem 100 tells us that there is a unique (up to equivalence) way to glue A to B with D as the leftmost portion of the glue.

By Lemma 3 to Theorem 81 we know that every vector with zeros in the first eight positions or in a fixed row of D occurs $2^{12-7} = 32$ times in the Golay code. Consider the set of all codewords in the Golay code with either zeros or a row of D in its first eight positions. In this way we obtain $8 \times 32 = 256$ codewords of C. Remove the first eight positions. This leaves a set of 256 binary vectors, called the *Nordstrom-Robinson* code, of length 16 whose minimum distance is 6. The Nordstrom-Robinson code is not a linear code (Problem 12), and it turns out that this is better than any linear code, i.e. $A(16, 6) = 256$ (see Table 2.2). But the Nordstrom-Robinson code really comes from a linear code anyway.

The code $\{B\}$ is a well-known code itself. It is called $R(1, 4)$, a first-order Reed-Muller code.

10.4   REED-MULLER CODES

Reed-Muller codes are an infinite family of codes which are defined recursively. Many things are known about them, including their minimum weights. Berlekamp [2] calls them weak codes which are easy to decode. At modest lengths, however, there are good Reed-Muller codes; they get weaker as their lengths increase.

If C_1 is a binary (n, k_1, d_1) code and C_2 is a binary (n, k_2, d_2) code, we construct a binary code C_3 of length $2n$ as follows: $C_3 = \{|\mathbf{u}|\mathbf{u} + \mathbf{v}|$ where $\mathbf{u}$ is in C_1, $\mathbf{v}$ is in $C_2\}$. Then (Problem 13) C_3 is a $(2n, k_1 + k_2, \min(2d_1, d_2))$ code. Further, if G_i is a generator matrix for C_i, $i = 1, 2$, then $\begin{pmatrix} G_1 & G_1 \\ 0 & G_2 \end{pmatrix}$ is a generator matrix for C_3 (Problem 14).

One way of defining Reed-Muller codes is recursively using this construction.

Reed-Muller codes, $R(r, m)$, are binary codes which exist at length $n = 2^m$ for $0 \le r \le m$. $R(m, m)$ is the whole space and $R(0, m)$ is the repetition code.

If $0 < r < m$, define $R(r + 1, m + 1)$ to be $\{|\mathbf{u}|\mathbf{u} + \mathbf{v}|$ where $\mathbf{u}$ is in $R(r + 1, m)$ and $\mathbf{v}$ is in $R(r, m)\}$. Let $G(r, m)$ denote a generator matrix of $R(r, m)$. Then we see that

$$G(r + 1, m + 1) = \begin{pmatrix} G(r + 1, m + 1) & G(r + 1, m) \\ 0 & G(r, m) \end{pmatrix}$$

is a generator matrix of $R(r + 1, n + 1)$.

Theorem 104. The dimension of $R(r, m)$ equals $1 + \binom{m}{1} + \cdots + \binom{m}{r}$. The minimum weight of $R(r, m)$ equals 2^{m-r}.

Proof. We leave it to Problem 17 to prove the statement about dimension by induction on m using the identity $\binom{m}{i} + \binom{m}{i+1} = \binom{m+1}{i+1}$.

Suppose the minimum weight of $R(r, m)$ is 2^{m-r}. Then the minimum weight of $R(r+1, m+1)$ equals $\min(2(2^{m-r-1}), 2^{m-r}) = 2^{m-r}$. We will see below that the formula is correct for $m = 2$ so it is correct for all m by induction.   Q.E.D.

It is interesting that one can write down a generator matrix for a specific $R(r, m)$ without having computed the generator matrices for smaller $R(r, m)$. We can show (Problem 18) that $R(r_1, m) \subset R(r_2, m)$ if $r_1 < r_2$ so we start with a basis of $R(0, m)$, namely **h**. We will call **h** v_0. We will then extend this to a basis of $R(1, m)$, then to a basis of $R(2, m)$ and so on.

Start with $m = 2$.

v_0	1	1	1	1
v_1	0	0	1	1
v_2	0	1	0	1
$v_1 v_2$	0	0	0	1

As noted v_0 is a basis of $R(0, 2)$ which has dimension 1 and $d = 4$. Now v_0, v_1, v_2 is a basis of $R(1, 2)$ which has dimension 3 and $d = 2$. Note that $v_1 v_2$ has ones in those positions in which both v_1 and v_2 are one. All four vectors are a basis of the whole space. This is not quite the basis we gave in our definition, but the rows of this basis are a permutation of the rows in the defining basis. This holds in general.

Consider now $m = 3$.

v_0	1	1	1	1	1	1	1	1
v_1	0	0	0	0	1	1	1	1
v_2	0	0	1	1	0	0	1	1
v_3	0	1	0	1	0	1	0	1
$v_1 v_2$	0	0	0	0	0	0	1	1
$v_1 v_3$	0	0	0	0	0	1	0	1
$v_2 v_3$	0	0	0	1	0	0	0	1
$v_1 v_2 v_3$	0	0	0	0	0	0	0	1

We notice that v_1 is chosen to have its first half zero, second half one, v_2 has its first quarter zero, second quarter one, third quarter zero, fourth quarter one, and so on. Again $v_i v_j$ has ones only where both v_i and v_j have ones and $v_1 v_2 v_3$ is only one where all three of v_1, v_2, and v_3 are one. Note that $R(1, 3)$ is equivalent to the extended Hamming code.

In addition to knowing the dimension and minimum weight of a Reed-Muller code, we can identify its dual code. Naturally this is another Reed-Muller code.

Theorem 105. $R(m - r - 1, m)$ and $R(r, m)$ are dual codes.

Proof. There are two things to prove: one is that the dimensions of these two codes add up to 2^m which we leave to Problem 20; the other is that these codes are orthogonal to each other.

We prove the orthogonality by induction on m. We can verify this easily for $m = 2$. Suppose it is true for all $R(r, m')$ where $m' < m$. Recall that

$$G(r, m) = \begin{pmatrix} G(r, m - 1) & G(r, m - 1) \\ 0 & G(r - 1, m - 1) \end{pmatrix}$$

and

$$G(m - r - 1, m) = \begin{pmatrix} G(m - r - 1, m - 1) & G(m - r - 1, m - 1) \\ 0 & G(m - r - 2, m - 1) \end{pmatrix}.$$

It is enough to show that these bases are orthogonal to each other.

Any row of $(G(r, m - 1)G(r, m - 1))$ is orthogonal to any row of $(G(m - r - 1, m - 1)G(m - r - 1, m - 1))$, as each of these rows is a repeated pair of vectors $(\mathbf{a}, \mathbf{a})$ where $\mathbf{a}$ has length 2^{m-1} and two such vectors are clearly orthogonal to each other. By the induction assumption the rows of $G(r, m - 1)$ are orthogonal to the rows of $G(m - r - 2, m - 1)$. Likewise for the rows of $G(r - 1, m - 1)$ and the rows of $G(m - r - 1, m - 1)$. As $R(m - r - 2) \subset R(m - r - 1)$, the rows of $G(r - 1, m - 1)$ are orthogonal to the rows of $G(m - r - 2, m - 1)$. We have actually checked enough rows to prove our point.   Q.E.D.

We have seen enough of Reed-Muller codes to get the feeling that these are codes with geometrical connections, and this is indeed true, but we will not explore these connections here. We just remark that, by means of their geometric nature, it can be shown that the group of each $R(r, m)$ contains the affine group, $AG(m, 2)$, of order $2^m(2^m - 1)(2^m - 2^2) \cdots (2^m - 2^{m-1})$. Punctured Reed-Muller codes are equivalent to cyclic codes.

We will spend just a bit of time on decoding Reed-Muller codes, called *Reed decoding*. Reed decoding of $R(r, m)$ is based on the fact that it is possible to construct 2^{m-r} check sums each involving 2^r bits of a received word where each received bit is used in only one check sum. This is a form of what is called *majority logic decoding*.

We illustrate this first for $R(1, 3)$ where we construct four check sums each involving two bits of a received word where each received bit is used in only one check sum. Notice that we are again decoding the single-error-correcting extended Hamming code but now by Reed-decoding. Recall the basis v_0, v_1, v_2, v_3. Let $v = (y_0, y_1, \ldots, y_7)$ be a received vector. If there are no errors, $v = a_0v_0 + a_1v_1 + a_2v_2 + a_3v_3$. It is not hard to see that

$$a_1 = y_0 + y_1 = y_2 + y_3 = y_4 + y_5 = y_6 + y_7$$
$$a_2 = y_0 + y_2 = y_1 + y_3 = y_4 + y_6 = y_5 + y_7$$
$$a_3 = y_0 + y_4 = y_1 + y_5 = y_2 + y_6 = y_3 + y_7.$$

Hence if a single error occurs, we can determine a_i, $i = 1, 2, 3$ by a majority count. We can find a_0 by taking a majority vote on all the y_i's, $i = 0, \ldots, 7$.

PROBLEMS

1. Show that the last four blocks in Table 10.1 are (modulo column permutations) in the $S(2, 3, 7)$ system that contains the first three blocks of the figure.

2. Show that any $(8, 4, 4)$ binary code is doubly even.

3. (a) Find a self-orthogonal binary $(8, 4, 2)$ code C.

   (b) Show directly that there are $\binom{8}{2}\binom{6}{2}\binom{4}{2}/4!$ codes equivalent to C.

   (c) Show that the group of C has order $2^4 \cdot 4!$

   (d) Prove that there are $3 \cdot 5 \cdot 9$ binary self-dual $(8, 4)$ codes.

4. If C is the Hamming $(8, 4, 4)$ code, find the order of the group of the $(16, 8)$ doubly even code C^2.

5. Show that the third, fourth, fifth, and sixth rows of A in the basis (I, A) of the ternary $(12, 6, 6)$ Golay code are determined up to equivalence given the first two rows.

6. Let C be the binary code generated by the blocks of a Steiner $S(5, 8, 24)$ system. We could have demonstrated Lemma 3 of Section

10.2 as follows. Suppose that C contains an octad v that is not a block. Choose five points in v. This determines a unique block b that must intersect v evenly since C is self-orthogonal. Hence v and b intersect in six points. Show that this determines a Steiner $S(5, 6, 8)$ system and that such a design is impossible.

7. Let C be the binary code generated by the blocks of a Steiner $S(5, 8, 24)$ system. Show that C cannot have any cosets of weight 6 or higher.

8. Show that (up to equivalence) octads 8, 9, 10 in Table 10.5 are uniquely determined.

9. Let C and D be equivalent codes. Let C' be the subcode of C consisting of all vectors in C that are 0 on some one coordinate and let D' be the subcode of D consisting of all vectors in D that are 0 on a fixed coordinate. Let C_i be the subcode of C consisting of all vectors in C that are 0 on the ith coordinate. Show that, if C_i is equivalent to C_j for any two unequal i and j, then C' is equivalent to D'.

10. In Section 10.3 show that the vector v_3 can be chosen as the fourth basis vector of B after h, v_1, and v_2 have been chosen.

11. After h, v_1, v_2, and v_3 are chosen as basis vectors of B, show that v_4 can be chosen as the fifth basis vector.

12. Show that the Nordstrom-Robinson code is not linear.

13. If C_1 is a binary (n, k_1, d_1) code and C_2 is a binary (n, k_2, d_2) code, let $C_3 = \{|u|u + v| \text{ where } u \text{ is in } C_1 \text{ and } v \text{ is in } C_2\}$. Show that C_3 is a $(2n, k_1 + k_2, \min(2d_1, d_2))$ code.

14. Let C_1, C_2, and C_3 be as in Problem 13. If G_i is a generator matrix for C_i, $i = 1, 2$ show that $\begin{pmatrix} G_1 & G_1 \\ 0 & G_2 \end{pmatrix}$ is a generator matrix for C_3.

15. Let C_1 and C_2 be extensions of the binary quadratic residue $(7, 4, 3)$ codes.

    (a) Show that C_1 and C_2 are $(8, 4, 4)$ codes and $C_1 \cap C_2 = \{h\}$.

    Consider the length 24 code C consisting of $\{|a + x|b + x|a + b + x|$ where a and b are in C_1 and x is in $C_2\}$.

    (b) Show that $\dim C = 12$ and the minimum weight of C is 8.

    (c) Deduce from this that C is equivalent to the Golay $(24, 12, 8)$ code. This construction of the Golay code is due to R. Turyn.

16. Let C_1, C_2, and C be as in Problem 15. Let G_i be generator matrices of C_i, $i = 1, 2$. Show that

$$\begin{pmatrix} G_1 & 0 & G_1 \\ 0 & G_1 & G_1 \\ G_2 & G_2 & G_2 \end{pmatrix}$$

is a generator matrix of C.

17. Prove that the dimension of $R(r, m)$ is $1 + \binom{m}{1} + \cdots + \binom{m}{r}$ by induction on m using the identity $\binom{m}{i} + \binom{m}{i+1} = \binom{m+1}{i+1}$.

18. Show that $R(r_1, m) \subset R(r_2, m)$ if $r_1 < r_2$.

19. Compute the dimensions and minimum weights of all the Reed-Muller codes of length 8.

20. Show that the sum of the dimensions of $R(m - r - 1, m)$ and $R(r, m)$ equals 2^m.

21. Compute the vectors v_0, v_1, v_2, v_3, v_4, v_{ij} ($i \neq j$, $i < j$, $i, j = 1, \ldots, 4$), $v_1v_2v_3$, $v_1v_2v_4$, $v_1v_3v_4$, $v_2v_3v_4$, and $v_1v_2v_3v_4$ for the Reed-Muller codes of length 16.

22. Find the check sums for $R(1, 4)$. How many errors can this code correct?

23. Do Problem 22 for $R(2, 4)$.

Appendix

This appendix is intended to gather those facts in linear algebra that are used in coding theory and also to accustom students to vector spaces over a finite field rather than over the real or complex numbers. Only a fraction of the material covered in a linear algebra course is actually used here. It is most important to have a firm grasp of the concepts of independence, dependence, and dimension.

We assume that the definitions of a group (Section 4.1) and a field (Section 3.1) are known. If not, these sections should be read first. The following defines a *vector space V over a field F*. We let $+$ and $\cdot$ be the operations in F whose identity elements are 0 and 1. We call the elements in F *scalars*. Let V be an abelian group with addition denoted by $+$ and an identity element called **0** (this is the zero vector, which is different from the zero scalar). We suppose that we can multiply any vector **v** by any scalar α, denoted by $\alpha\mathbf{v}$, and that $\alpha\mathbf{v}$ is again a vector in V. The following conditions are assumed to hold for all **v** and **w** in V and for all α and β in F:

(i) $\alpha(\mathbf{v} + \mathbf{w}) = \alpha\mathbf{v} + \alpha\mathbf{w}$.

(ii) $(\alpha + \beta)\mathbf{v} = \alpha\mathbf{v} + \beta\mathbf{v}$.

(iii) $(\alpha\beta)\mathbf{v} = \alpha(\beta\mathbf{v})$.

(iv) $1\mathbf{v} = \mathbf{v}$.

An example of a vector space is the set of all binary 7-tuples with addition given by $(a_1, \ldots, a_7) + (b_1, \ldots, b_7) = (a_1 + b_1, \ldots, a_7 + b_7)$ where the a_i's and b_i's assume the values 0 and 1 and $0 + 0 = 1 + 1 = 0, 1 + 0 = 0 + 1 = 1$. Clearly F is the field of two elements, $GF(2)$. Another example of a vector space is the Hamming $(7, 3)$ code C_4 (Section 2.4). If we let $F = GF(3)$, the set of all 4-tuples with components 0, 1, and 2 is a vector space.

A set S of vectors in a vector space V over a field F is a *subspace* of V if S is itself a vector space. For example, the Hamming code C_4 is a subspace of the space of all binary 7-tuples, the first example above. The $(4, 2)$

ternary code C_2, which consists of the scalar multiples of the following vectors, $(0,0,0,0)$, $(0,1,2,1)$, $(1,0,2,2)$, $(1,2,0,1)$, and $(1,1,1,0)$, is a subspace of the space of all 4-tuples over $GF(3)$. This subspace contains nine vectors.

If $v_1, \ldots, v_r$ are vectors in V, then a *linear combination* of $v_1, \ldots, v_r$ is a vector of the form $\alpha_1 v_1 + \alpha_2 v_2 + \cdots + \alpha_r v_r$ where the α_i's are in F. If $v_1, \ldots, v_r$ are in V, then the space they *span* is the set of all their linear combinations and is denoted by $\langle v_1, \ldots, v_r \rangle$. We call this a space because it is a subspace of V (Problem 2). If we let $v_1 = (0,1,2,1)$ and $v_2 = (1,0,2,2)$, then C_2 is $\langle v_1, v_2 \rangle$ (Problem 3). If we let $v_3 = (1,2,0,1)$, then C_2 still is $\langle v_1, v_2, v_3 \rangle$ (Problem 4).

Let S_1 and S_2 be subspaces of V. Then the *sum* of S_1 and S_2, denoted by $S_1 + S_2$, is the set of all $u + v$ where u is in S_1 and v is in S_2. The *intersection* of S_1 and S_2, denoted by $S_I \cap S_2$, is the set of all vectors in both S_1 and S_2. It is not hard to show that both $S_1 + S_2$ and $S_1 \cap S_2$ are subspaces of V (Problem 5).

A set of vectors $v_1, \ldots, v_r$ are called *dependent* if there are scalars $\alpha_1, \ldots, \alpha_r$, not all 0, so that $\alpha_1 v_1 + \alpha_2 v_2 + \cdots + \alpha_r v_r = 0$. For example, the binary vectors $(1,1,0)$, $(0,1,1)$, and $(1,0,1)$ are dependent as their sum is the zero vector. A set of vectors $v_1, \ldots, v_r$ that are not dependent are called *independent*. If $v_1, \ldots, v_r$ are independent, then $\alpha_1 v_1 + \cdots + \alpha_r v_r = 0$ implies that $\alpha_1 = \cdots = \alpha_r = 0$. Any two of the three binary vectors above are independent.

Theorem A1. If $v_1, \ldots, v_k$ span a vector space V and $w_1, \ldots, w_r$ are an independent set of vectors in V, then $r \leq k$.

Proof. Suppose not. Then $r > k$. Since $v_1, \ldots, v_k$ span V,

$$w_1 = \alpha_{11} v_1 + \cdots + \alpha_{1k} v_k$$
$$w_2 = \alpha_{21} v_1 + \cdots + \alpha_{2k} v_k$$
$$\vdots$$
$$w_k = \alpha_{k1} v_1 + \cdots + \alpha_{kk} v_k$$
$$w_{k+1} = \alpha_{(k+1)1} v_1 + \cdots + \alpha_{(k+1)k} v_k.$$

Since $w_1 \neq 0$, some $\alpha_{1i} \neq 0$. We can suppose it is α_{11}. Then we have the following set of equations.

$$\gamma_1 w_1 = v_1 + \cdots + \beta_{1k} v_k$$
$$w_2 - \gamma_2 w_1 = \beta_{22} v_2 + \cdots + \beta_{2k} v_k$$
$$\vdots$$
$$w_k - \gamma_k w_1 = \beta_{k2} v_2 + \cdots + \beta_{kk} v_k$$
$$w_{k+1} - \gamma_{k+1} w_1 = \beta_{(k+1)2} v_2 + \cdots + \beta_{(k+1)k} v_k$$

where $\gamma_1 = \gamma_{11}^{-1}$, $\gamma_2 = (\alpha_{11}^{-1}\alpha_{21})$, $\beta_{22} = (\alpha_{22} - \alpha_{11}^{-1}\alpha_{21}\alpha_{12})$, and so on. By the independence of the w_i, all the vectors on the left side of the equations above are nonzero. If we look at the second equation now, some β_{2i} is nonzero. Again without loss of generality we can suppose it is β_{22} and we obtain a new set of equations with the first equation the same, the second β_{22}^{-1} times the second equation above, and the ith equation, for $i \geq 3$, involving combinations of w_i, w_1, and w_2 on the left and combinations of $v_3, \ldots, v_k$ on the right. Since the coefficient of w_i is 1 and the w's are independent, no vector on the left is 0. We can continue in this fashion, removing v_i's from the right, until eventually we have on the left a linear combination of $w_1, \ldots, w_{k+1}$, which cannot be 0, by the independence of the w's and the fact that the coefficient of w_{k+1} is 1, and we have 0 on the right. This contradiction proves the theorem.

Theorem A2. If two finite sets of independent vectors span a space V, then there are the same number of vectors in each set.

Proof. If k is the number of vectors in one set and r is the number of vectors in the other set, then by Theorem A1, $k \leq r$ and $r \leq k$.   Q.E.D.

We are only interested in vector spaces that are spanned by a finite number of vectors, so we assume this from now on. We say that a set of vectors in V is a *basis* of V if they are independent and span V.

Theorem A3. Let V be a vector space over a field F. Then the following statements hold.

(i) V has a basis.

(ii) Any two bases of V contain the same number of vectors.

(iii) If B is a basis of V, every vector in V has a unique representation as a linear combination of vectors in B.

Proof. To demonstrate (i), we let $v_1 \neq 0$ be in V. If $V = \langle v_1 \rangle$, we are finished. If not, there is a vector v_2 in V not in $\langle v_1 \rangle$. If $V = \langle v_1, v_2 \rangle$, we are finished. If not, we continue until we obtain a basis of V. This process must terminate by our assumption that V is spanned by a finite number k of vectors and the fact that the number of vectors in the set we are building cannot exceed k by Theorem A1.

Statement (ii) is a direct consequence of Theorem A2. Let $B = \{b_i\}$, $i = 1, \ldots, k$, be a basis of V. Since the vectors in B span V, any v in V can be written as $\alpha_1 b_1 + \cdots + \alpha_k b_k$. If v is also equal to $\beta_1 b_1 + \cdots + \beta_k b_k$, then $\alpha_1 \mathbf{b}_1 + \cdots + \alpha_k \mathbf{b}_k = \beta_1 \mathbf{b}_1 + \cdots + \beta_k \mathbf{b}_k$ and since the $\mathbf{b}_i$'s are independent, $\alpha_i = \beta_i$, $i = 1, \ldots, k$. Hence statement (iii) holds.   Q.E.D.

The *dimension* of a vector space V, denoted by dim V, is the number of vectors in any basis. By the last theorem, this is well defined.

Theorem A4. If S and T are subspaces of V, then dim S + dim T = dim($S + T$) + dim($S \cap T$).

Proof. Clearly $S \cap T$ is a subspace of S, T, and $S + T$. Let $(a_1, \ldots, a_k)$ be a basis of $S \cap T$. We can extend this to a basis of S (Problem 12), say $\{a_1, \ldots, a_k, b_{k+1}, \ldots, b_{k+i}\}$, and also to a basis of T, say $\{a_1, \ldots, a_k, c_{k+1}, \ldots, c_{k+j}\}$. Then it can be shown that $\{a_1, \ldots, a_k, b_{k+1}, \ldots, b_{k+i}, c_{k+1}, \ldots, c_{k+j}\}$ is a basis of $S + T$ (Problem 14).

If M is a matrix whose elements are contained in a field F, then the *row rank* of M, denoted by $\rho(M)$, is defined to be the dimension of the subspace spanned by the rows of M. The *column rank* of M is defined to be the dimension of the subspace spanned by the columns of M. These concepts are important in the study of codes, as we often specify a code by a generator matrix G and the dimension of the code is clearly $\rho(G)$. However, we also talk about information positions and redundancy positions. The maximal number of information positions is the column rank of G, so it is perhaps worth a bit of effort to show that these two ranks associated with a matrix are equal.

An $n \times n$ matrix A is called *nonsingular* if $\rho(A) = n$. This means that the rows of A are linearly independent. A fact that we mention without proof is that A is nonsingular iff $|A| \neq 0$. A useful fact for a nonsingular matrix A is that $\rho(AB) = \rho(B)$ if AB is defined and $\rho(B) = \rho(BA)$ if BA is defined (both AB and BA are defined if B is also $n \times n$). This is usually proven in a linear algebra course, so we omit its proof.

If M is a matrix, the following operations on its rows are called *elementary operations*.

(i) Permuting rows.

(ii) Multiplying a row by a nonzero scalar.

(iii) Adding a scalar multiple of one row to another row.

Clearly the elementary operations do not change the row space of M. Each elementary operation on M can be represented by premultiplying M by a nonsingular matrix (Problem 15) called an *elementary matrix*.

A matrix M with $\rho(M) = k$ is said to be in *row-echelon form* if, after possibly permuting its columns,

$$M = \begin{pmatrix} I & A \\ 0 & 0 \end{pmatrix}$$

where I is the $k \times k$ identity matrix. If the section of zeros is absent, M is a generator matrix in standard form of a code (see 1.2).

Lemma. If M is any matrix, there is a sequence of elementary matrices, $E_1, \ldots, E_r$ so that $E_1 \ldots E_r M = E$ where E is in row-echelon form.

Proof. This is not difficult to see in general; we content ourselves with an example. Let

$$M = \begin{pmatrix} 0 & 2 & 1 & 2 \\ -1 & 0 & 1 & 1 \\ 3 & 2 & 1 & 4 \end{pmatrix}$$

and consider the row space of M to be over the field of rational numbers. First we permute the first rows, getting

$$M_1 = \begin{pmatrix} -1 & 0 & 1 & 1 \\ 0 & 2 & 1 & 2 \\ 3 & 2 & 1 & 4 \end{pmatrix}.$$

Then we multiply the first row by -1, getting

$$M_2 = \begin{pmatrix} 1 & 0 & -1 & -1 \\ 0 & 2 & 1 & 2 \\ 3 & 2 & 1 & 4 \end{pmatrix}.$$

We now subtract three times the first row from the third row yielding

$$M_3 = \begin{pmatrix} 1 & 0 & -1 & -1 \\ 0 & 2 & 1 & 2 \\ 0 & 2 & 4 & 7 \end{pmatrix}.$$

We now subtract the second row from the third row, resulting in

$$M_4 = \begin{pmatrix} 1 & 0 & -1 & -1 \\ 0 & 2 & 1 & 2 \\ 0 & 0 & 3 & 5 \end{pmatrix}.$$

We multiply the second row by $\frac{1}{2}$ and follow this with multiplying the third row by $\frac{1}{3}$, giving the row-echelon form

$$E = \begin{pmatrix} 1 & 0 & 0 & \frac{2}{3} \\ 0 & 1 & 0 & \frac{1}{6} \\ 0 & 0 & 1 & \frac{5}{3} \end{pmatrix}.$$

Corollary. If k columns of M are independent, then after elementary operations, M can be transformed to a matrix with the identity on these k columns.

Theorem A5. The row rank of a matrix M, $\rho(M)$, equals its column rank.

Proof. Suppose that $\rho(M) = k$. By the lemma there are elementary matrices, $E_1, \ldots, E_r$ so that $E_1 \ldots E_r M = E$, a matrix in row-echelon form. Since $\rho(E_1 \ldots E_r M) = \rho(E_2 \ldots E_r M) = \cdots = \rho(M)$ as each E_i is nonsingular, $\rho(E)$ is k also. Thus E has k columns, each of which consists of exactly one 1 and all the rest 0's. It is clear that these k columns are a basis for the column space of E. Hence $\rho(E^T) = k$. But $\rho(E^T) = \rho(M^T E_r^T \cdots E_1^T) = \rho(M^T E_r^T \cdots E_2^T) = \cdots = \rho(M^T)$ since each E_i^T is nonsingular. Since $\rho(M^T)$ is the column rank of M and this is k, the theorem is demonstrated.

Until now the items we have covered would be included in most elementary linear algebra courses. The next topic, the inner product, is somewhat different. Usually an elementary course would discuss inner products but they would be only over the reals or complexes and some of the facts there do not hold over an arbitrary field, for example, over finite fields, the cases of interest here.

Let V be a vector space over a field F. An *inner product*, denoted by $\cdot$, is a function on pairs of vectors in V with values in F satisfying the following properties for all $\mathbf{u}$ and $\mathbf{v}$ in V and scalars α, β, and γ in F.

(i) $\mathbf{u} \cdot \mathbf{v} = \mathbf{v} \cdot \mathbf{u}$.

(ii) $(\alpha\mathbf{u} + \beta\mathbf{v}) \cdot \mathbf{w} = \alpha(\mathbf{u} \cdot \mathbf{w}) + \beta(\mathbf{v} \cdot \mathbf{w})$.

(iii) If $\mathbf{u} \cdot \mathbf{v} = 0$ for all $\mathbf{v}$ in V, then $\mathbf{u} = 0$.

Axioms (i) and (ii) above are sometimes referred to by saying that the inner product is a symmetric, bilinear function from $V \times V$ to F and axiom (iii) says that this function is nondegenerate.

For example, let V be the space of all binary n-tuples and let $\mathbf{u} = (u_1, \ldots, u_n)$, $\mathbf{v} = (v_1, \ldots, v_n)$ be vectors in V. Then $\mathbf{u} \cdot \mathbf{v} = \sum_{i=1}^{n} u_i v_i \pmod 2$ is an example of an inner product. A similar example can be obtained by taking V to be the space of all n-tuples over a finite field F. Then if $\mathbf{u} = (u_1, \ldots, u_n)$ and $\mathbf{v} = (v_1, \ldots, v_n)$ are vectors in V, $\mathbf{u} \cdot \mathbf{v} = \sum_{i=1}^{n} u_i v_i$ evaluated in F is an inner product.

Two vectors $\mathbf{u}$ and $\mathbf{v}$ are said to be *orthogonal* to each other if $\mathbf{u} \cdot \mathbf{v} = 0$. If C is a subspace of V, then it is easy to see (Problem 18) that the set of all vectors in V that are orthogonal to each vector in C is a subspace, which we call the space orthogonal to C and denote by $C^\perp$.

Theorem A6. If $\mathbf{u}$ is orthogonal to every vector in a set S, then $\mathbf{u}$ is in $\langle S \rangle^\perp$.

We leave the proof of this to Problem 19.

Theorem A7. If S and T are subspaces of V, then $(S^\perp \cap T^\perp) = (S + T)^\perp$.

Proof. Any vector that is orthogonal to $S + T$ is clearly orthogonal to both S and T. Hence $(S + T)^\perp \subseteq (S^\perp \cap T^\perp)$. If a vector is orthogonal to both S and T, then it is orthogonal to any linear combination of vectors from S and T so that $(S^\perp \cap T^\perp) \subseteq (S + T)^\perp$.   Q.E.D.

It is quite possible, for instance when looking at spaces over finite fields, for C to be contained in $C^\perp$. When this happens, C is called *self-orthogonal*. An example of this is given by the binary $(7, 3)$ code C_4, whose basis $\mathbf{c}_1, \mathbf{c}_2, \mathbf{c}_3$ we give so that this fact can be verified. $\mathbf{c}_1 = (0, 0, 0, 1, 1, 1, 1)$, $\mathbf{c}_2 = (0, 1, 1, 0, 1, 1, 0)$, and $\mathbf{c}_3 = (1, 0, 1, 0, 1, 0, 1)$.

The next theorem is very important in coding. Its proof is based on a well known identity for linear transformations, namely $\dim \text{kernel} + \dim \text{range} = \dim \text{image}$. As we do not try to cover linear transformations in this brief account, we omit the proof.

Theorem A8. If C is a subspace of V, then $\dim C + \dim C^\perp = \dim V$.

Corollary. $C^{\perp\perp} = C$.

Proof. By the definition of $\perp$, $C \subseteq C^{\perp\perp}$. By the theorem, $\dim C = \dim V - \dim C^\perp = \dim C^{\perp\perp}$.

We now cover a few items that might prove useful in Chapter 8 on weight distributions. One vector space that is needed there is the space of solutions to a set of linear equations. Let a_{ij} and c_i, $i = 1, \ldots, m$, $j = 1, \ldots, n$, be scalars in a field F and let $x_1, \ldots, x_n$ be indeterminants. Then a set of m *linear equations* in n unknowns has the following form.

$$a_{11}x_1 + a_{12}x_2 + \cdots + a_{1n}x_n = c_1$$

$$a_{21}x_1 + a_{22}x_2 + \cdots + a_{2n}x_n = c_2 \tag{1}$$

$$\vdots$$

$$a_{m1}x_1 + a_{m2}x_2 + \cdots + a_{mn}x_n = c_m.$$

The $m \times n$ matrix (a_{ij}) is called the *coefficient matrix* of the system of equations. A *solution* to the system is a vector $(b_1, \ldots, b_n)$ where the b_i's are scalars so that each equation $a_{i1}b_1 + \cdots + a_{in}b_n = c_i$, $i = 1, \ldots, m$, holds. If $c_1 = \cdots = c_m = 0$, the system is called *homogeneous*; otherwise it is *nonhomogeneous*. The following type of space arises in considering solutions to nonhomogeneous equations. If W is a subspace of a vector space V and $\mathbf{v}$ is a vector in V, then the set of all vectors of the form $\mathbf{v} + \mathbf{w}$, $\mathbf{w}$ in W, is called an *affine space*. In general, it is not a vector space. We have called it a coset in Chapter 2.

Theorem A9. (i) The set of all solutions to a homogeneous system of m equations in n unknowns with coefficient matrix A is a vector space of dimension equal to $n - \rho(A)$. (ii) Let $\mathbf{v}$ be a solution to a nonhomogeneous system (1) and let W be the space of solutions to the homogeneous system we obtain by letting $c_1 = \cdots = c_m = 0$. Then any solution to (1) is given by $\mathbf{v} + \mathbf{w}$ where $\mathbf{w}$ is in W.

Proof. For (i) let $\mathbf{w} = (w_1, \ldots, w_n)$ be one solution to the homogeneous system and let $\mathbf{z} = (z_1, \ldots, z_n)$ be another; then it is immediate that $\alpha\mathbf{w} + \beta\mathbf{z}$ are also solutions. The statement about dimensions follows from Theorem A8. We leave the proof of (ii) to Problem 20. While the solutions to the homogeneous system are a vector space, the solutions to the nonhomogeneous system are an affine space.

Corollary. If $m = n$ and $\rho(A) = n$, a homogeneous system of n equations in n unknowns with coefficient matrix A has a unique solution. If $m = n$ and $\rho(A) = n$, a nonhomogeneous system of n equations in n unknowns with coefficient matrix A that has a solution has a unique solution.

Proof. The condition that $\rho(A) = n$ is equivalent to $|A| \neq 0$, which is often stated in this theorem. If $m = n$ and $\rho(A) = n$, the homogeneous system has the solution $0 = (0, \ldots, 0)$ and by the theorem the solution space has dimension 0 so that this is the unique solution. The statement about the nonhomogeneous system follows from the unique solution for the homogeneous system and part (ii) of the theorem.

Corollary. If $\mathbf{v}_1$ and $\mathbf{v}_2$ are solutions to the nonhomogeneous system of equations, then $\alpha\mathbf{v}_1 + \beta\mathbf{v}_2$ is also a solution to the nonhomogeneous system whenever $\alpha + \beta = 1$.

Proof. By the theorem, $\mathbf{v}_2 = \mathbf{v}_1 + \mathbf{w}$ where $\mathbf{w}$ is in W. Hence $\alpha\mathbf{v}_1 + \beta\mathbf{v}_2 = \alpha\mathbf{v}_1 + \beta(\mathbf{v}_1 + \mathbf{w}) = \mathbf{v}_1 + \beta\mathbf{w}$ is also a solution by part (ii) of the theorem.

PROBLEMS

1. If V is a vector space over a field F, show that $0\mathbf{v} = \mathbf{0}$ for all $\mathbf{v}$ in V.

2. Show that the span of a set of vectors in a vector space is itself a subspace.

3. Show that C_2 is the space spanned by $\mathbf{v}_1 = (0, 1, 2, 1)$ and $\mathbf{v}_2 = (1, 0, 2, 2)$.

4. Show that C_2 is spanned by the vectors $\mathbf{v}_1$ and $\mathbf{v}_2$ given in Problem 3 and $\mathbf{v}_3 = (1, 2, 0, 1)$.

5. If S_1 and S_2 are subspaces of V, show that both $S_1 + S_2$ and $S_1 \cap S_2$ are subspaces of V.

6. Show that any set of vectors that contains a dependent set of vectors is dependent.

7. Show that any set of vectors that is contained in an independent set of vectors is independent.

8. Show that if $\mathbf{v}_1, \ldots, \mathbf{v}_r$ is a dependent set of vectors, then some $\mathbf{v}_i$, $1 \leq i \leq r$, is contained in the span of $\mathbf{v}_1, \ldots, \mathbf{v}_{i-1}$.

9. If $\{\mathbf{v}_1, \ldots, \mathbf{v}_r\}$ is an independent set of vectors, show that $\{\mathbf{v}_1, \mathbf{v}_2 - \alpha_2\mathbf{v}_1, \ldots, \mathbf{v}_r - \alpha_r\mathbf{v}_1\}$ is also an independent set of vectors for any scalars $\alpha_2, \ldots, \alpha_r$.

10. If $\{\mathbf{v}_i\}$, $i = 1, 2, 3$, span a vector space V and $\{\mathbf{w}_i\}$, $i = 1, \ldots, 4$, are vectors in V, show that the $\{\mathbf{w}_i\}$ are dependent using the method of Theorem A1.

11. Show that any set of r vectors in a k-dimensional vector space must be dependent if $r > k$.

12. Show that any independent set of vectors in a space V is contained in a basis of V.

13. Show that any k independent vectors in a k-dimensional vector space constitute a basis.

14. If $\{a_1, \ldots, a_k\}$ is a basis of $S \cap T$, $\{a_1, \ldots, a_k, b_{k+1}, \ldots, b_{k+i}\}$ is a basis of S, and $\{a_1, \ldots, a_k, c_{k+1}, \ldots, c_{k+j}\}$ is a basis of T, then $\{a_1, \ldots, a_k, b_{k+1}, \ldots, b_{k+i}, c_{k+1}, \ldots, c_{k+j}\}$ is a basis of $S + T$.

15. Show that each elementary operation on M can be expressed by premultiplying M by a nonsingular matrix.

16. Let

$$M = \begin{pmatrix} 0 & 1 & 0 & 0 & 2 \\ 2 & 3 & 1 & 4 & 0 \\ 2 & 1 & 0 & 1 & 1 \\ 5 & 0 & 0 & 3 & 4 \end{pmatrix}.$$

Find a sequence of elementary operations so that premultiplying M by the corresponding elementary matrices results in a matrix in row-echelon form. Let the scalars be in the field of rational numbers.

17. Show that $\mathbf{w} \cdot (\alpha\mathbf{u} + \beta\mathbf{v}) = \alpha(\mathbf{w} \cdot \mathbf{u}) + \beta(\mathbf{w} \cdot \mathbf{v})$.

18. If C is a subspace of V, show that the set of all vectors in V that are orthogonal to every vector in C is a subspace.

19. Prove Theorem A6.

20. Prove part (ii) of Theorem A9.

References

1. E. F. Assmus, Jr., and H. F. Mattson, Jr., "New 5-designs," *J. Comb. Theory* **6** (1966), 122–151.
2. E. R. Berlekamp, *Algebraic Coding Theory*, McGraw-Hill, New York, 1968.
3. E. R. Berlekamp, F. J. MacWilliams, and N. J. A. Sloane, "Gleason's theorem on self-dual codes," *IEEE Trans. Info. Theory* **18** (1972), 409–414.
4. I. F. Blake and R. C. Mullin, *The Mathematical Theory of Coding*, Academic Press, New York, 1975.
5. R. C. Bose and D. K. Ray-Chaudhuri, "On a class of error correcting binary group codes," *Info. and Control* **3** (1960), 68–79, 279–290.
6. P. J. Cameron and J. H. van Lint, *Graph Theory, Coding Theory and Block Designs*, London Math. Soc. Lecture Note Series, No. 19, Cambridge University Press, London, 1975.
7. A. M. Gleason, "Weight polynomials of self-dual codes and the MacWilliams identities," Actes Congres Internl. de Mathematique, 3 1970, Gauthier-Villars, Paris, 1971, pp. 211–215.
8. J. M. Goethals, "On the Golay perfect binary code," *J. Comb. Theory* **11** (1971), 178–186.
9. J. H. van Lint, *Coding Theory*, Springer, New York, 1971.
10. J. H. van Lint, "A survey of perfect codes," *Rocky Mountain J. Math.* **5** (1975), 199–224.
11. S. Lin, *An Introduction to Error-Correcting Codes*, Prentice-Hall, Englewood Cliffs, N. J., 1970.
12. S. P. Lloyd, "Binary block coding," *Bell Syst. Tech. J.* **36** (1957), 517–535.
13. F. J. MacWilliams, "A theorem on the distribution of weights in a systematic code," *Bell Syst. Tech. J.* **42** (1963), 79–94.
14. F. J. MacWilliams, "Permutation decoding of systematic codes," *Bell Syst. Tech. J.* **43** (1964), 485–505.
15. F. J. MacWilliams and N. J. A. Sloane, *The Theory of Error-Correcting Codes*, Vols. I and II, North-Holland, Amsterdam, 1977.
16. F. J. MacWilliams, N. J. A. Sloane, and J. G. Thompson, "On the existence of a projective plane of order 10," *J. Comb. Theory* **14A** (1973), 66–78.
17. C. L. Mallows, A. M. Odlyzko, and N. J. A. Sloane, "Upper bounds for modular forms, lattices, and codes," *J. Algebra* **36** (1975), 68–76.

18. R. J. McEliece, *The Theory of Information and Coding*: *A Mathematical Framework for Communication*, Addison-Wesley, Reading, Mass., 1977.

19. W. W. Peterson and E. J. Weldon, Jr., *Error-Correcting Codes*, M.I.T. Press, Cambridge, Mass., 1972.

20. V. Pless, "Power moment identities on weight distributions in error-correcting codes," *Info. and Control* **6** (1963), 147–152.

21. V. Pless, "On the uniqueness of the Golay codes," *J. Comb. Theory* **5** (1968), 215–228.

22. V. Pless, "Symmetry codes over $GF(3)$ and new five-designs," *J. Comb. Theory* **12** (1972), 119–142.

23. V. Pless, "A classification of self-orthogonal codes over $GF(2)$," *Discrete Math.* **3** (1972), 209–246.

24. V. Pless and J. N. Pierce, "Self-dual codes over $GF(q)$ satisfy a modified Varshamov bound," *Info. and Control* **23** (1973), 35–40.

25. V. Pless and N. J. A. Sloane, "On the classification and enumeration of self-dual codes," *J. Comb. Theory* **18A** (1975), 313–335.

26. V. Pless, N. J. A. Sloane, and H. N. Ward, "Ternary codes of minimum weight 6, and the classification of the self-dual codes of length 20," *IEEE Trans. Info. Theory* **26** (1980), 305–316.

27. E. Prange, "The use of information sets in decoding cyclic codes," *IEEE Trans. Info. Theory* **8** (5) (1962), 55–59.

28. C. E. Shannon, "A mathematical theory of communication," *Bell Syst. Tech. J.* **27** (1948), 379–423, 623–656.

29. A. Tietäväinen, "On the nonexistence of perfect codes over finite fields," *SIAM J. Appl. Math.* **24** (1973), 88–96.

SECOND EDITION REFERENCES

30. E. R. Berlekamp, *Algebraic Coding Theory*, Revised 1984 Edition, Aegean Park Press, Laguna Hills, Calif., 1984.

31. R. E. Blahut, *Theory and Practice of Error Control Codes*, Addison-Wesley, Reading, Mass., 1984.

32. R. A. Brualdi, V. Pless, and J. S. Beissinger, "On the MacWilliams Identities for linear codes," *Linear Algebra and Its Applications* **107** (1988), 181–189.

33. J. H. Conway and N. J. A. Sloane, *Sphere Packings, Lattices and Groups*, Springer, New York, 1988.

34. R. Hill, *A First Course in Coding Theory*, Clarendon Press, Oxford, 1986.

35. M. J. E. Golay, "Notes on digital coding," *Proc. IEEE* **37** (1949), 657.

36. H. Koch, "On self-dual, doubly-even codes of length 32," *J. Comb. Theory* **51A** (1989), 63–76.

37. E. Lander, *Symmetric Designs: An Algebraic Approach*, Cambridge University Press, London, 1983.

38. R. Lidl and H. Niederreiter, *Finite Fields*, Addison-Wesley, Reading, Mass., 1983.

39. S. Lin and D. J. Costello, *Error Control Coding: Fundamentals and Applications*, Prentice-Hall, N.J., 1983.

40. J. H. van Lint, *Introduction to Coding Theory*, Springer, New York, 1982.

41. J. H. van Lint and R. M. Wilson, "On the minimum distance of cyclic codes," *IEEE Trans. Info. Theory* **32** (1986), 23–40.

42. C. L. Mallows and N. J. A. Sloane, "An upper bound for self-dual codes," *Infor. and Control* **22** (1973), 188–200.

43. V. Pless, "Decoding the Golay codes," *IEEE Trans. Info. Theory* **32** (1986), 561–567.

Index

DATE DUE